THE LIFE AND THE DOCTRINES OF

PHILIPPUS THEOPHRASTUS BOMBAST OF HOHENHEIM

KNOWN BY THE NAME OF

PARACELSUS

AND

THE SUBSTANCE OF HIS TEACHINGS

CONCERNING COSMOLOGY, ANTHROPOLOGY, PNEUMATOLOGY, MAGIC AND SORCERY, MEDICINE, ALCHEMY AND ASTROLOGY, PHILOSOPHY AND THEOSOPHY

EXTRACTED AND TRANSLATED FROM HIS RARE AND EXTENSIVE WORKS AND FROM SOME UNPUBLISHED MANUSCRIPTS

BY

FRANZ HARTMANN, M. D.

SECOND EDITION, REVISED AND ENLARGED, 1896.

RE-PRINTED WITH NEW FORMATTING, 2016.

www.kshetrabooks.com

The Life and Doctrines of Paracelsus
First Edition, 1891
Second Edition, Revised and Enlarged, 1896
Third Edition, "Theosophical Publishing House," 1910

Re-print (with new formatting)

© Copyright 2016
All rights reserved.

ISBN: 978-1539832881

Contents

Preface v
Chapter 1: The Life of Paracelsus 1
    The Writings of Paracelsus 12
Chapter 2: Explanation's of Terms Used by Paracelsus 17
Chapter 3: Cosmology 29
Chapter 4: Anthropology. The Generation of Man 39
    Woman and Marriage 45
    The Constitution of Man 47
    Death 54
Chapter 5: Pneumatology 59
Chapter 6: Magic and Sorcery 71
Chapter 7: Medicine 87
    The Virtues of a Physician 88
    The Four Pillars of Medicine 89
    The Archaeus 95
    The Mumia 97
    Sympathetic Cures 98
    Occult Properties of Plants 99
    The Magnet 99
    Anatomy 101
    Physiology 102
    Therapeutics 103
    Paramirum; or, The Book of the Causes and the Beginning of Diseases—The Five Causes 103
    The Practice of Medicine 119
    The Three Substances 120
    Arcana (Mysteries) 122
Chapter 8: Alchemy and Astrology 125
    The Seven Planets 126
    Sulphur, Mercury and Salt 129
    Charms 130
    The Electrum Magicum 132
    Palingenesis 133
    Homunculi 133
Chapter 9: Philosophy and Theosophy 137
    Knowledge 139
    Spiritual Regeneration 140
    Faith 142
    Reincarnation 143
    "The Philosopher's Stone" 143
    The Church 144
    Unselfishness 146
Appendix 149
    Adepts 149

    Creation..149
    Generation...150
    Initiation..150
    Mediumship..151
    Occult Phenomena...151
    Thought-Transfer..152
    Spirits of the Departed..152
    The Elixir of Life..153
    The Primum Ens...154
    Primum Ens Sanguinis..155
    The Alcahest..155
    Zenexton...155
Notes..157

"The beginning of wisdom is the
beginning of supernatural power."
—Paracelsus

Preface

Recent researches in the ethereal realms of Mysticism, Metaphysics, and transcendental Anthropology have proved beyond a doubt the existence of a great number of apparently mysterious and occult facts, whose causes cannot be explained by a science whose means for investigation are limited by the imperfections of sensual perception, and whose researches must necessarily come to a stop where physical instruments cease to be of any service. Invisible things cannot be seen, neither can that which is imponderable be weighed with scales; but invisible and imponderable things, such as the cosmic ether, the light producing power of the sun, the vital power of plants and animals, thought, memory, imagination, will, psychological influences affecting the state of the mind or producing a sudden change of feeling, to mention, are nevertheless facts, and other things too numerous and exist in spite of the incapacity of teachers of anatomy or chemistry to explain them. If a reasonable sceptic says that such things do not exist, he can only mean to say that they do not exist relatively to his knowledge; because, to deny the possibility of the existence of anything of which we know nothing would imply that we imagined ourselves to be in possession of all the knowledge that exists in the world, and believed that nothing could exist of which we did not know. A person who peremptorily denies the existence of anything which is beyond the horizon of his understanding because he cannot make it harmonise with his accepted opinions is as credulous as he who believes everything without any discrimination. Either of these persons is not a freethinker, but a slave to the opinions which he has accepted from others, or which he may have formed in the course of his education, and by his special experiences in his (naturally limited) intercourse with the world. If such persons meet with any extraordinary fact that is beyond their own experience, they often either regard it with awe and wonder, and are ready to accept any wild and improbable theory that may be offered to them in regard to such facts, or they sometimes reject the testimony of credible witnesses, and frequently even that of their own senses. They often do not hesitate to impute the basest motives and the most silly puerilities to honourable persons, and are credulous enough to believe that serious and wise people had taken the trouble to play upon them "practical jokes" and they are often willing to admit the most absurd theories rather than to use their own common sense.

It seems almost superfluous to make these remarks, as perhaps none of our readers will be willing to be classified into either of these two categories; but nevertheless the people to whom they may be applied are exceedingly numerous, and by no means to be found only among the ignorant and uneducated. On the contrary, it seems that now, as at the time of the great Paracelsus, the three (dis)graces of dogmatic science—self-conceit, credulity, and scepticism—go still hand in hand, and that their favourite places of residence are public auditories and the private visiting-rooms of the learned.

It is difficult for the light of truth to penetrate into a mind that is crammed full of opinions to which it tenaciously clings, and only those who accept the opinions of others, not as their guides, but only as their assistants, and are able to rise on the wings of their own unfettered genius into the region of independent thought, may receive the truth. Our modern age is not without such minds. The world is moving in spirals, and our greatest modern philosophers are nearing a place in their mental orbit where they come again into conjunction with minds like Pythagoras and Plato. Only the ignorant schoolboy believes that he knows a great deal more than Socrates and Aristotle because he may have learned some modern opinions in regard to a few superficial things, or some modern inventions, with which the philosophers of old may not have been acquainted; but if our modern scientists know more about steam-engines and telegraphs than the ancients did, the latter knew more about the powers that move the world, and about the communication of thought at a distance without the employment of visible means. If the anatomist of today knows more about the details of the anatomy of the physical body than the ancients, the ancients knew more about the attributes and the constitution of that power which organises the physical body, and of which the latter is nothing more than the objective and visible representative. Modern science may be successful in producing external appearances or manifestations with which the ancients were not acquainted; the initiates into ancient sciences could create internal causes of which modern science knows nothing whatever, and which the latter will have to learn if it desires to progress much further. There no resting-place in the evolution of the world. There is only progression and retrogression, rising or falling. If we falter at the door to the realm of the invisible, and dare not enter the temple where the mysterious workshop of Nature exists, we will sink still more into the mire of illusion, and lose still more of the faculties necessary to perceive the things of the soul. A member which not used atrophies; a faculty that is not actively employed is lost. If our whole time and attention is taken up by the illusions of sense, we will lose the power to perceive that which is supersensual; the more we look at the surface, the less will we know of the kernel; the more we sink into matter, the more will we become unconscious of the spirit which is the life of all things.

But, fortunately for humanity, each evil carries its own remedy in its bosom, each action is followed by a reaction, and the progression of the world resembles the movements of a pendulum that swings from one side to the other, while it at the same time moves forward. Ages of bigotry are followed by periods of thought that may end in ages of scepticism; centuries of scientific or religious ignorance, intolerance, and superstition lead to revolutions of thought that may, again, end in atheism and crime; but each swing of the pendulum raises humanity a step higher on the ladder of progression. When it reaches the point of gravity, it would stop unless pushed on by the impulse from one or the other extreme.

It seems that our age is nearing that neutral point again. Blind "Materialism" has expended its powers; it may still have many pretended followers, but very few that believe in it in their hearts. If there were any persons who sincerely believed in it, and followed its teachings to its last logical consequences, they would necessarily end their days in jail or be driven to suicide; but the great majority of the advocates of Materialism like the bigots of old theology, feel and think differently from what they say: they deal out their theories to others, but do not desire to use them themselves. Doubt, the great enemy of true faith, is also the enemy of dogmatic ignorance; it destroys all self-confidence, and therefore impedes not only the power to do good in those that are good, but it also weakens the poison of those that do evil. The eyes of a world that stepped out from a night of bigotry into the light of day were dazzled and blinded for a while by the vain glitter of a pile of rubbish and broken pots that had been collected by the advocates of material science, who palmed it off for diamonds and precious stones; but the world has recovered from the effect of the glare, and realised the worthlessness of the rubbish, and it again seeks for the less dazzling but priceless light of the truth. Treasures that have long been buried and hidden away from the sight of those that were neither able to realise nor to appreciate their value are now brought to light; pearls of ancient wisdom are brought from the East; fountains of knowledge that have been for centuries closed up are again opened, and a flood of light is thrown over things that appeared impossible, mysterious, and occult.

As we dive into the ancient mysteries a new world opens before us. The more we begin to understand the language of the Adepts, the more grows our respect for their wisdom. The more we become able to grasp their ideas, the more grows our conception of man.

The anatomy, physiology, and psychology which they teach make of man something immeasurably greater than the puny and impotent being known to modern science as a compound of bones, muscles, and nerves. Modern science attempts to prove that man is an animal; the teachings of the Adepts show that he may be a god. Modern science invests him with the power to lift his own weight; ancient science invests him with the power to control the destiny of the world. Modern science allows him to live for a very limited number of years; ancient science teaches that he has always existed, and will never cease to exist if he desires to live. Modern science deals with the instrument that the real man uses as long and as often as he comes into relationship with the world of phenomena, and she mistakes that instrument for the man; the Adepts show us the true nature of the essential man, to whom one earthly existence is nothing more than one of the many incidents of his eternal career.

There is an invisible universe within the visible one, a world of causes within the world of effects. There is force within matter, and the two are one, and are dependent for their existence on a third, which is the mysterious cause of their existence. There is a world of soul within a world of matter, and the two are one, and caused by the world of spirit. And within these worlds are other worlds, visible and invisible ones. Some are known to modern science; of others she does not even know that they exist; for, as the material worlds of suns and planets and stars, the worlds of animate and inanimate beings, from man, the lord of creation, down to the microscopic world with its countless inhabitants, can only be seen by him who is in the possession of the powers necessary for their perception, likewise the world of the soul and the realms of the spirit can only be known to him whose inner senses are awakened to life. The things of the body are seen through the instrumentality of the body, but the things of the soul require the power of spiritual perception.

It is very natural that those who have not developed the power of spiritual perception will not believe in its existence, because for them this faculty does not exist. Therefore the outward reasoner is like a man who keeps his eyes closed, and calls for proofs of the existence of that which he cannot see; while he who is able to see with the eye of the soul or the intellect requires no other proof that the things which he sees exist, and he is rightfully entitled to speak authoritatively of his experience in regard to that which is invisible to the majority, just as a man who has returned from a previously unexplored country is entitled to speak authoritatively about the things which he has seen, and to describe his experiences; while, as a matter of course, every listener has the right to accept that which appears to him reasonable, and to reject whatever goes beyond his capacity to understand; but to deny the power of spiritual perception because one does not possess it himself is as foolish and arrogant as if a blind man were to deny to others the power to see.

This power of spiritual perception, potentially contained in every man, but developed in few, is almost unknown to the guardians of science in our modern civilisation, because learning is often separated from wisdom, and the calculating intellect seeking for worms in the dark caverns of the earth cannot see the genius that floats towards the light, and it cannot realise his existence. And yet this ancient science, which the moderns ignore, is perhaps as old as the world. It was known to the ancient prophets, to the Arhats and Rishis of the East, to initiated Brahmins, Egyptians, and Greeks. Its fundamental doctrines are found in the Vedas as well as in the Bible. Upon these doctrines rest the fundaments of the religions of the world. They formed the essence of the secrets that were revealed only to the initiated in the inner temple where the ancient mysteries were taught, and whose disclosure to the vulgar was forbidden under the penalty of torture and death. They were the secrets known to the ancient sages, and to the Adepts and Rosicrucians of the Middle Ages, and upon a partial understanding of their truths rests the system of modern Freemasonry.

But it is a great error to suppose that the secrets of the Alchemists can all be communicated by words or signs, or be explained to any one who may be trusted with them. The rendering of an explanation requires the capacity to understand on the part of the receiver, and where that power is absent all explanations, be they ever so clear, will be in vain. It would be of little use to explain the nature of a palm-tree to an Eskimo, who living among icebergs, never saw a plant, or to describe the construction of a dynamo-machine to an Australian savage. A man entirely ignorant of all spiritual comprehension, however well his intellectuality be developed, will be in the same condition regarding the understanding of spiritual things as the savage in regard to that which belongs to modern civilisation. In the spiritual as well as in the sensual kingdom the perception is first, and then comes the understanding. The greatest mysteries are within our own self. He who knows himself thoroughly knows God and all the mysteries of His nature. The doctrines resulting from true contemplation are not to be confounded with speculative philosophy, that reasons from the known to that which it cannot know, trying by the flickering light of logic to grope its way into the darkness, and to feel the objects which it cannot see. These doctrines were taught by the children of light, who possessed the power to see. Such men were the great religious reformers of all ages, from Confucius and Zoroaster down to Jacob Boehme and Eckartshausen, and their teachings have been verified by every one whose purity of mind and whose power of intellect have enabled him to see and to understand the things of the spirit.

Some of their doctrines refer to morals and ethics, others are of a purely scientific character; but both aspects of their teachings are intimately connected together, because beauty cannot be separated from truth. They both form the two pages of a leaf in the book of universal Nature, whose understanding confers upon the reader not merely opinions but knowledge, and renders him not only learned but illuminated with wisdom.

Among those who have taught the moral aspect of the secret doctrine, there are none greater than Buddha, Plato, and Jesus of Nazareth; of those who have taught its scientific aspect there have been none more profound than Hermes Trismegistus, Sankaracharya, Pythagoras, and Paracelsus. They obtained their knowledge not merely from following the prescribed methods of learning, or by accepting the opinions of the "recognised authorities" of their times, but they studied Nature by her own light, and becoming illuminated by the light of Divine Nature, they became lights themselves, whose rays illuminate the world of mind. What they taught has been to a certain extent verified and amplified by the teachings of Eastern Adepts, but many things about which the latter have to this day kept a well-guarded silence were revealed by Paracelsus three hundred years ago. Paracelsus threw pearls before the swine, and was scoffed at by the ignorant, his reputation was torn by the dogs of envy and hate, and he was treacherously killed by his enemies. But although his physical body returned to the elements out of which it was formed, his genius still lives; and as the eyes of the world become better opened to an understanding of spiritual truths, he appears like a star on the mental horizon, whose light is destined to illuminate the world of occult science, and to penetrate deep into the hearts of the coming generation, to warm the soil out of which the science of the coming century will grow.

Chapter 1: The Life of Paracelsus

The dawn of the sixteenth century called into existence a new era of thought, and was the beginning of the most stupendous and important accomplishments of those times—the reformation of the Church. The world awoke again from its long sleep in mental torpitude during the Middle Ages, and shaking off the incubus of Papal suppression, it breathed freely once more. As the shadows of night fly at the approach of the day, so clerical fanaticism, superstition, and bigotry began to fade away, because Luther, in the name of the Supreme Power of the Universe, spoke again the Divine command: "Let there be light!" The sun of truth began again to rise in the East, and although his light may afterwards have been obscured by the mists and vapours rising from fields on which dogmas and superstitions were undergoing the process of putrefaction, nevertheless it was penetrating enough to extend its beneficial influence over the subsequent hours of that day. It shone through the murky atmosphere of sectarian bigotry, and sent its rays into doubting minds. Free thought and free investigation, having shaken off the chains with which they were bound down for centuries by the enemies of religious liberty, broke the door of their dungeon, and rose again to heaven to drink from the fountain of truth. Free inquiry took the place of blind credulity; reason rose victorious out of its struggle with blind belief in clerical authority. Spirits that had been bound to cold and dead forms were set free, and began to expand and take their natural shapes; and truths that had been monopolised and held captive for centuries by an exclusive caste of priests, became the common property of all that were able to grasp them.

Such a great struggle for liberty on the battlefield of religious thought could not take place without causing a commotion in other departments where mind was at work. In the department of science there could be seen a general struggle of the new against the old, of reason against sophistry, and of young truths against errors that bad become venerable through age. Logic battled against belief in antiquated authorities; and new constellations, composed of stars of the first magnitude, began to rise, sending their rays into the deepest recesses of thought. Luther overthrew the barrier of ecclesiastical hierarchy; Melanchthon and Erasmus liberated speech; Cardanus lifted the veil off the goddess of Nature; an Copernicus, like Joshua of old, bade the sun to stand still, and, obedient to his command, the sun stood still, and the planetery system was seen to move in the grooves in which it was ordained by the wisdom of the Supreme.

One of the greatest and illuminated minds of that age was Philippus Aureolus Theophrastus Bombast, of Hohenheim. He was born November 26 in the year 1493, in the vicinity of a place called Maria-Einsiedeln,[1] being a village about two hours' walk from the city of Zurich, in Switzerland. His father, William Bombast, of Hohenheim, was one of the descendants of the old and celebrated family Bombast, and they were called of Hohenheim after their ancient residence known as Hohenheim, a castle near the village of Plinningen, in the vicinity of Stuttgart, in Würtemberg. He was a relative of the Grand

Master of the Order of the Knights of St. John of these times, whose name was George Bombast of Hohenheim. He established himself, in his capacity of a physician, near Maria-Einsiedeln; and in the year 1492 he married the matron of the hospital belonging to the abbey of that place, and the result of their marriage was Theophrastus, their only child. It may be mentioned that Paracelsus, in consideration of the place of his birth, has also been called Helvetius Eremita, and furthermore we sometimes find him called Germanus, Suevus, and Arpinus. His portrait, in life-size, can still be seen at Salzburg, painted on the wall of his residence (Linzer Street, No. 365, opposite the church of St. Andrew). Other portraits of Paracelsus are to be found in Huser's edition of his works, and in the first volume of Hauber's "Bibliotheca Magica." The head of Paracelsus, painted by Kaulbach in his celebrated picture, at the Museum at Berlin, called "The Age of Reformation," is idealised, and bears little resemblance to the original.

In his early youth Paracelsus obtained instructions in science from his father, who taught to him the rudiments of alchemy, surgery, and medicine. He always honoured the memory of his father, and always spoke in the kindest terms of him, who was not only his father, but also his friend and instructor. He afterwards continued his studies under the tuition of the monks of the convent of St. Andrew—situated in the valley of Savon—under the guidance of the learned bishops, Eberhardt Baumgartner, Mathias Scheydt of Rottgach, and Mathias Schacht of Freisingen. Having attained his sixteenth year, he was sent to study at the University of Basel. He was afterwards instructed by the celebrated Johann Trithemius of Spanheim, abbot of St. Jacob at Würzburg (1461-1516), one of the greatest adepts of magic, alchemy, and astrology, and it was under this teacher that his talents for the study of occultism were especially cultivated and brought into practical use. His love for the occult sciences led him to enter the laboratory of the rich Sigismund Fugger, at Schwatz, in Tyrol, who, like the abbot, was a celebrated alchemist, and able to teach to his disciple many a valuable secret.

Later on, Paracelsus travelled a great deal. He visited Germany, Italy, France, the Netherlands, Denmark, Sweden, and Russia, and it is said that he even went to India, because he was taken prisoner by the Tartars and brought to the Khan, whose son he afterwards accompanied to Constantinople. Every reader of the works of Paracelsus who is also acquainted with the recent revelations made by the Eastern Adepts, cannot fail to notice the similarity of the two systems, which in many respects are almost identical, and it is therefore quite probable that Paracelsus during his captivity in Tartary was instructed in the secret doctrine by the teachers of occultism in the East. The information given by Paracelsus in regard to the sevenfold principles of man, the qualities of the astral body, the earth-bound elementaries, etc., was then entirely unknown in the West; but this information is almost the same as the one given in "Isis Unveiled", "Esoteric Buddhism", and other books recently published, and declared to have been given by some Eastern Adepts. Paracelsus, moreover, wrote a great deal about the Elementals, or spirits of Nature, but in his description of them he substituted for the Eastern terms such as were more in harmony with the German mythological conceptions of the same, for the purpose of bringing these subjects more to the understanding of his countrymen, who were used to the Western method of thought. It is probable that Paracelsus stayed among the Tartars between 1513 and 1521, because, according to Van Helmont's account, he came to

Chapter 1: The Life of Paracelsus

Constantinople during the latter year,[2] and received there the Philosopher's Stone.

The Adept from whom Paracelsus received this stone was, according to a certain *aureum vellus* (printed at Rorschach, 1598), a certain Solomon Trismosinus (or Pfeiffer), a countryman of Paracelsus. It is said that this Trismosinus was also in possession of the Universal Panacea; and it is asserted that he had been seen, still alive, by a French traveller, at the end of the seventeenth century.

Paracelsus travelled through the countries along the Danube, and came to Italy, where he served as an army surgeon in the Imperial army, and participated in many of the warlike expeditions of these times. On these occasions he collected a great deal of useful information, not only from physicians, surgeons, and alchemists, but also by his intercourse with executioners, barbers, shepherds, Jews, gipsies, midwives, and fortune-tellers. He collected useful information from the high and the low, from the learned and from the vulgar, and it was nothing unusual to see him in the company of teamsters and vagabonds, on the highways and at public inns—a circumstance on account of which his narrow-minded enemies heaped upon him bitter reproach and vilifications. Having travelled for ten years—sometimes exercising his art as a physician, at other times teaching or studying alchemy and magic,[3] according to the custom of those days—he returned at the age of thirty-two again to Germany, where he soon became very celebrated on account of the many and wonderful cures which he performed.

In the year 1525 Paracelsus went to Basel; and in 1527, on the recommendation of Oxcolampadius, he was appointed by the City Council a professor of physic, medicine, and surgery, receiving a considerable salary. His lectures were not—like those of his colleagues—mere repetitions of the opinions of Galen, Hippocrates, and Avicenna, the exposition of which formed the sole occupation of the professors of medicine of those times. His doctrines were essentially doctrines of his own, and he taught them independently of the opinions of others, gaining thereby the applause of his students, and horrifying his orthodox colleagues by his contravention of their established custom of teaching nothing but what could be well supported by old and accepted authorities, irrespective of whether or not it was compatible with reason and truth.

He held at the same time the office of city physician, and in that capacity he offered a resolution to the City Council of Basel to the effect that the apothecaries of that city should be subjected to his supervision, and that he should be permitted to examine whether or not the compounders of medicines understood their business, and to ascertain whether they had a sufficient quantity of pure and genuine drugs on hand, so that he might prevent them from asking exorbitant prices for their goods.

The consequence of this measure was, as might have been expected, that he drew upon himself the concentrated hatred of all the druggists and apothecaries; and the other physicians and professors, jealous of his success in teaching medicine and curing diseases, joined in the persecution, under the pretext that his appointment as a professor at the university had been made without their consent, and that Paracelsus was a stranger, of whom "nobody knew where he came from," and furthermore that they did not know whether or not he was "a real doctor." But perhaps all these annoyances and vilifications would have had no serious consequences if he had not made the members of the City Council his enemies by writing a severe publication against a decision which he considered very unjust, and which was rendered in favour of a certain Canonicus Cornelius of Lichtenfels, whom he had saved from death after the latter had been given up to die by the other physicians, and who had acted very ungratefully towards him.

The consequence of his hasty action was, that he had to leave Basel secretly and hurriedly in July 1528, to avoid unpleasant complications.[4]

After this event Paracelsus resumed his strolling life, roaming—as he did in his youth —over the country, living in village taverns and inns, and travelling from place to place.

Numerous disciples followed him, attracted either by a desire for knowledge or by a wish to acquire his art and to use it for their own purposes. The most renowned of his followers was Johannes Oporinus, who for three years served as a secretary and *famulus* to him, and who afterwards became a professor of the Greek language, and a well-known publisher, bookseller, and printer at Basel. Paracelsus was exceedingly reticent in regard to his secrets, and Oporinus afterwards spoke very bitterly against him on that account, and thereby served his enemies. But after the death of Paracelsus he regretted his own indiscretion, and expressed great veneration for him.

Paracelsus went to Colmar in 1528, and came to Esslingen and Nuremberg in the years 1529 and 1530. The "regular physicians" of Nuremberg denounced him a quack, charlatan, and impostor. To refute their accusations he requested the City Council to put some patients that had been declared incurable under his care. They sent him some cases of elephantiasis, which he cured in a short time and without asking any fee. Testimonials to that effect may be found in the archives of the city of Nuremberg.

But this success did not change the fortune of Paracelsus, who seemed to be doomed to a life of continual wanderings. In 1530 we find him at Noerdlingen, Munich, Regensburg, Amberg, and Meran; in 1531 in St Gall, and in 1535 at Zurich. He then went to Maehren, Kaernthen, Krain, and Hongary, and finally landed in Salzburg, to which place he was invited by the Prince Palatine, Duke Ernst of Bavaria, who was a great lover of the secret arts. In that place Paracelsus obtained at last the fruits of his long labours and of a widespread fame.

But he was not destined to enjoy a long time the rest he so richly deserved, because already, on the 24th of September 1541, he died, after a short sickness (at the age of forty-eight years and three days), in a small room of the inn called the "White Horse", near the quay, and his body was buried in the graveyard of St. Sebastian. There is still a mystery in regard to his death, but the most recent investigations go to confirm the statement made by his contemporaries, that Paracelsus during a banquet had been treacherously attacked by the hirelings of certain physicians who were his enemies, and that in consequence of a fall upon a rock, a fracture was produced on his skull, that after a few days caused his death. A German physician, S. Th. von Soemmering, examined the skull of Paracelsus, which on account of its peculiar formation could not easily be mistaken, and noticed a fracture going through the temporal bone, which, by reason of the age and frequent handling of the skull, had become enlarged in size so as to be easily seen, and he believes that such a fracture could only have been produced during the lifetime of Paracelsus, because the bones of a solid but old and desiccated skull would not be likely to separate in that manner.

Certain it is that Paracelsus was not killed on the spot, but that at the time of his death he was in possession of his mental faculties and reasoning powers, as is shown by the documents containing his last will and testament, which were written down on the 20th of September 1541, at noon, in the presence of Melchior Spaech, city-judge of Hallein; Hans Kalbssor, notary-public of Salzburg; and several other persons of prominence.

The bones of Paracelsus were exhumed in the year 1572, at a time when the church was repaired, and reinterred near the back side of the wall that encloses the space in front of the chapel of St. Philippi Neri, an extension of the church of St. Sebastian, where his monument may be seen at the present time. The midst of a broken pyramid of white marble shows a cavity which contains his picture, and above it is a Latin inscription, saying:

> Philippi Theophrasti Paracelsi qui tantam orbis famam ex auro chymico adeptus est effigies et ossa donec rursus circumdabitur pelle sua.—JON. cap. xix.

Below the portrait are the following words:

> Sub reparatione ecclesiae MDCCLXXII, ex sepulchrali tabe eruta heic locata sunt.

The base of the monument contains the following inscription:

> Conditur hic Philippus Theophrastus insignia Medicinae Doctor qui dira illa vulnera Lepram Podagram Hydropsin aliaque insanabilia corporis contagia mirifica arte sustulit et bona sua in pauperes distribuenda locandaque honoravit. Anno MDXXXXL Die xxiv. Septembris vitam cum morte mutavit.

Below this inscription may be seen the coat-of-arms of Paracelsus, representing a beam of silver, upon which are ranged three black balls, and below are the words:

> Pax vivis requies aeterna sepultis.

A translation of the above inscription into German may be seen on a black board on the left side of the monument. The two latter inscriptions have evidently been taken from the original monument, but the one around the portrait was added in 1572.

Thus were the earthly remnants of Paracelsus disposed of; but an old tradition says—and those who are supposed to know confirm the tale—that his astral body having already during physical existence become self-conscious and independent of the physical form, he is now a living Adept, residing with other Adepts of the same Order in a certain place in Asia, from whence he still—invisibly, but nevertheless effectually—influences the minds of his followers, appearing to them occasionally visible and tangible shape.

Paracelsus left very few worldly goods at the time of his death, but the inheritance which he left in the shape of his writings is rich and imperishable. This extraordinary man —one of the most remarkable ones of all times and all peoples—found many enthusiastic followers; but the number of those who envied, and therefore hated, him was still greater. He had many enemies, because he overthrew the customary old-fogeyism of the orthodox physicians and speculative philosophers of his age; he proclaimed new, and therefore unwelcome, ideas; and he defended his mode of thinking in a manner that was rather forcible than polite.

One-sided culture could see in Paracelsus nothing else but an enthusiast, a fanatic, and noise-maker; his enthusiastic followers, on the other hand, looked upon him as a god and a monarch of all mysteries and king of the spirits. It was his destiny to be misjudged by his friends as well as by his enemies, and each side exaggerated his qualities—the one his virtues, the other his faults. He was denounced and vilified by one set of ignoramuses, and his qualities extolled by another, and the two camps roused each other into a frenzy by their inordinate praises and vile denunciations, whose exaggerations were evident to every one but themselves. Those historians who have criticised the character of Paracelsus severely, forgot to take into consideration the customs and fashions of the time in which he lived, the character of his surroundings, and his restless wanderings. Now, as the battle of contending opinions has ceased to rage, we may take a dispassionate view of the past, and after studying his works and the writings of his critics and biographers, we will arrive at the conclusion that he was one of the greatest and most sublime characters of all times. His works contain inexhaustible mines of knowledge and an extraordinary amount of germs out of which great truths may grow if they are attended to by competent cultivators, and a great deal that is at present misunderstood and rejected will by future inquirers be drawn to the light, and be cut into some of the noblest blocks in the spiritual Temple of Wisdom.

The writings of Paracelsus are especially distinguished by the short and concise manner in which his thoughts are expressed. In this regard they may be compared to some of the writings of Thales, Heraclitus, Pythagoras, Anaxagoras, and Hippocrates. There is no ambiguity in his expressions, and if we follow the roads which he indicated, progressing at the same time along the path of physical science, we shall find the richest of treasures buried at the places that he pointed out with his magic wand.

Paracelsus was a Christian in the true meaning of that word, and he always attempted to support the doctrines he taught by citations from the Bible. He asks: "What is a philosophy that is not supported by spiritual (internal) revelation? Moses did not attempt to teach physics; he wrote in a theological sense calculated to impress the feelings and awaken the faith of the simple-minded, and perhaps he may not have understood physics himself. The scientist, unlike the theologian, does not put any trust in his feelings, but believes only in his experiments, because physical science deals with phenomena and not with faith. The Hebrews, moreover, did not know much about natural science, and as a people they have always been more ignorant than others in that respect."

"Faith is a luminous star that leads the honest seeker into the mysteries of Nature. You must seek your point of gravity in God, and put your trust into an honest, divine, sincere, pure, and strong faith, and cling to it with your whole heart, soul, sense, and thought—full of love and confidence. If you possess such a faith, God (Wisdom) will not withhold His truth from you, but He will reveal His works to you credibly, visibly, and consolingly."

"Everything that happens takes place through the will of the Supreme. Conscience is the state which we have received from God, in which we should see our own image, and according to the dictates of which we should act, without attempting to discover reasons in the guidance of our life in regard to morals and virtues. We should do that which our conscience teaches, for no other reason but because our conscience teaches it. He who does not burn himself will not be burned by God, and God provided him with a conscience into which he may put his implicit trust. To learn from others, to accept the opinion of others, to act in a certain manner because others are acting in that way, is temptation.

Therefore faith in the things of the earth should be based upon the holy Scripture and upon the teachings of Christ, and it will then stand upon a firm basis. Therefore we shall put the foundation and the corner-stone of our wisdom upon three principal points, which are: first, Prayer, or a strong desire and aspiration for that which is good. It is necessary that we should seek and knock, and thereby ask the Omnipotent Power within ourselves, and remind it of its promises and keep it awake; and if we do this in the proper form and with a pure and sincere heart, we shall receive that for which we ask, and find that which we seek, and the doors of the Eternal that have been closed before us will be opened, and what was hidden before our sight will come to light. The next point is Faith: not a mere belief into something that may or may not be true, but a faith that is based upon soul-knowledge, an unwavering confidence, a faith that may move mountains and throw them into the ocean, and to which everything is possible, as Christ has Himself testified. The third point is Imagination. If this power is properly kindled in our soul, we will have no difficulty to make it harmonise with our faith. A person who is sunk into deep thought, and, so to say, drowned in his own soul, is like one who has lost his senses, and the world looks upon him as a fool. But in the consciousness of the Supreme he is wise, and he is, so to say, the confidential friend of God, knowing a great deal more of God's mysteries than all those that receive their superficial learning through the avenues of the senses; because he can reach God through his soul, Christ through faith, and attract the Holy Ghost through an exalted imagination. In this way we may grow to be like the apostles, and to fear neither death nor prison, neither suffering nor torture, neither fatigue nor hunger, nor anything else."

But with all his piety Paracelsus was no bigot. He was an enemy of hypocrisy, ceremonial service, and pious ostentation. He says "If you pray publicly, to what purpose will it serve? It will only be the beginning and the cause of idolatry, and therefore it has been prohibited by Christ."

He did not teach that we should ignore or treat with contempt all external forms of religion, and imagine ourselves superior to them; but he taught that we should try to outgrow and rise above all externalism, and become members of the true inner Church of Christ. Therefore he says: "Let us depart from all ceremonies, conjurations, consecrations, etc., and all similar delusions, and put our heart, will, and confidence solely upon the true rock. We must continually knock and remind God in us to fulfill His promises. If this is done sincerely, without hypocrisy, with a true and pious heart, we will then obtain that for which we seek. "If we abandon selfishness, the door (of our higher consciousness) will be opened for us, and that which is mysterious will be revealed." (*Philosophia Occulta*)

"Salvation is not attained by fasting, neither by wearing a particular kind of clothing, nor by beating one's self. Such things are all superstition and hypocrisy. God, from the beginning of the world, has created all things holy and pure, and they need not be consecrated by man. God Himself is holy, and all that He made out of His own holy will is also holy. It is for us, by becoming holy, to recognise the holiness of God in all things." (*Philosophia Occulta*)

During the time of the Reformation, when the mental atmosphere was in a state of great commotion, when everybody contended either for Luther or for the Pope, Paracelsus stood above the quarrelling parties, and rejected all sectarianism, for he said:

"Among all sects there is none which possesses intellectually the true religion. We must read the Bible more with our heart than with our brains, until at some future time the true religion will come into the world." His sympathies, however, went with the liberal Protestants, and he expressed himself in regard to the action of Luther as follows: "The enemies of Luther are to a great extent composed of fanatics, knaves, bigots, and rogues. Why do you call me a 'Medical Luther'? You do not intend to honour me by giving me that name, because you despise Luther. But I know of no other enemies of Luther but those whose kitchen prospects are interfered with by his reforms. Those whom he causes to suffer in their pockets are his enemies. I leave it to Luther to defend what he says, and I shall be responsible for what I may say. Whoever is Luther's enemy will deserve my contempt. That which you wish to Luther you wish also to me; you wish us both to the fire."

Such were the true characteristics of this great man. The accusations brought against him by his opponents show that his faults have been so grossly exaggerated that the very absurdity of the charges brought against him renders such statements incredible and harmless. He has been represented as a drunkard, and this accusation has been based upon a passage occurring in a letter which he wrote to some students of the University of Zurich, and in which he addresses them as *Combibones optimi*. It seems, however, more probable that the partnership in drinking alluded to in this expression was meant to refer to the "wine" of Wisdom rather than to any more material liquid; moreover, the contents of that letter are very serious and pathetic, and show no indication of frivolity or a love for debauch. It has also been ascertained that Paracelsus up to his twentieth year never drank any intoxicating drinks, and even if it should be found that he afterwards drank wine, such a fact could easily be explained by the general custom of those times, according to which even the most honourable and respected persons (Luther included) were in the habit of "drinking each other's health." If we, moreover, take into consideration the quantity and quality of his works, which were all written within a period of time covering fifteen years, we may be permitted to conclude that he could not have accomplished such a work in a state of that continual intoxication in which, according to the statement of his enemies, he must have remained. "Therefore," says Arnold in his "History of Churches and Heretics," (vol. ii. cap. xxii.) "the report is disproved by the fact that a man who is a glutton and a drunkard could not have been in possession of such divine gifts."

Paracelsus has been accused of vanity and boasting, and the fact is, that he was proud of the attributes or accomplishments manifested in him; but he did not glorify his own person, only the spirit that exalted his soul. Seeing himself surrounded by ignorance, misjudged and misrepresented, but conscious of his own strength, he asserted his rights. He maintained that the value of the truths he taught would be appreciated in due time, and his prophecy has proved to be true. It was this consciousness of his superior power that inspired him to exclaim: "I know that the monarchy (of mind) will belong to me, that mine will be the honour. I do not praise myself, but Nature praises me, for I am born of Nature and follow her.[5] She knows me and I know her."

His language is not that of a boaster, but rather that of a general who knows that he will be victorious, when he writes: "After me, ye, Avicenna, Galenus, Rhases, Montagnana, and others! You after me, not I after you, ye of Paris, Montpelier, Suevia,

Meissen, and Cologne; ye of Vienna, and all that come from the countries along the Danube and Rhine, and from the islands of the ocean; you Italy, you Dalmatia, you Sarmatia, Athens, Greece, Arabia, and Israelita! Follow me! It is not for me to follow you, because mine is the monarchy. Come out of the night of ignorance! The time will come when none of you shall remain in his dark corner who will not be an object of contempt to the world, because I shall be the monarch, and the monarchy will be mine."[6]

This is not the language of vanity and self-conceit; it is rather the language either of wisdom or of folly, because extremes resemble each other. Paracelsus was proud of the spirit that spoke through him; but personally he was modest and self-sacrificing, and he well knew that a man would be a useless thing if he were not overshadowed by the spirit of the Supreme. He says: "Remember that God has put a mark upon us, consisting in our shortcomings and diseases, to show to us that we have nothing to pride ourselves about, and that nothing comes within the reach of our full and perfect understanding; that we are far from knowing absolute truth, and that our own knowledge and power amount to very little indeed."

Personal vanity and ostentation were not the elements to be found in the character of Paracelsus—they were the customs of the physicians of that age; but it is a daily occurring fact, that he who exposes and denounces the faults of others appears to the superficial observer as boasting of his own superiority, although no such motive may prompt him. And as Paracelsus was not slow to criticise the ignorance of the "learned", it was necessarily supposed by the vulgar that he looked upon himself as more learned than all others, and they had not the capacity to know whether or not he was justified in such an estimate of himself. He was, however, far superior in medical skill to all his colleagues, and performed apparently miraculous cures among many patients that had been pronounced incurable by the leading doctors—a fact that has been proved by Erasmus of Rotterdam, a most careful and scientific observer. Among such patients were not less than eighteen princes, on whom the best physicians had tried their arts and failed. In his thirty-third year he was already an object of admiration for the laity, and an object of professional jealousy for the physicians. He also incurred the wrath of the latter by treating many of the poorer classes without pay, while the other physicians unrelentingly claimed their fees. The most common reward for his labour was ingratitude, and this he earned everywhere, not only in the houses of the moderately wealthy, but also among the rich; for instance, in the house of the Count Philippus of Baden, whose case had been given up as hopeless by his physicians. Paracelsus cured the count in a short time, who in return showed great penuriousness towards him. Moreover, the ingratitude of that prince caused great joy to the enemies of Paracelsus, and gave them a welcome opportunity to ridicule and slander him more than ever.

Accusations of a different order are brought against him, referring to the bluntness of his style of writing, which was not always refined or polite. It should, however, be remembered that such a style of speaking and writing was universally used in those times, and objectionable expressions were adopted by all, not excluding Luther, the great Reformer, who, in spite of his genius, was a mortal man. Paracelsus was a great admirer of Luther, and even surpassed him in enthusiasm for religious and intellectual freedom. Luther seemed to him to be still too conservative. He believed that such a gigantic revolution in the world of mind could not be accomplished with meekness and condescension, but that it required firmness, tenacity, and an unbending will. He says of himself: "I know that I am a man who does not speak to every one only that which might please him, and I am not used to give submissive answers to arrogant questions. I know my ways, and I do not wish to change them; neither could I change my nature. I am a rough man, born in a rough country; I have been brought up in pine woods and I may have inherited some knots. That which seems to me polite and amiable may appear unpolished to another, and what seems silk in my eyes may be but homespun to you."

Great abuse has been heaped upon Paracelsus by his enemies on account of his restless and roaming way of living. He acquired his knowledge, not in the comfortable manner in which the great majority of scientists acquire theirs, but he travelled all over the country on foot, and went wherever he expected to find something that might be useful to know. He writes: "I went in search of my art, often incurring danger of life. I have not been ashamed to learn that which seemed useful to me even from vagabonds, executioners, and barbers. We know that a lover will go a long way to meet the woman he adores: how much more will the lover of wisdom be tempted to go in search of his divine mistress!" (*Paragranum:* Preface)

He says: "The knowledge to which we are entitled is not confined within the limits of our own country, and does not run after us, but waits until we go in search of it. No one becomes a master of practical experience in his own house, neither will he find a teacher of the secrets of Nature in the corners of his room. We must seek for knowledge where we may expect to find it, and why should the man be despised who goes in search of it? Those who remain at home may live more comfortably, and grow richer than those who wander about; but I neither desire to live comfortably, nor do I wish to become rich. Happiness is better than riches, and happy is he who wanders about, possessing nothing that requires his care. He who wants to study the book of Nature must wander with his feet over its leaves. Books are studied by looking at the letters which they contain; Nature is studied by examining the contents of her treasure-vaults in every country. Every part of the world represents a page in the book of Nature, and all the pages together form the book that contains her great revelations."

So little has Paracelsus been understood by the profane, that even to this day he is supposed to have advocated the very superstitions which he tried to destroy. For instance, far from encouraging the superstitious practices of the star-gazers, he says: "The planets and stars on the sky neither build up a man's body, nor do they endow him with virtues and vices, or any other qualities whatsoever. The course of Saturn lengthens or shortens nobody's life; and although Nero was of a martial temperment, he was not the child of Mars, nor Helena the daughter of Venus. If there had never been any moon on the sky, there would be nevertheless people inclined to lunacy. The stars force us to nothing, they incline us to nothing; they are free for themselves, and we are free for ourselves. It is said that a wise man rules over the stars; but this does not mean that he rules over the stars in the sky, but over the powers that are active in his own mental constitution, and which are symbolised by the visible stars in the sky." (*Philosophia Occulta*)

Paracelsus did not read or write much. He says that for ten years he never read a book, and his disciples testify that he dictated his works to them without using any memoranda or manuscripts. On taking an inventory of his goods after his death, a Bible, a Biblical Concordance, a Commentary to the Bible, and a written book on Medicine were all the books that could be found in his possession. Even earlier than Luther, he had publicly burned a Papal bull, and with it the writings of Galen and Avicenna. He says: "Reading never made a physician. Medicine is an art, and requires practice. If it were sufficient to learn to talk Latin, Greek, and Hebrew to become a good physician, it would also be sufficient for one to read Livius to become a great commander-in-chief. I began to study my art by imagining that there was not a single teacher in the world capable to teach it to me, but that I had to acquire it myself. It was the book of Nature, written by the finger of God, which I studied—not those of the scribblers, for each scribbler writes down the rubbish that may be found in his head; and who can sift the true from the false? My accusers complain that I have not entered the temple of knowledge through the 'legitimate door'. But which one is the truly legitimate door? Galenus and Avicenna or Nature? I have entered through the door of Nature: her light, and not the lamp of an apothecary's shop, has illuminated my way."

Great stress was laid by his accusers upon the fact that he wrote the greater part of his books and taught his doctrines in the German language, and not, as was then customary, in Latin. But this was one of his most important acts; because in so doing he produced a reformation in science similar to the one that Luther produced in the Church. He rejected the time-honoured use of the Latin language, because he believed that the truth could as well be expressed in the language of the country in which he lived. This daring act was the beginning of free thought in science, and the old belief in authorities began to weaken. It is probable that Paracelsus would never have attained his knowledge if he had permitted his mind to be fettered and imprisoned by the idle formalities that were connected with a scientific education at that time.

Here it may not be improper to add a few opinions concerning Theophrastus Paracelsus from persons of repute:

Jordanus Brunus says: "The highest merit of Paracelsus is, that he was the first to treat medicine as a philosophy, and that he used magical remedies (hypnotism, suggestion, etc.) in cases where the physical substances were not sufficient."

J. B. van Helmont: "Paracelsus was a forerunner of the true medicine. He was sent by God, and endowed with divine knowledge. He was an ornament for his country, and all that has been said against him is not worthy to be listened to."

Opposed to this there are the opinions of certain "authorities", whose memory does not longer exist, but who may be quoted as specimens of learned ignorance:

Libanius: "Opera Paracelsi sunt cloaca, monstrosa, jactantia rudiate, temeritate conflata."

K. G. Neumann: "No one can take up a book of Theophrastus without becoming convinced that the man was insane."

Very recently one medical authority, while acknowledging publicly the high merits of Paracelsus, said that the consequence of the promulgation of his doctrines was the growth of a sickly mysticism. This may be true, but Paracelsus cannot be blamed for the inability of those who do not understand him; we may just as well make Jesus Christ responsible for the introduction of the Inquisition and other follies that arose from a misinterpretation of what He taught.

It is true that it is very difficult, if not altogether impossible, to understand the writings of Paracelsus without possessing a certain amount of spiritual insight and intuition. The writings of Paracelsus deal especially with metaphysical and not with corporeal things. Thus, for instance, when he speaks of "Sulphur", he, like other Alchemists of his times, refers to a certain active energy or form of the will, for which even modern science has not yet invented a name, and for which the term "Sulphur" is a symbol, in the same sense as "Mercury" is a symbol for intelligence, "Salt" for substance, "Venus" for love, and so forth. One would therefore vainly inquire at the chemist's shop for the "sulphur" of Paracelsus, for he says: "If any one wanted to thoroughly describe the sulphur, and if it were proper to do so, which it is not, paper alone would not be sufficient for that purpose. To the sulphur belongs a good worker and artist, well experienced and capable to think profoundly; not a mere talker and theorist, who is only great in preaching but does not act. He who knows how to use the sulphur (his own power) will be able to produce more miracles than I can describe. He who does not know the sulphur knows nothing, and can accomplish nothing, neither of medicine nor of philosophy, nor about any of the secrets of Nature." (*Vom Schwefel*, vol. vii. p. 182)

This is merely to show that the language of Paracelsus has to be taken in an allegorical and mystical sense, which was well understood by the Alchemists of his time, but for which modern erudition has no comprehension; because with the knowledge of spiritual mysteries and secret powers of Nature, the meaning of the symbols representing those things has also been lost. It is therefore not surprising to see that Paracelsus is very little understood even by his admirers, and that the majority of his researchers seem to be far more concerned about his person than about his philosophy.

Moreover, Paracelsus uses a terminology of his own. He deals in his writings with many subjects, for which his language had no appropriate terms.[7] He therefore invented a great many words of his own to express his meaning, and only few of his words have obtained the right of citizenship in our language. To facilitate the study of the works of Paracelsus, his disciples, Gerhard Dorn, Bernhard Thurneyssen, and Martin Ruland, composed dictionaries to explain the meaning of such curious terms. The one compiled by Ruland, entitled "Lexicon Alchemicum" (Prague, 1612), is the most complete. Guilhelmus Johnson published the same under his own name at London in 1660, and it has been incorporated into the greatest collection of alchemical writings, the "Bibliotheca Chymica Curiosa," by J. T. Mangets (Geneva, 1702). Another "Dictionarium Paracelsicum" was written by a certain Bailiff, and added to the Geneva publication. But as all these books have become very rare, and can only be obtained with difficulty and at a great expense, we therefore add below a complete list of his favourite terms, for the benefit of those who may wish to read his complete works.

The Writings of Paracelsus

Paracelsus wrote personally not a great deal. He usually dictated that which he desired to be put into writing to his disciples. The greatest part of his works is therefore in the handwriting of his disciples. Few of the works of Paracelsus were printed during his lifetime. Those that were printed consist of his seven books, "De Gradibus et Compositionibus

Receptorum et Naturalium," Basel, 1526; and of his "Chirurgia Magna," printed at Ulm, 1536. The rest of his writings did not become known publicly until after his death, and it is to be regretted that his disciples and followers—such as Adam von Bodenstein, Alexander von Suchten, Gerhard Dorn, Leonhard Thurneyssen, Peter Severinus, Oswald Crall, Melchior Schennemann, and others—delivered them in such a state of confusion to the printer, that frequently entire pages were missing, and it was very difficult to put those that were to be had into some order.

Separate editions of the works of Paracelsus were published by Hieronymus Feierabend in Frankfurt, by Arnold Byrkmann in Cologne, and by Peter Barna in Basel. Simultaneously a great many spurious prints and writings, falsely attributed to Paracelsus, were put into circulation, as appears from a note by Antiprassus Siloranus, who says that Paracelsus wrote 35 books on Medicine, 235 on Philosophy, 12 on Politics, 7 on Mathematics, and 66 on Necromancy. If we remember that Paracelsus was engaged in literary labours for only fifteen years, it appears self-evident that Siloranus referred in his note to all the books and papers that were put into circulation, and attributed to Paracelsus by the public.

John Huser, doctor of medicine at Grossglogau, undertook a critical examination of such works, on the request of the Archbishop Prince Ernst of Cologne. He collected with great labour all the autographs of Paracelsus and the original manuscripts of his disciples, such as could be found; he put them into order, and revised and published them at Cologne in a general edition during the years 1589 and 1590. That collection contains the following works:

I. WORKS ON MEDICINE.

1. Paramirum de Quinque Entibus Omnium Morborum (Paramirum of the Five Causes of Disease). (*Autograph of Paracelsus*)
2. Opus Paramirum Secundum (2 Second Book, Paramiruno). (*Autograph.*)
3. Liber de Generatione Hominis (Book of the Generation of Man).
4. Liber Paragranum (Paragranum). (*Autograph.*)
5. Liber Paragranum Secundum (Paragranum, Second Book. (*Autograph.*)
6. Chronica des Landes Kaernthen (History of the Country of Kaernthen).
7. Defensiones und Verantwortung wegen etlicher Verunglimpfung seiner Misgoenner (Defence and Answer respecting some Misrepresentations made by his Enemies).
8. Labyrintbus medicorum errantium (The Labyrinth of the Wandering Physician).
9. Das Buch vom Tartaro, das ist vom Ursprung des Sands und Steins (The Book of Tartarus—i.e., of the Origin of Stones in the Bladder).
10. Epistel der Landschaft Kaernthen an Theophrastum (Letter of the Country of Kaernthen to Theophrast).
11. De viribus membrorum (Of Organic Powers).
12. De primis tribus essentiis (Of the Three First Elements).
13. Vom Ursprung und Heilung der natuerlichen Pestilenz (Of the Cause and Cure of the Ordinary Pest).
14. Ein Buechlein von der Pestilenz an dir Stadt Sterzingen (Letter about the Pest to the Town of Sterzingen).

15. Zwei Buecher vom Ursprung und Ursach der Pest (Two Books on the Cause and Origin of the Pest).
16. Drei andere Buecher von der Pestilenz (Three more Books on the Pest).
17. Eltiche Collectanea de Peste (Collections of Notes on the Pest). (*Autograph.*) (*MS. of Montanus.*)
18. De Morbis ex Tartaro oriundis (On Diseases coming from the Tartarus). (*MS. of Montanus.*)
19. Theophrasti Epistola ad Erasmum Rotterdamum (Theophrastus' Letter to Erasmus of Rotterdam). (*MS. of Montanus.*)
20. Erasmi Rotterdami Responsio (His Answer). (*MS. of Montanus.*)
21. Liber de Teteriis (Book on Jaundice). (MS. of Montanus.)
22. Liber quatuordecim paragraphorum (Book of Fourteen Paragraphs). (*Autograph of Paracelsus.*)
23. Von den tartarischen Krankheiten (On Tartaric Diseases). (*Autograph of Paracelsus.*)
24. Von den Krankheiten die den Menschen der Vernunft herauben (On Diseases causing Insanity). (*Autograph of Paracelsus.*)
25. Von Krummen und lahmen Gliedern (On Contracted and Paralysed Members). (*Autograph of Paracelsus.*)
26. Von den astralischen Krankheiten (Diseases caused by Astral Influences). (*Autograph of Paracelsus.*)
27. Vom Padagra (On Gout). (Autograph of Paracelsus.)
28. Andere zwei Buecher vom Podagra (Two more Books on Gout). (*Print.*)
29. Vom Ursprung, Ursach und Heilung des Morbi Caduci und Epilepsy (On the Cause, Origin, and Cure of Nervous Diseases and Epilepsy). (*MS.*)
30. De Caduco matricis (On Displacements of the Uterus). (*MS.*)
31. Von den Bergkrankheiten (Diseases in Mountainous Regions). (*MS.*)
32. Theorica Schemata seu Typi (On Types of Diseases). (*Autograph.*)
33. Practicae particularis sen Curationis morborum Tartareonum (Cure of Tartaric Diseases). (*Fragment.*)
34. Etliche Consilia Medica (Some Written Consultations). (*MS.*)
35. Etliche Fragmenta Medical (Medical Fragments). (*MS.*)
36. De Sanitate et Aegritudine (Health and Disease). (*Autograph.*)
37. De Stercore et Aegritudinibus en hoc oreundis (Excrementive Substances and Diseases caused by them). (*Autograph.*)
38. De anatomia oculorumm et eorum affectionibus (The Eye: Its Anatomy and Diseases). (*Autograph.*)
39. Auslegung primae sectionis Aphorismorum Hippocrates (Explanation of the First Sections of Hippocrates' Aphorisms). (*Sources not mentioned.*)
40. De modo phlebotomandi (How to Let Blood). (*Sources not mentioned.*)
41. De urinis et pulsibus (Diagnostics from Urine and Pulse). (*Sources not mentioned.*)
42. De modo pharmacandi (Pharmaceutics). (*Sources not mentioned.*)
43. Archidoxorum Libri X (The Book of Archidoxes). (*Autograph.*)
44. De Renovatione (Renewal). (*Autograph.*)

45. De Vita longa (Long Life). (*German.*) (*Autograph.*)
46. De Vita longa (Ditto). (*Latin.*)
47. Some fragments in German (Various Fragments). (*MS.*)
48. De praeparationibus libri duo (Preparations of the Second Book). (*MS.*)
49. Process den Spiritum Vitrioli zu machen (How to make Spirit of Vitriol). (*MS.*)
50. De natura rerum (The Essential Nature of Things). (*MS.*)

II. ALCHEMY.

51. De Tinctura Physica ("Curative Tincture"). (*MS.*)
52. Liber Vexationum (Vexations). (*MS.*)
53. Thesaurus Alchemistarum (Alchemical Treasures). (*MS.*)
54. De Cementis (Cements). (*Autograph.*)
55. Cementum super Venerem et Marte (A Cement for Venus and Mars). (*Autograph.*)
56. Das Manuale de Lapide Philosophorum (Manual of the Philosopher's Stone). (*MS.*)
57. Ratio extrahendi ex omnibus metallis Mercurium, Sulphur, et Crocum (How to Extract of all Metals their Mercury, Sulphur, and Crocus). (*MS.*)
58. Intimatio Theophrasti (Advice of Theophrastus). (*MS. of Aporinus.*)

III. VARIOUS WRITINGS

59. De gradibus rerum naturalium (Of the Various Grades of Things). (*MS. of Aporinus.*)
60. Herbarius (On Plants). (*Autograph.*)
61. Von den fuenf natuerlichen Dingen (On the Five Natural Things). (*Autograph.*)
62. Zwei Tractate vom Terpenthin und Honig (Two Tracts on Turpentine and Honey). (*MS. of Montanus.*)
63. Vom Ebenholz, von Bruechen und Praeparation der Mumie (Ebony-Wood, Ruptures, Preparation of the Mumia). (*MS. of Montanus.*)
64. De virtutibus herbarum (The Virtues of Plants). (*MS. of Aporinus.*)
65. Liber Principiorum (The Books of Beginnings). (*MS. of Montanus.*)
66. De Thermis (Mineral Springs). (*MS. of Oporinus.*)
67. Vom Bade Pfeffers (The Baths of Pfeffers). (*MS. of Montanus.*)
68. De gradibus et compositionibus (Gradations and Compositions). (*MS. of Montanus.*)
69. Scholia in libros de gradibus (Remarks about Gradations). (*MS. of Montanus.*)
70. Fragmenta (Fragments).
71. Fragmenta aliquod de re Herbaria (Fragments treating of Plants). (*Autograph.*)

IV. NATURAL HISTORY AND PHILOSOPHY.

72. Philosophia ad Athenienses (Letters to the Athenians). (*Print.*)
73. Opus anatomicum (Anatomy). (*Autograph.*)
74. Philosophia degenerationibus et fructibus quatuor elementarum (Doctrine of the Products and Fruits of the Four Elements). (*Print.*)
75. Philosophia de generatione hominis (On the Generation of Man). (*Print.*)
76. De meteoris (Meteors). (*Autograph.*)

77. Aliud opusculum de meteoris (More about Meteors). (*Autograph.*)
78. Liber meteorum tertius (Third Book on Meteors). (*MS. of Montanus.*)
79. De generatio metallorum (The Generation of Metals). (*Ditto.*)
80. Von den natuerlichen Waeasern (Natural (Thermal) Springs).

V. MAGIC.

81. De divinibus operibus et secretis naturae (The Divine Works and Secrets of Nature). (*Autograph.*)
82. De sagis earumque operibus (Sorcerers and Witches and their Arts). (*Autograph.*)
83. De Daemonicis et Obsessis (Devils and Obsessions). (*Autograph.*)
84. De somniis (Dreams). (*Autograph.*)
85. De sanguine ultra mortem (The State of the Blood after Death). (*Autograph.*)
86. De animalium hominum post mortem apparentibus (Souls of Men appearing after Death). (*Autograph.*)
87. De virtute imaginativa (The Virtue of Imagination). (*Autograph.*)
88. De characteribus (Characters). (*Autograph.*)
89. De Homunculis et Monstris (Homunculi and Monsters). (*Autograph.*)
90. De Philosophia occulta (Occult Philosophy). (*MS. of Montanus.*)
91. De Imaginationibus (Imaginations). (*MS. of Montanus.*)
92. Philosophia Paracelsi (The Philosophy of Paracelsus). (*MS. of Montanus.*)
93. Vom Fundamente und Ursprung der Weisheit und Kuenste (The Foundation and Origin of Wisdom and Arts). (*Other Manuscript.*)
94. Fragmenta (Fragments). (*Other Manuscript.*)
95. Philosophia sagax (Critical Philosophy). (*Other Manuscript.*)
96. Erklaerung der ganzen Astronomie (Explanation of Astronomy). (*MS. of Montanus.*)
97. Practica in Scientiam Divinationis (Instructions in the Science of Divination). (*Autograph.*)
98. Erklaerung der natuerlichen Astronomie (Natural Astronomy). (*Autograph.*)
99. Fragmenta (Fragments). (*Autograph.*)
100. Das Buch Azoth seu de ligno Vitae (The Book Azoth, or the Tree of Life). (*Ms.*)
101. Archidoxes Magicae (seven books) (Fundamental Doctrines of Magic). (*Ms.*)
102. Auslegung von 30 magischen Figuren (Explanation of Thirty Magic Figures). (*Autograph.*)
103. Prognostication zukuenftiger Geschichten auf 24 Jahre (Prophecies for Twenty-four Years). (*Print.*)
104. Vaticinium Theophrasti (The Predictions of Theophrast). (*MS. of Montanus.*)
105. Verbesserte Auslegung Theophrasti (Explanations). (*MS. of Montanus.*)
106. Fasciculus Prognosticationum Astrologicarum (Astrological Predictions).

Chapter 2: Explanation's of Terms Used by Paracelsus

Including some other Terms frequently used by Writers on Occultism.

"Since the days of the unlucky medieval philosophers, the last to write upon these secret doctrines of which they were the depositaries, few men have dared to brave persecution and prejudice by placing their knowledge upon record. And these few have never as a rule written for the public, but only for those of their own and succeeding times who possessed the key to their jargon. The multitude, not understanding them or their doctrines, have been accustomed to look upon them as either charlatans or dreamers."—H. P. Blavatsky: *Isis Unveiled*, vol. i.

A

ABESSI, or REBIS.—Refuse; dead matter; excrementitious substances.

ADECH.—The inner (spiritual) man; the lord of thought and imagination, forming subjectively all things in his mind, which the exterior (material) man may objectively reproduce. Either of the two acts according to his nature, the invisible in an invisible, and the visible one in a visible manner, but both act correspondingly. The outer man may act what the inner man thinks, but thinking is acting in the sphere of thought, and the products of thought are transcendentally substantial, even if they are not thrown into objectivity on the material plane. The inner man is and does what he desires and thinks. Whether or not his good or evil thoughts and intentions find expression on the material plane is of less importance to his own spiritual development than to others who may be affected by his acts, but less by his thoughts.

ADMISURAL.—Earth (literally and allegorically).

ADROP, AZANE, or AZAR.—"The Philosopher's Stone." This is not a stone in the usual sense of that term, but an allegorical expression, meaning the principle of wisdom on which the philosopher who has obtained it by practical experience (not the one who is merely speculating about it) may fully rely, as he would rely on the value of a precious stone, or as he would trust to a solid rock upon which to build the foundation of his (spiritual) house.

ACTHNA.—An invisible, subterrestrial fire, being the matrix from which bituminous substances take their origin, and sometimes producing volcanic eruptions. It is a certain state of the "soul" of the earth, a mixture of astral and material elements, perhaps of an electric or magnetic character.[1]

ACTHNICI.—Elemental spirits of fire; spirits of Nature. They may appear in various shapes, as fiery tongues, balls of fire, etc. They are sometimes seen in "spiritual stances."[2]

A'KASA.—An Eastern term. Living primordial substance, corresponding to the conception of some form of cosmic ether pervading the solar system. Everything visible is, so to say, condensed A'kasa, having become visible by changing its supra-ethereal state into a concentrated and tangible form, and everything in nature may be resolved again into A'kasa, and be made invisible, by changing the attractive power that held its atoms together into repulsion; but there is a tendency in the atoms that have once constituted a form, to rush together again in the previous order, and reproduce the same form; and a form may therefore, by making use of this law, be apparently destroyed and then reproduced. This tendency rests in the character of the form preserved in the Astral Light.

ALCAHEST.—An element which dissolves all metals, and by which all terrestrial bodies may be reduced into their *Ens primum*, or the original matter (A'kasa) of which they are formed. It is a power which acts upon the Astral forms (or souls) of all things, capable of changing the polarity of their molecules, and thereby to dissolve them. The power of Will is the highest aspect of the true Alcahest. In its lowest aspect it is a visible fluid able to dissolve all things, not yet known to modern chemistry.

ALCHEMY.—A science by which things may not only be decomposed and recomposed (as is done in chemistry), but by which their essential nature may be changed and raised higher, or be transmuted into each other. Chemistry deals with dead matter alone, but Alchemy uses life as a factor. Everything is of a threefold nature, of which its material and objective form is its lowest manifestation. There is, for instance, immaterial spiritual gold, ethereal fluid and invisible astral gold, and the solid visible, material and earthly gold. The two former are, so to say, the spirit and soul of the latter, and by employing the spiritual powers of the soul we may induce changes in them that may become visible in the objective state. Certain external manipulations may assist the powers of the soul in their work; but without the possession of the latter the former will be perfectly useless. Alchemical processes can therefore only be successfully undertaken by one who is an Alchemist by birth or by education. Everything being of a threefold nature, there is a threefold aspect of Alchemy. In its higher aspect it teaches the regeneration of the spiritual man, the purification of the mind, thought, and will, the ennobling of all the faculties of the soul. In its lowest aspect it deals with physical substances, and as it leaves the realm of the living soul, and steps down to hard matter, it ends in the science of modern chemistry of the present day.

ALCOL.—The substance of a body free from all earthly matter; its ethereal or astral form.

ALUECH.—The pure spiritual body (the Atma).

ANATOMY.—The knowledge of the parts of which a thing is composed; not merely of its physical organs and limbs, but of its elements and principles. Thus the knowledge of the sevenfold constitution of the universe embraces the anatomy of the Macrocosm.

ANIADUS.—The spiritual activity of things.

ANIADUM.—The spiritual (re-born) man; the activity of man's spirit in his mortal body; the Seat of Spiritual Consciousness.

ANIADA.—The activities that are caused by astral influences, celestial powers; the activity of imagination and phantasy.

ANYODEL.—The spiritual life; the subjective state into which the higher essence of the soul enters after death, and after having lost its grosser parts in Kama-loca. It corresponds to the conception of Devachan.

AQUASTOR.—A being created by the power of the imagination—i.e., by a concentration of thought upon the A'kasa by which an ethereal form may be created (Elementals, Succubi and Incubi, Vampires, etc.). Such imaginary but nevertheless real forms may obtain life from the person by whose imagination they are created, and under certain circumstances they may even become visible and tangible.

ARCHATES, or ARCHALLES.—The element of the mineral kingdom.

ARCHAEUS.—The formative power of Nature, which divides the elements and forms them into organic parts. It is the principle of life; the power which contains the essence of life and character of everything.

ARES.—The spiritual principle; the cause of the specific character of each thing.

ASTRA.—States of mind, either in the mind of man or in the universal mind. Each mental state in the mind of man corresponds to a similar condition in the mental atmosphere of the world, and as the mind of man acts upon the universal mind, so that mental atmosphere reacts upon him.

ASTRAL BODY.—The invisible ethereal body of man or of any other thing; the physical form being merely the material expression of the astral body, which builds up the external form.

ASTRAL LIGHT.—The same as the Archaeus. A universal and living ethereal element, still more ethereal and highly organised than the A'kasa. The former is universal, the latter only cosmic—viz., pertaining to our solar system. It is at the same time an element and a power, containing the character of all things. It is the storehouse of memory for the great world (the Macrocosm), whose contents may become re-embodied and reincarnated in objective forms; it is the storehouse of memory of the little world, the Microcosm of man, from which he may recollect past events. It exists uniformly throughout the interplanetary spaces, yet it is more dense and more active around certain objects on account of their molecular activity, especially around the brain and spinal cord of human beings, which are surrounded by it as by an aura of light It is this aura around the nerve-cells and nerve-tubes by which a man is enabled to catch impressions made upon the astral aura of the cosmos, and thereby to "read in the Astral Light". It forms the medium for the transmission of thought, and without such a medium no thought could be transferred to a distance. It may be seen by the clairvoyant, and as each person has an astral aura of his own, a person's character may be read in his Astral Light by those who are able to see it. In the case of a child who has not yet generated any special characteristics, that emanating aura is milk-white; but in the adult there is always upon this fundamental colour another one, such as blue, green, yellow, red, dark-red, and even black. Every living nerve has its astral aura, every mineral, every plant or animal, and everything of life, and the glorified body of the spirit is made to shine by its light.

ASTROLOGY.—The science of the "stars"; i.e., of the mental states in the mind. It is not to be confounded with modern physical astronomy.

ASTRUM.—This term is frequently used by Paracelsus, and means the same as Astral Light, or the special sphere of mind belonging to each individual, giving to each thing its own specific qualities, constituting, so to say, its world.

AVITCHI.—An Eastern term. A state of ideal spiritual wickedness; a subjective condition; the antitype of Devachan or Anyodei.

AZOTH.—The creative principle in Nature; the universal panacea or spiritual life-giving air. It represents the Astral Light in its aspect as the vehicle of the universal essence of life; in its lowest aspect the electrifying power of the atmosphere—Ozone, Oxygen, etc.

B

BERYLLUS.—A magic mirror or crystal in whose Astral aura apparitions may be seen by the clairvoyant. *Berillistica ars:* art of divining by means of seeing in crystals, magic mirror, flowing water, looking into cups, into stones, etc., all of which methods are calculated to render the mind passive, and thereby to enable it to receive the impressions that the Astral light may make upon the mental sphere of the individual by detracting the attention from external and sensual things, the inner man is made conscious and receptive for its subjective impressions.

BRUTA.—Astral force manifested in animals; second sight in animals; power of animals to discover instinctively poisonous or curative medicines, etc.

C

CABALLI, CABALES, LEMURES.—The astral bodies of men who died a premature death—that is to say, who were killed or killed themselves before their natural term of life was over. They may be more or less self-conscious and intelligent, according to the circumstances in which they lived and died. They are the earth-bound suffering souls of the dead, wandering in the sphere of the earth's attraction (Kania-loca) until the time arrives when they would have died according to natural law, when the separation of their higher principles from the lower ones takes place. They imagine to perform bodily actions, while in fact they have no physical bodies, but act in their thoughts; but their bodies appear to them as real as ours appear to us. They may under certain necessary conditions communicate with man through "mediums", or directly through a man's own mediumistic organisation.

CHAOMANTIA.—Divination by aerial visions; clairvoyance; second sight.

CHERIO.—"Quint-essence." The essence or fifth principle of a thing; that which constitutes its essential qualities, freed of all impurities and non-essentials.

CLISSUS.—The hidden specific power contained in all things; the life-force which in vegetables mounts from the roots into the trunk, leaves, flowers, and seeds, causing the latter to produce a new organism.

CORPUS INVISIBILE.—The invisible body; the animal soul (Kama rupa); the medium between material forms and the spiritual principle; a substantial, ethereal, but under ordinary circumstances invisible thing; the lower astral form.

CORPORA SUPERCOELESTIA. Forms that can only be seen by the highest spiritual perception; they are not ordinary astral forms, but the refined and intelligent elements of the same.

D

DERSES.—An occult exhalation of the earth, by means of which plants are enabled to grow. Carbonic acid gases, etc., are its vehicles.

DEVACHAN.—An Eastern term. A subjective state of happiness of the higher principles of the soul after the death of the body. (See ANYODEI.) It corresponds to the idea of Heaven, where each individual monad lives in a world which it has created by its own thoughts, and where the products of its own spiritual ideation appear substantial and objective to it.

DIVINATO.—The act of foreseeing future events by means of the soul's own light; prophecy.

DIVERTELLUM.—The matrix of the elements, from which the latter generated.[3]

DURDALES.—Substantial but invisible beings, residing in trees (Dryades); elemental spirits of nature.

E

EDELPHUS.—One who divines from the elements of the air, earth, water, or fire.

ELEOTRUM MAGICUM.—A composition of seven metals, compounded according to certain rules and planetary influences; a preparation of great magic power, of which magic rings, mirrors, and many other things may be made.

ELEMENTALS.—Spirits of Nature. Substantial but (for us) invisible beings of an ethereal nature, living in the elements of air, water, earth, or fire. They have no immortal spirits, but they are made of the substance of the soul, and are of various grades of intelligence. Their characters differ widely. They represent in their natures all states of feeling. Some are of a beneficial and others of a malicious nature.

ELEMENTARIES.—The astral corpses of the dead, from which the spiritual part has departed, but in which, nevertheless, intellectual activity may have remained; the ethereal counterpart of the once living person, which will sooner or later be decomposed into its astral elements, as the physical body is dissolved into the elements to which it belongs. These elementaries have under normal conditions no consciousness of their own; but they may receive vitality from a mediumistic person, and thereby for a few minutes be, so to say, galvanised back into life and (artificial) consciousness, when they may speak and act and apparently remember things as they did during life. They very often take possession of Elementals, and use them as masks to represent deceased persons and to mislead the credulous. The Elementaries of good people have little cohesion and evaporate soon; those of wicked persons may exist a long time; those of suicides, etc., have a life and consciousness of their own as long as the division of principles has not taken place.[4] These are the most dangerous.

ELEMENTUM.—The invisible element or basic principle of all substances that may be either in a solid (earthly), liquid (watery), gaseous (airy), or ethereal (fiery) state. It does not refer to the so-called simple bodies or elements in chemistry, but to the invisible basic substance out of which they are formed.

ERODINIUM.—A pictorial or allegorical representation of some future events; visions and symbolic dreams that may be produced in various ways. There are three classes of dreams from which may arise four more mixed states of dreams. The three pure classes are: 1. Dreams that result from physiological conditions; 2. Dreams that result from psychological conditions and astral influences; 3. Dreams that are caused by spiritual agency. Only the latter are worthy of great consideration, although the former may occasionally indicate important changes in the planes to which they belong; for instance, a dream of a nail being driven into the head may predict apoplexy, etc.

EVESTRUM.—The Thought body of Man; his conscious ethereal counterpart, that may watch over him and warn him of the approach of death or of some other danger. The more the physical body is active and conscious of external things, the more is the Thought body stupefied; the sleep of the body is the awakening of the Evestrum. During that state it may communicate with the Evestra of other persons or with those of the dead. It may go to certain distances from the physical body for a short time; but if its connection with that body is broken, the latter dies.

F

FIRMAMENT.—The soul-sphere of the Macrocosmos, respectively that of the Microcosmos.

FLAGAE.—Spirits knowing the secrets of man; familiar spirits; spirits that may be seen in mirrors and reveal secret things.

G

GAMATHEI, or GAMAHEU.—Stones with magic characters and pictures, possessing powers received from astral influences. They may be made by art or in a natural manner. Amulets, charms.

GIGANTES.—Elementals having the human form, but of superhuman size. They live like men, and are mortal, though invisible under ordinary circumstances.

GNOMI, PYGMAEI, CUBITALL.—Little Elementals having the human form and the power to extend their form. They live in the element of the earth, in the interior of the earth's surface, in houses and dwellings constructed by themselves.

H

HOMUNCULI.—Artificially made human beings, generated from the sperm without the assistance of the female organism (Black magic).

HOMUNCULI IMAGUNCULAE.—Images made of wax, clay, wood, etc., that are used in the practice of black magic, witchcraft, and sorcery, to stimulate the imagination and to injure an enemy, or to affect an absent person in an occult manner at a distance.

I

ILECH PRIMUM, ILEIAS, ILEADUS.—The first beginning; primordial power; causation.

ILECH SUPERNATURALE.—The union of the superior and inferior astral influences.

ILECH MAGNUM.—The specific healing power of medicine.

ILECH CRUDUM.—The combination of a body out of its three constituent principles, represented by salt, sulphur, and mercury, or body, soul, and spirit; respectively the elements of earth, water, and fire.

ILEIADES.—The element of the air the vital principle.

ILIASTER.—The hidden power in Nature, by means of which all things grow and multiply; primordial matter; materia prima; A'kasa. *Iliaster primus*: life; the balsam of Nature. *Il. segundus*: the power of life inherent in matter. *Il. tertius*: the astral power of man. *II. quartus:* perfection; the power obtained by the mystic process of squaring the circle.

IMAGINATIO.—The plastic power of the soul, produced by active consciousness, desire, and will.

IMPRESSIONES.—Effects of a passive imagination, which may give rise to various bodily affections, diseases, malformations, stigmata, monsters (hare-lips, acephali, etc.), moles, marks, etc.

INCUBUS and SUCCUBUS.—Male and female parasites growing out of the astral elements of man or woman in consequence of a lewd imagination. 2. Astral forms of dead persons (Elementaries), being consciously or instinctively attracted to such persons, manifesting their presence in tangible if not visible forms, and having carnal intercourse with their victims. 3. The astral bodies of sorcerers and witches visiting men or women for immoral purposes. The Incubus is male, and the Succubus female.

K

KAMA-LOCA.—An Eastern term. Region of Desire. The soul-sphere (third and fourth principle) of the earth not—necessarily on the earth's surface—where the astral remnants of the deceased putrefy and are decomposed. In this region the souls of the deceased that are not pure live (either consciously or in a state of torpor) until their Kama-rupas (bodies of desire) are laid off by a second death, and they themselves having been disintegrated, the division of the higher principles takes place. The lower principles being disposed of, the spirit, with his purified affections and the powers he may have acquired during his earthly existence, enters again into the state of Devachan. Kama-Loca corresponds to the Hades of the Greeks, and to the purgatory of the Roman Catholic Church—the *Limbus*. (See ELEMENTARIES.)

L

LEFFAS. Astral bodies of plants. They may be rendered visible out of the ashes of plants after the latter have been burned. (See PALINGENESIS, in the Appendix.)

LEMURES.—Elementals of the air; Elementaries of the deceased; rapping and tipping spirits, producing physical manifestations.

LIMBUS (*Magnus*).—The world as a whole; the spiritual matrix of the universe; Chaos, in which is contained that out of which the world is made.

M

MAGIC.—Wisdom; the science and art of consciously employing invisible (spiritual) powers to produce visible effects. Will, love, and imagination are magic powers that every one possesses, and he who knows how to develop them and to use them consciously and effectually is a magician. He who uses them for good purposes practices white magic. He who uses them for selfish or evil purposes is a black magician.[5] Paracelsus uses the term Magic to signify the highest power of the human spirit to control all lower influences for the purpose of good. The act of employing invisible powers for evil purposes he calls Necromancy, because the Elementaries of the dead are often used as mediums to convey evil influences. Sorcery is not Magic, but stands in the same relation to Magic as darkness to light. Sorcery deals with the forces of the human and animal soul, but Magic with the supreme power of the spirit.

MAGISTERIUM.—The medicinal virtue of medicinal substances, preserved in a vehicle.

MANGONARIA.—A magic power by which heavy bodies may be lifted without any great physical effort; magical suspension levitation. It is usually accomplished by changing their polarity in regard to the attraction (gravity) of the earth.

MATRICES.—The vehicles of things; elementary bases.

MELOSINAE.—Elemental spirits of water, usually appearing in female forms, but which may also take the forms of fishes or snakes. They have souls, but no spiritual principle; but they may obtain the latter by entering into a union with man. (The fourth principle uniting with the fifth.) The human shape is their true form; their animal forms are assumed. They are also called Undines.

METAPHYSICS.—The science of that which is "supersensual" but not purely spiritual; consequently the knowledge of the astral plane, the ethereal elements in the organism of man and of Nature, the anatomy and physiology of the "inner man," the correlation of spiritual energies, etc. etc.

MACROCOSMOS.—The Universe; the great world, including all visible and invisible things.

MICROCOSMOS.—The little world. Usually applied to Man. A smaller world is a Microcosmos if compared with a larger one. Our Solar System is a Microcosm in comparison with the Universe, and a Macrocosm if compared with the Earth. Man is a Microcosm in comparison with the Earth, and a Macrocosm if compared with an atom of matter. An atom of matter is a Microcosm, because in it are all the potentialities out of which a Macrocosm may grow if the conditions are favourable. Everything contained in a Microcosm in a state of development is contained in the Microcosm in germ.

MONSTRA.—Unnatural—usually invisible beings, that may spring from corruption or from unnatural sexual connection, from the from the effects of a morbid (astral) putrefaction of sperma, or imagination. All such and similar things may pass from the merely subjective into the objective state; because "objective" and "subjective" are relative terms, and refer rather to our capacity to perceive them, than to any essential qualities of their own. What may be merely subjective to a person in one state of existence may be fully objective to one in another state: for instance, in delirium tremens and insanity, subjective hallucinations appear objective to the patient.

MUMIA.—The essence of life contained in some vehicle. (Prana, Vitality; clinging to some material substance.) Parts of the human, animal, or vegetable bodies, if separated from the organism, retain their vital power and their specific action for a while, as is proved by the transplantation of akin, by vaccination, poisoning by infection from corpses, dissection wounds, infection from ulcers, etc. (Bacteria are such vehicles of life.) Blood, excrements, etc., may contain vitality for a while after having been removed from the organism, and there may still exist some sympathy between such substances and the vitality of the organism; and by acting upon the former, the latter may be affected.[6]

MYSTERIUM MAGNUM.—Original matter; the matter of all things; the ultimate essence; essentiality of the inner nature; specific quality of the semi-material part of things. All forms come originally from the Mysterium magnum, and all return to it in the end; the Parabrahman of the Vedantins.

MYSTICISM AND MYSTIC KNOWLEDGE.—Mystical is that which is mysterious and occult, and therefore not generally known. Mysticism generally refers to a morbid craving for gratifying a curiosity to know all about spooks, witchcraft, black magic, etc.; true mystic knowledge is soul-knowledge, and is based upon the development of the power of the soul to distinguish between that which is real, eternal and permanent, and that which is illusive, temporal, and subject to change.

N

NECROCOMICA.—Visions of future events in the air.

NECROMANTIA.—Sorcery; witchcraft; the art of employing the unconscious Elementaries of the dead by infusing life into them, and employing them for evil purposes.

NECTROMANTIA (NECTROMANCY).—The perception of the interior (the soul) of things; psychometry; clairvoyance.

NENUFARENL.—Elementals of the air. Sylphs.

NYMPHAE.—Elementals of water-plants.

O

OCCULTISM.—The science that deals with things that transcend sensual perception and are generally little known. It deals especially with effects that cannot be explained by the universally known laws of Nature, but whose causes are still a mystery to those who have not penetrated deep enough into the secrets of Nature to understand them correctly. What may be occult to one person may be fully comprehensible to another. The more the spirituality and intelligence of man grows, and the more it becomes free of the attractions of sense, the more will his perceptive power grow and expand, and the less will the processes of Nature appear occult to him.

P

PARAGRANUM (from *para* = over, and *granum* = kernel).—The science that deals with the very heart of things, taking into account their mysterious origin.

PARAMIRUM (from *para* = over, and *mirare* = admire).—The science which deals with that which is spiritual, wonderful, elevating, holy, and admirable in Nature.

PENATES or PENNATES, LARES, HERCII, ETESII, MEILICHII.—Spirits of the elements of fire, as well as imps, hobgoblins, etc., attached to particular places, haunted houses, etc. They may produce noises, "physical manifestations," stone-throwing, etc.

PENTACULA.—Plates of metal with magic symbols written or engraved upon them. They are used as charms, amulets, etc., against diseases caused by evil astral influences.

PHANTASMATA.—Creations of thought; "spirits" living in solitary places (they may be produced by the imagination of man, and be able to communicate with him); hallucinations.

PRAESAGIUM.—Omen; signs of future events.

PYGMAEI.—Spirits of the Element of the Earth; being the products of a process of organic activity going on in that element, by which such forms may be generated. They are dwarfs and quite microscopical beings, ever at war with the Gnomes.

R

RUPA.—An Eastern term. Form. *Kama-rupa*, form caused by desire; *Mayavi-rupa*, illusive form caused by the will and imagination of a person who consciously projects his own astral reflection as that of any other form.

S

SAGANI.—Elementals or spirits of Nature.
SAHMANDRI.—Salamanders; spirits living in the element of fire.
SALT, SULPHUR, AND MERCURY.—The three constituent states or principles of the cosmos, corresponding to Substance, Energy, and Consciousness.
SCAIOLAE.—Spiritual powers, qualities, virtues, depending on the quality and quantity of the elements that produce them. Such powers are thought, love, hate, imagination, hope, fear, etc.
SIDEREAL BODY.—The same as the astral soul or the body formed by thought.
SOMNIA.—1. Dreams. 2. The invisible astral influences that one person may exercise over another in his dream. A person may thus make another person dream what he desires him to perceive; or the astral body of one sleeping person may converse with that of another; or such astral bodies of living persons may be impressed or be made to promise to do certain things after awakening, and they will then keep such promises when they awake.
SPIRIT.—This term is used very indiscriminately, a fact that may cause great confusion. In its true meaning spirit is a unity, a one living universal power, the source of all life; but the word spirit and spirits is also used very often to signify invisible, but nevertheless substantial things forms, shapes, and essences, elementals and elementaries, shades, ghosts, apparitions, angels, and devils.
SPIRITISM.—The dealing with spooks, ghosts, elementals, etc., and believing them to be the immortal spirits of departed human beings.
SPIRITUALISM.—The science of that which is spiritual, the contrary of "materialism"; the understanding of religious truths, based upon spirituality.
SPIRITUS VITAE. The vital force; a principle taken from the elements of whatever serves as a nutriment, or which may be imparted by "magnetism."
SPIRITUS ANIMALIS.—Astral power, by which the will of the inner principles in man is executed on the sensual and material plane; instincts.
SYLPHES.—Elementals residing in mountainous regions (not in the air).
SYLVESTRES.—Elementals residing in forests; the Dusii of St. Augustine; fauns.
SYRENES.—Singing elementals. Melusinae, attracted to and often keeping in the waters; half women, half fishes.

T

THEOSOPHIA.—Supreme wisdom, acquired by practical experience, by which it is eminently distinguished from merely speculative philosophy. Theosophy, or divine self-knowledge, is therefore not to be confounded with theosophical doctrines that are the result of theosophical knowledge; to say nothing about the idle dreams and vagaries which are often dealt out under the name of "theosophy," and which have brought this term into general disrepute.

TRARAMES.—An invisible power that may communicate with man through sounds, voices, ringings of bells, noises, etc.

U

UMBRATILES.—Shadows; astral appearances becoming visible and sometimes tangible (modern spiritistic form manifestations);[7] the Scin-lecca, or wraith, or the German Doppelgaenger of a person. They may become visible by attracting ethereal material elements from the body of a medium, or any other person in whom there is little cohesion of his lower elements in consequence of some disease, or on account of inherited peculiarities of his organisation; or they may attract them from the surrounding atmosphere. Their life is borrowed from the medium, and if it were prevented to return to the medium, the latter would be paralysed or die. (See EVESTRUM.)

V

VAMPIRES.—Astral forms living at the expense of persons from whom they draw vitality and strength. They may be either the astral bodies of living persons, or of such that have died, but which still cling to their physical bodies buried in the grave, attempting to supply them with nutriment drawn from the living, and thereby to prolong their own existence. Such cases are especially well known in the south-east of Europe—Moldavia, Servia, Russia, etc. (Vourdalak).[8]

X

XENI NEPHIDEI.—Elemental spirits that give men occult powers over visible matter, and then feed on their brains, often causing thereby insanity.[9] A great number of physical mediums have become insane from this cause.

Y

YLIASTER. Primordial matter out of which the universe has been formed in the beginning of time.

Chapter 3: Cosmology

The power that was active in the formation of the world was God; the Supreme Cause and Essence of all things, being not only the Father of the Son, but of all created things that ever were, that are, or will be; the Yliaster,[1] the primordial and original Cause of all existence. This Power is, was, and will be the eternal Constructor of the world, the "Carpenter" of the universe, the Sculptor of forms. *Creation took place through the inherent Will of that Creative Power being expressed in the "Word"*;[2] or Fiat (active and efficient thought), in the same manner as if a house would come into existence by a breath.[3] The cause of the beginning of creation was in the eternal inherent activity of the immaterial Essence, and all things were invisibly or potentially contained in the First Cause, or God.

When creation took place the Yliaster divided itself; it, so to say, melted and dissolved, and developed out of itself the Ideos or Chaos (Mysterium magnum, Iliados, Limbus major, or Primordial Matter). This Primordial Essence is of a monistic nature, and manifests itself not only as vital activity, a spiritual force, an invisible, incomprehensible, and indescribable power; but also as vital matter, of which the substance of living beings consists.[4] In the Limbus or Ideos of primordial matter, invested with the original power of life, without form, and without any conceivable qualities—in this, the only matrix of all created things, the substance of all things is contained. It is described by the ancients as the Chaos, and has been compared to a receptacle of germs, out of which the Macrocosmos, and afterwards by division and evolution in Hysteria specialia,[5] each separate being came into existence. All things and all elementary substances were contained in it, *in potentia*,[6] but not *in actu*, in the same sense as in a piece of wood a figure is contained, which may be cut out by an artist, or as heat is contained in a pebble, that may manifest its essence as a spark if struck with a piece of steel.[7]

The Magnus Limbus is the nursery out of which all creatures have grown, in the same sense as a tree may grow out of a small seed; with the difference, however, that the great Limbus takes its origin from the Word of God, while the Limbus minor (the terrestrial seed or sperm) takes it from the earth. The great Limbus is the seed out of which all beings have come, and the little Limbus is each ultimate being that reproduces its form, and that has itself been produced by the great. The little Limbus has all the qualifications of the great one, in the same sense as a son has an organisation similar to that of his father. "As it is above, so it is below."

As creation took place and the Yliaster dissolved, Ares, the dividing, differentiating, and individualising power of the Supreme Cause, began to act. All production took place in consequence of separation. There were produced out of the Ideos the elements of Fire, Water, Air, and Earth, whose birth, however, did not take place in a material mode or by simple separation, but spiritually and dynamically, just as fire may come out of a pebble or a tree come out of a seed, although there is originally no fire in the pebble nor a tree in the seed. "Spirit is living and Life is Spirit, and Life and Spirit produce all things, but they are essentially one and not two. The tongue talks, and yet it does not talk, for it is the Spirit that talks by means of the tongue, and without the Spirit the tongue would be silent, because the flesh alone cannot talk." The elements, too, have each one its own Yliaster, because all the activity of matter in every form is only an effluvium of the same fountain. But as from the seed grow the roots with their fibres, afterwards the stalk with its branches and leaves, and lastly the flowers and seeds; likewise all beings were born from the elements, and consist of elementary substances out of which other forms may come into existence, bearing the characteristics of their parents.[8] The elements, as the mothers of all creatures, are of an invisible spiritual nature, and have souls.[9] They all spring from the Mysterium magnum, which is eternal life, and therefore the spiritual elements, and all the beings that have been formed of such elements, must be eternal; just as a flower consists of elements similar to those of the plant on which it grows.

"Nature being the Universe, is one, and its origin can only be one eternal Unity. It is an organism in which all natural things harmonise and sympathise with each other. It is the Macrocosm. Everything is the product of one universal creative effort; the Macrocosm and man (the Microcosm) are one. They are one constellation, one influence, one breath, one harmony, one time, one metal, one fruit."[10] (*Philosophia ad Athenienses*)

There is nothing dead in Nature. Everything is organic and living, and consequently the whole world appears to be a living organism. "There is nothing corporeal which does not possess a soul hidden in it. There exists nothing in which is not a hidden principle of life. Not only the things that move, such as men and animals, the worms of the earth, and the birds of the air and the fishes in the water, but all corporeal and essential things have life."

There is no death in Nature, and the dying of the beings consists in their return into the body of their mother; that is to say, in an extinction and suppression of one form of existence and activity, and in a re-birth of the same thing into another and more interior world, in a new form, possessed of new faculties that are adapted to its new surroundings. "Two factors are discernible in each thing—its body (form) and its Activity (qualities). The latter is nothing else but an effluence of the Supreme Cause because everything exists from the beginning in God, into whose unmanifested state all things will return in the end, and from whose power they all receive their qualities, or whatever they deserve on account of their capacity to receive or attract it.

Life is an universal omnipresent principle, and nothing is without life: "It cannot be denied that the air gives life to all corporeal things, such as grow from the earth and are born of it; but the special life of each thing is a spiritual being, an invisible and intangible spirit. There is nothing corporeal which has not within itself a spiritual essence, and there is nothing which does not contain a life hidden within. Life is something spiritual. Life is not only in that which moves, such as men and animals, but in all things; for what would be a corporeal form without a spirit?" "The form may be destroyed; but the spirit remains and is living, for it is the subjective life. There are as many spirits and lives as there are bodily forms. Therefore there are celestial, infernal, and terrestrial spirits, spirits of human beings, of metals, stones, plants, etc. The spirit is the life and the balsam within all corporeal things." (*Vita Rerum,* iv.) In some forms life acts slowly—for instance, in stones; in others (organised beings) it acts quickly. Each element has its own peculiar living existences, belonging to it exclusively.[11] Such existences or beings, living in the invisible elements, are the elemental spirits of Nature. They are beings of the Mysteria specialia, soul-forms, which will return into their chaos, and who are not capable of manifesting any higher spiritual activity because they do not possess the necessary kind of constitution in which an activity of a spiritual character can manifest itself. Otherwise they live like animals, or even like human beings, and they propagate their species. By the knowledge of ether (A'kasa) we may come into contact with such beings, and there are some of them that know all the mysteries of the elements.[12]

"Matter is, so to say, coagulated smoke, and is connected with spirit by an intermediate principle which it receives from the Spirit. This intermediate link between matter and spirit belongs to all three kingdoms of Nature. In the mineral kingdom it is called Stannar or Trughat,[13] in the vegetable kingdom Leffas;[14] and it forms, in connection with the vital force of the vegetable kingdom, the *Primum Ens*, which possesses the highest medicinal properties.[15] This invisible ethereal body may be resurrected and made visible from the ashes of plants and animals by alchemical manipulations. The form of the original body may thus be made to appear and disappear.[16] In the animal kingdom this semi-material body is called Evestrum, and in human beings it is called the Sidereal Man. Each living being is connected with the Macrocosmos and Microcosmos by means of this intermediate element or Soul, belonging to the Mysterium magnum, from whence it has been received, and whose form and qualities are determined by the quality and quantity of the spiritual and material elements."

As all things come from the same source, containing the primordial substance of all things, they are all intimately related to each other and connected with each other, and are essentially and fundamentally a unity. Any difference existing between two dissimilar things arises only from a difference in the forms in which the primordial essence manifests its activity. Such a difference is caused by the different grades through which such forms have passed in the progress of their evolution and development.

> [NOTE.—If we compare the teachings of the Eastern sages with the cosmology taught by Paracelsus, and substitute the Sanscrit or the Tibetan terms used by the former for those invented by the latter, we find the two systems almost, if not wholly, identical. According to the Eastern sages, there is a ceaseless activity going on during the state of Pralaya (the night of Brahm), in that incomprehensible eternal First Cause that may be looked upon in one of its many aspects as being Matter, Motion, and Space, in an absolute sense, which is beyond the grasp of our relative conception. Its motion is the unconscious latent life inherent in it. This is the Yliaster of Paracelsus, the "root of Matter," or Mulaprakriti of the Vedantins, out of which Prakriti (Matter) and Purusha (Space) become manifest as body and form. In this, *The Absolute, Infinite*, and Unconditioned, being the endless aggregation of everything conditioned and finite, the germs or potentialities of all things are contained. It is the Limbus Chaos of Paracelsus, and the germs contained in it are developed by the action of the Universal Mind, Dyan-Chohans, and the power of Wisdom, Fo-hat—to use the Tibetan words. Thus the Universe may be said to be a product of Cosmic Ideation and Cosmic Energy, acting, not at

random or in an arbitrary manner, but according to a certain order produced by previous causes, which are themselves the effects of other causes, and which constitute the Law. The existence of this inevitable and unchangeable law is frequently alluded to by Paracelsus. He says, for instance, in his book, "De Origine Morborum Invisibilium": "Does not holy writ say that God spoke: Am I not the God who made the dumb and the deaf, the blind and the seeing? What else does this mean, but that he is the creator of all things, of good and of evil?" The writings of the Buddhists teach the same doctrine, saying that there is only One Power, *Swabhavat*. It cannot act otherwise than according to the law of cause and effect, and that makes a useful tree grow as well as a useless stone in the bladder, according to the causes that have been produced by previous effects. Each act and each thought has a cause, and the cause of the cause is the Law.]

Man, as such, is the highest being in existence, because in him Nature has reached the culmination of her evolutionary efforts. In him are contained all the powers and all the substances that exist in the world, and he constitutes a world of his own. In him wisdom may become manifest, and the powers of his soul—good as well as evil—may be developed to an extent little dreamed of by our speculative philosophers. "In him are contained all the Coelestia, Terrestria, Undosa, and Aeria"—that is to say, all the forces and beings and forms that may be found in the four elements out of which the Universe is constructed. Man is the Microcosm containing in himself the types of all the creatures that exist in the world, "and it is a great truth, which you should seriously consider, that there is nothing in heaven or upon the earth which does not also exist in Man, and God who is in heaven exists also in man, and the two are but One." Each man in his capacity as a member of the great organism of the world can be truly known only if looked upon in his connection with universal Nature, and not as a separate being isolated from Nature. Man is dependent for his existence on Nature, and the state of Nature depends on the condition of mankind as a whole. If we know Nature we know Man, and if we know Man we know Nature. "Whoever desires to be a practical philosopher ought to be able to indicate heaven and hell in the Microcosm, and to find everything in Man that exists in heaven or upon the earth; so that the corresponding things of the one and the other appear to him as one, separated by nothing else but the form. He must be able to turn the exterior into the interior, but this is an art which he can only acquire by experience and by the light of Nature, which is shining before the eyes of every man,[17] but which is seen by few mortals."

The science which deals with the comparison of the Microcosm and Macrocosm for the purpose of elucidating the nature of the two (which are in reality one), and to bring to an understanding the rational principle governing their activity, is called by Paracelsus, *Astronomia*, and this term is not to be confounded with modern physical Astronomy, or the science of the revolutions of the suns and planets in cosmic space, neither does it refer to the mathematical astrological science of the sixteenth century. The Astronomy of Paracelsus means wisdom, or a direct recognition of the truth, caused by a just appreciation and comprehension of the relationship existing between the Macrocosmos and the Microcosmos, "whereby the nature of man becomes known through an understanding of the upper sphere of the great world, as well as by investigating the lower sphere of his little world, as if they were apparently (what they are essentially) one Firmament,[18] one Star, one Being, although appearing temporarily in a divided form and shape."[19]

The sphere of the Universal Mind is the upper firmament and the sphere of the individual mind the lower firmament, but the two are intimately connected together and are essentially one. "It is the knowledge of the upper (outer) firmament that enables us to know the lower (inner) firmament in Man, and which teaches in what manner the former continually acts upon and interrelates with the latter." Upon this knowledge the true science of Astrology is based.

Each, however—the Microcosmos as well as the Macrocosmos—are to be looked upon as having each a separate and independent existence, and as being independent of each other, each one by reason of the individuality of its own inherent power, notwithstanding the fact that both have the same origin and the same life; for the one primordial power has become differentiated in each separate form, and its originally homogeneous action has become modified by the special qualities that have been acquired by the forms in which it manifests itself. "As the sky with its stars and constellations is nothing separate from the All but includes the All, so is the 'firmament' of Man not separate from Man; and as the Universal Mind is not ruled by any external being, likewise the firmament in Man (his individual sphere of mind) is not subject to the rule of any creature, but is an independent and powerful whole."[20]

The practical application of Astronomia (mental science) is called Magic, a science which by investigating the parts of the whole leads to a comparison of their ideal relations and connections, and consequently to a recognition of their inner nature. "Hidden things (of the soul) which cannot be perceived by the physical senses, may be found through the sidereal body, through whose organism we may look into Nature in the same way as the sun shines through a glass. The inner nature of everything may therefore be known through Magic in general, and through the powers of the inner (or second) sight."[21] "These are the powers by which all secrets of Nature may be discovered, and it is necessary that a physician should be instructed and become well versed in this art, and that he should be able to find out a great deal more about the patient's disease by his own inner perception than by questioning the patient. For this inner sight is the Astronomy of Medicine, and as physical Anatomy shows all the inner parts of the body, such as cannot be seen through the skin, so this magic perception shows not only all the causes of disease, but it furthermore discovers the elements in medicinal substances in which the healing powers reside."[22] "That which gives healing power to a medicine is its 'Spiritus' (an ethereal essence or principle), and it is only perceptible by the senses of the sidereal man. It therefore follows that Magic is a teacher of medicine far preferable to all written books. Magic power alone (that can neither be conferred by the universities nor created by the awarding of diplomas, but which comes from God) is the true teacher, preceptor, and pedagogue, to teach the art of curing the sick. As the physical forms and colours of objects, or as the letters of a book, can be seen with the physical eye, thus the essence and the character of all things may be recognised and become known by the inner sense of the soul."[23]

"I have reflected a great deal upon the magical powers of the soul of man, and I have discovered a great many secrets in Nature, and I will tell you that he only can be a true physician who has acquired this power. If our physicians did possess it, their books might be burnt and their medicines be thrown into the ocean, and the world would be all the more benefited by it. Magic inventrix finds everywhere what is needed, and more than will be required. The soul does not perceive the external or internal physical construction of herbs and roots, but it intuitively perceives their powers and virtues, and recognises at once their *signatum*.

"This signatum (or signature) is a certain organic vital activity, giving to each natural object (in contradistinction to artificially made objects) a certain similarity with a certain condition produced by disease, and through which health may be restored in specific diseases in the diseased part. This signatum is often expressed even in the exterior form of things, and by observing that form we may learn something in regard to their interior qualities, even without using our interior sight. We see that the internal character of a man is often expressed in his exterior appearance, even in the manner of his walking and in the sound of his voice. Likewise the hidden character of things is to a certain extent expressed in their outward forms. As long as man remained in a natural state, he recognised the signatures of things and knew their true character; but the more he diverged from the path of Nature, and the more his mind became captivated by illusive external appearances, the more this power became lost.

"A man who wholly belongs to himself cannot belong to anything else. Man has the power of self-control, and no external influences can control him if he exercises this power. The influences of the Macrocosm cannot so easily impress their action upon a rational, wise, and passionless man as they do upon animals, vegetables, and minerals, which they impregnate to such an extent that their characters may be seen in the forms, colours, and shapes, and be perceived by the odour and taste of such objects. Some of these external signs are universally known; for instance, the age of an elk is indicated by the number of the ends and the shape of its horns; other symbols may require a special study for their true interpretation."[24] (*De Natura Rerum*)

This science, resulting from a comparison of the external appearance of a thing and its true character, is called by Paracelsus their Anatomy. There are even to this day a great many vegetable medicines used in the prevailing system of Medicine whose mode of action is not known, and for whose employment no other reason has been given but that the exterior shapes of such plants correspond to a certain extent to the form of the organs upon which they are supposed to be acting beneficially, and because experience has supported such a belief.

"Each plant is in a sympathetic relation with the Macrocosm, and consequently also with the Microcosm, or, in other words, with Constellation and Organism (for the activity of the organism of man is the result of the actions of the interior constellation of stars existing in his interior world), and each plant may be considered to be a terrestrial star. Each star in the great firmament, and in the firmament of man, has its specific influence, and each plant likewise, and the two correspond together. If we knew exactly the relations between plants and stars, we might say: This star is 'Stella Rorismarini,' that plant is 'Stella Absynthii,' and so forth. In this way a *herbarium spirituale sidereum* might be collected, such as every intelligent physician, who understands the relationship existing between matter and mind, should possess,[25] because no man can rationally employ remedies without knowing their qualities, and he cannot know the qualities of plants without being able to read their signatures. It is useless for a physician to read the books of Dioscorides and Macar, and to learn from hearsay the opinion of others who may be his inferiors in wisdom. He ought to look with his own eyes into the book of Nature and become able to understand it; but to do this requires more than mere speculation and to ransack one's brain; and yet without that art nothing useful can be accomplished."

Perhaps this might be made clearer by expressing the same idea in modern language, and saying: Each thing is a state of mind, because the whole world is mind. Each thing is a materialised thought (a "star"), and represents the character of the thought expressed in it; and as one thought acts upon another, so the mental state represented by a certain plant may act favourably upon a certain state of the patient's mind, and thus react upon the body. The peculiar qualities of a plant are those which are symbolised by its form; all that is required to know it, is the faculty of recognising its character. As there is a state and influence which is called "love," "hate," etc., so there are states of mind represented in outward forms of plants, such as *Hypericon perforatum, Sambucus, Juniperus, etc. etc.* Each form is only the materialised part and external expression of the character of the "spirit" or the "aura" which it represents, in the same way as each star in the sky is only the visible part or the materialised kernel of the "spirit" which it represents, and whose sphere extends as far as its influence, just as the sphere of a rose extends as far as its odour. The character builds the form, and the form expresses the character.

But this harmony existing between the form and the character is furthermore remarkable in certain other conditions and qualities, which are often of more importance to a physician than the external shapes: "If the physician understands the anatomy of medicines and the anatomy of diseases, he will find that a concordance exists between the two. There is not only a general relationship existing between the Macrocosm and the Microcosm, but a separate and intimate interrelation and interaction exist between their separate parts, each part of the great organism acting upon the corresponding part of the small organism in the same sense as the various organs of the human body are intimately connected and influencing each other, and manifesting a sympathy with each other that may continue to exist even after such organs have been separated from the trunk." There is a great sympathy existing between the stomach and the brain, between the mammae and the uterus, between the lungs and the heart.[26] There is, furthermore, a great sympathy existing between the mind and the thoughts and the organs of the human body. Such a sympathy exists between the thoughts and the plants, between stars and stars, between plants and plants, and between the plants and the organs of the human body, in consequence of which relationship each body can produce certain changes in the activity of life in another body that is in sympathy with the former. Thus may the action of certain specific medicines in certain diseases be explained. As a bar of magnetised iron induces magnetism in another bar of iron, but leaves copper and brass unaffected, likewise a certain plant, possessing certain powers, will induce certain similar vital ethers to become active in certain organs if the plant and the organ are related to the same "star". Certain plants, therefore, act as antidotes in certain diseases, in the same manner as fire will destroy all things that have not the power to resist it. The neutralisation, destruction, or removal of any specific elements producing disease, the change of an unhealthy and abnormal action of the vital currents into a normal and healthy state, constitutes the basis of the therapeutic system of Paracelsus. His object was to re-establish in the diseased organism the necessary equilibrium, and to restore the lost vitality, by attracting the vital principles from living objects and powers. Remedies containing the required quality of that principle in the greatest quantity were most apt to replace such lost powers and to restore health.[27]

The organisms—that is to say, the material forms of invisible principles—take their origin from the soul of the world, symbolised as "water".[28] This doctrine of Paracelsus is therefore the same as the ancient doctrine of Thales, and as the old Brahminical doctrine according to which the world came into existence from an egg (allegorically speaking) laid in water (the soul) by Brahm (Wisdom). He says that by the decomposition of that essence a "mucilage" is formed, containing the germs of life, out of which, by *generatio aequivoca*, first the lower and afterwards the higher organisms are formed.

We see, therefore, that the doctrine of Paracelsus bears a great resemblance to the one advocated by the greatest modern philosophers, such as Haeckel and Darwin; with this difference, however, that Paracelsus looks upon the continually evolving forms as necessary vehicles of a continually progressing living spiritual principle, seeking higher modes for its manifestation, while many of our modern speculative philosophers look upon the intelligent principle of life as non-existing, and upon life as being merely a manifestation of chemical and physical activity of dead matter in an incomprehensible and causeless state of development.[29] They see only one half of the truth.

No animal ever grew to be a man, but the divine man, becoming incarnated in human-like animal forms, caused these forms to become the human beings, such as we know them at present upon our earth.

"According to the biblical account, God created the animals before He created man. The animal elements, instincts, and desires existed before the Divine Spirit illuminated them and made them into man. The animal soul of man is derived from the cosmic animal elements, and the animal kingdom is therefore the father of the animal man. If man is like his animal father, he resembles an animal; if he is like the Divine Spirit that lives within his animal elements, he is like a god. If his reason is absorbed by his animal instincts, it becomes animal reason; if it rises above his animal desires, it becomes angelic. If a man eats the flesh of an animal, the animal flesh becomes human flesh; if an animal eats human flesh, the latter becomes animal flesh. A man whose human reason is absorbed by his animal desires is an animal, and if his animal reason becomes enlightened by wisdom he becomes an angel."

"Animal man is the son of the animal elements out of which his soul was born, and animals are the mirrors of man. Whatever animal elements exist in the world exist in the soul of man, and therefore the character of one man may resemble that of a fox, a dog, a snake, a parrot, etc. Man need not, therefore, be surprised that animals have animal instincts that are so much like his own; it might rather be surprising for the animals to see that their son (animal man) resembles them so closely. Animals follow their animal instincts, and in doing so they act as nobly and stand as high in Nature as their position in it permits them, and they do not sink thereby below that position; it is only animal man who sinks below the brute. Animals love and hate each other according to the attraction or repulsion of their animal elements: the dog loves the dog and hates the cat, and men and women are attracted to each other by their animal instincts, and love their young ones for the same reason as the animals love theirs; but such a love is animal love—it has its purposes and its rewards, but it dies when the animal elements die. Man is derived from the dog, and not the dog from the man. Therefore a man may act like a dog, but a dog cannot act like a man. Man may learn from the animals, for they are his parents; but the animals can learn nothing useful to them from man. The spider makes a better web than man, and the bee builds a more artistic house. He may learn how to run, from the horse; to swim, from the fish; and to fly, from the eagle. The animal world is taught by Nature, and it is divided into many classes and species, so that it may learn all the natural arts. Each species has forms that differ from those of another species, so that it may learn that art for which it is adapted by Nature; but man, as a whole, has only one kind of form, and is not divided, and therefore the animal soul of man is not divided, but all the animal elements are combined in it, the reason of man selecting what it likes.

"A man who loves to lead an animal life is an animal ruled by his interior animal heaven.[30] The same stars (qualities) that cause a wolf to murder, a dog to steal, a cat to kill, a bird to sing, etc., make a man a singer, an eater, a talker, a lover, a murderer, a robber, or a thief. These are animal attributes, and they die with the animal elements to which they belong; but the divine principle in man, which constitutes him a human being, and by which he is eminently distinguished from the animals, is not a product of the earth, nor is it generated by the animal kingdom, but it comes from God, it is God, and is immortal, because, coming from a divine source, it cannot be otherwise than divine. Man should therefore live in harmony with his divine parent, and not in the animal elements of his soul. Man has an Eternal Father who sent him to reside and gain experience within the animal elements, but not for the purpose of being absorbed by them, because in the latter case man would become an animal, while the animal principle would have nothing to gain," and would thus be led individually to speedy annihilation. (*De Fundamento Sapientiae*)

What, then, can be the true object of human life, except to attain the consciousness of one's own true and divine state, and to realise that one is not an animal, but a godlike being inhabiting a human animal form. All the divine powers are latent in man's divine nature. If he once realises what he actually is, he will be able to use them and be himself a creator of forms.

Chapter 4: Anthropology. The Generation of Man

"All that Aristoteles and his followers have written about the generation of man, is not based upon observation or reading within the light of nature, but consists merely of theories which they have invented and elaborated with a great deal of cunning and trouble. It is merely phantastry and devoid of truth; for although the light of nature has not refused them anything, it has also given them nothing. What we teach is not the result of opinion and speculation, but of actual experience. Our philosophy has not originated in the realm of the imagination, but is copied from the book of nature itself. We believe that for the terrestrial man there is no nobler enjoyment than to know the laws of nature; but we reject that kind of smartness and cunning which invents systems of so-called philosophy, based upon arguments which have no foundation in truth. All that these writers can talk about is the sensual world, such as they perceive with their senses; but we claim that this world of external appearances is only the fourth part of the actual world; not that the world were still three times bigger than it appears to us, but that there are still three-fourths of it of which we are unconscious. We say that there is a world within the (element of) water, and that it has its own inhabitants; and another world within the (element of) the earth; and there are *volcanic* people, who live in the fourth part of the world, in the element of the fire." (*De Generatio Hominis*)

"There are creatures having within themselves the seed for their propagation, such as minerals and plants, and all that has no self-consciousness; and there are others endowed with consciousness and life, without any seed in them, namely, animals and human beings."[1]

Man is made out of three substances, or seeds, or "mothers." His spiritual seed is from God, and God is his mother; his astral elements are developed under the influences of the constellation (the astral plane), and his mother is, therefore, the soul of the world; his visible body is formed and born out of the elements of the visible world, and thus the terrestrial world is its mother.

"If the whole man were made only out of the seed of his parents, he would resemble his parents in every respect. A chestnut-tree bears chestnuts, and from each of its fruits can grow nothing else but a chestnut-tree; but the mixture of seeds is the cause that a son may be very unlike his father. The seed (*tincture*) from the brain of the father and that from the brain of the mother make only one brain in the child, but that *tincture* among the two which is the strongest will predominate and characterise the child."

Man receives his spirit and body not from his father and mother, but from God and from nature, acting through the instrumentality of his parents. His soul and body are formed in his mother, but do not originate in her. The *three substances* or elements which go to make up the constitution of man are universal; man is merely a centre or *focus* through which they act.

There are beings who live exclusively in only one of these elements, while man exists in all three. Each of these elements is visible and tangible to the beings living therein, and its qualities may be known to its inhabitants. Thus the *Gnomes* may see all that is going on in the interior of the earthly shell surrounding our planet, this shell being as air for them; the *Undines* thrive and breathe in their watery world; the *Sylphs* live in the air like a fish in the water, and the *Salamanders* are happy in the element of the fire. A person in whose organisation the element of earth preponderates will have great talents for agriculture and mining; a soul sympathising especially with the watery element will endow the person with a taste for a seafaring life, etc.

Spirit is perceptible to spiritual existences, and the thoughts of mortals consequently appear visible and material to spirits; the Soul essence, with its currents and forms, may be seen and felt by the Elementals and beings that live in the realm of the soul; and they are, also, capable of reading such thoughts as are not of a too refined and spiritual character to be discerned by them, and to perceive the states of feelings of men by the colours and impressions produced in the auras of the latter; but they cannot perceive divine and spiritual things. Matter, in the state in which it is known to us, is seen and felt by means of the physical senses; but to beings who are not provided with such senses, material things are as invisible and intangible as spiritual things are to those who have not developed the power of spiritual perception.

The Spiritual Essence of Man comes from the highest emanation of God. It is gifted with divine wisdom and with divine power; and if the higher elements constituting the normal man become conscious of the possession of divine gifts, and learn to realise their powers and how to employ them, they will be, so to say, superhuman, and may rightly be called Divine Beings, or Sons of the Almighty. Whenever a child is conceived, a word proceeds, like a ray from God, which provides the future man with a Spirit.[2] This Spirit, however, is not absorbed immediately by the new-born child, but becomes incarnate gradually, as the man grows and attains reason and intelligence.[3] Many men and women live, and marry, and die without ever coming into full possession of (or without entering into a firm connection with) that divine ray of wisdom that can alone transform them into immortal human beings; because, although the powers and essences that go to make up their astral souls may be much more enduring in their form than their physical bodies, still these powers will become exhausted and these essences be decomposed into their elements in due time, and there is nothing that endures to the end except the Spirit of God, that may become manifest in man by assimilating the more refined essences of the soul. If no such assimilation takes place—in other words, if the individual during his life does not become wise and good and spiritually enlightened—the divine ray will, at the death of the person, return again to the source from whence it came; but that individual's personality[4] will only remain as an impression in the astral light. There are two kinds of intelligence in man: the higher and the lower intelligence. It is only the human (superhuman) intelligence that can combine and unite itself with the spirit. The lower or animal intellect, however clever it may be, and however much learning it may possess, will be lost, because it is not spiritual. It is the spirit or life alone that can hold forms together and prevent their dissolution and their return into chaos. Pure spirit has no personality, but exists impersonal in and as God. Every birth produces a new person, but not a new spiritual ray. The spirit survives, but the personality of man, as such, will be lost. Only those elements belonging to his personality that will be absorbed by the spirit will survive with the latter. The cement that unites the soul with the spirit is love, and the love of God is, therefore, the highest good attainable by mortal man.

"The animal kingdom is not without reason and intellect, and in many of its arts, such as swimming, flying, &c, even superior to man; but the Spirit of God is far superior to the reasoning intellect, and by means of this spirituality man may rise above the animal plane. Therefore there is a great difference between the external and the internal man; for the intellectuality of the former perishes, while the wisdom of the latter remains." (*De Fundamento Sapientiae*)

The astral Soul-essence of Man is formed by the ethereal or astral influences coming from the souls of the world and of the planets and stars, especially from the soul (or astral body) of the planet whereon he lives. As the soul of each man and of each animal has its peculiar qualities that distinguish it from others, so the soul of each planet, each sun, each world, has its peculiar characteristics, and sends out its beneficial or its destructive influences, pervading cosmic space, acting upon the Microcosm of man, and producing finally visible results.[5] These astral elements are the organisers of the soul of man. They are the builders of the temple in which the spirit resides, and being energised by them, the soul of man attracts by physiological processes the elements of the earth, and forms tissues, muscles, and bones, and becomes visible and tangible to other similarly constituted beings as the material or animal body of man.[6]

Man may therefore be looked upon as a twofold being—a visible and an invisible man (or as having a material and a spiritual aspect), linked together by an astral soul. "The form of a corporeal thing is one thing, and that which produces the form is another thing; the form of a thing arises from the form of the mystery (character). If a builder wants to build a house, the form of the house exists in his mind before he executes the building, even if it is seen by no one except by the builder himself." (*De Podagris,* II.) The visible man consists of such originally invisible elements as have become visible in his body; the invisible man consists of feelings and thoughts whose origin is in the Macrocosm, and their light is reflected and impresses itself upon matter. Man is therefore the quintessence of all the elements, and a son of the universe, or a copy in miniature of its Soul, and everything that exists or takes place in the universe, exists and can take place in the constitution of man. The congeries of forces and essences making up the constitution of what we call *man*, is the same as the congeries of forces and powers that on an infinitely larger scale is called the Universe. Everything in the Universe reflects itself in man, and may come to his consciousness; and this circumstance enables man, when he knows himself, to know the Universe, and to perceive not only that which exists invisibly in the Universe, but to foresee and prophesy future events. On this intimate relationship between the Universe and Man depends the harmony by which the Infinite becomes intimately connected with the Finite, the immeasurably great with the small. It is the golden chain of Homer, or the Platonic ring.[7]

The object of man's existence is *to be a real Man*, including all that this term implies; i.e., to re-establish the harmony which originally existed between him and the divine state before the separation took place which disturbed the equilibrium, and which caused the first emanation of the divine essence to be absorbed by the third material emanation and to sink into matter. To re-establish this harmony, Man may bring the will of God to perfect expression in his nature, by learning to know within himself the will of God and being obedient to it, and thereby his own nature and finally even the whole of the Macrocosm, will become spiritualised and be rendered paradisaical. The individual qualities and temperaments of men will be developed to a certain extent, independently of their surroundings, by the power of the *Ens seminis*, a formative power (potency of matter). Adam and Eve (the spiritual dual male and female essence) have received their body through the "creatures" (elemental or astral essences), and through the *Ens seminis*, and through this never-ceasing supply men and women will come into existence until the end of the world.[8] If there were no planets and stars, and if there never had been any in existence, nevertheless the children of Adam and Eve would be born and have their particular temperaments. One may be melancholy, another choleric, a third sanguine or bilious, etc. Such qualities of men come from the *Ens proprietatis*, and not from any astral influences, for the temperaments, tastes, inclinations, and talents form no part of the body; that is to say, they give no complexion, colour, or form to it—they are the attributes of the *Ens proprietatis*.[9]

Although, speaking in a general sense, the Microcosm and the Macrocosm bear to each other a similar relationship as the chicken in the egg bears to its surrounding albumen, nevertheless the action of the Macrocosm upon the Microcosm is only an external condition of life, called by Paracelsus, *Digest*. No man or any mortal being can exist without the influence of the Astra, but they do not come into existence through them. A seed thrown into the soil may grow and produce a plant, but it could not accomplish this if it were not acted upon by the sun, nor could the soil itself produce a seed, no matter how long the sun would shine upon it. Paracelsus explains the origin of the qualities of the external conditions of life as being produced by the mutual attractions and interactions existing between the Macrocosmos and the Microcosmos, and by the harmony of both spheres (the upper and lower mind), of which either is formed in accordance with the other. The common basis of both—which is, so to say, their common receptacle of germs —is called *Limbus*. "Man being formed out of the Limbus, and the Limbus being universal, and therefore the mother of all things, it follows that all things, including man, have the same origin, and each thing is attracted to its own original by reason of this mutual relationship."[10]

"If man were not formed in such a manner and out of the whole ring and of all its parts, but if each man were made out of a separate piece of the world essentially distinct from others, he would not be capable to receive the influences residing in the whole. But the soul of the great world has the same divisions, proportions, and parts as the soul of man, and the material body of man receives the material body of Nature in the same sense as the son receives 'the blood' of his father."

A relationship similar to the one existing between the Macrocosm and the Microcosm exists between man and woman, and between woman and the uterus, and between the uterus and the foetus.

"The whole of the Microcosm is potentially contained in the *Liquor Vitae* (Prana), a nerve-fluid comparable to the fluidic brain-substance, and in which is contained the nature, quality, character, and essence of beings, and which ethereal life-fluid in man may be looked upon as an invisible or hidden man so to say, his ethereal counterpart or reflection." (*De Generatio Hominis*)

"From this nerve-aura or liquor vitae, in the process of the generation of man, the *semen* separates itself in a manner comparable to the separation of the foam or froth from a fermenting liquid, or as the quintessence (the fifth principle) of all things separates itself from the lower elements. This semen, however, is not the spermia or the visible seminal fluid of man, but rather a semi-material principle contained in the sperma, or the *aura seminalis*, to which the sperma serves as a vehicle.[11] The physical sperma is a secretion of the physical organs, but the *aura seminalis* is a product (or emanation) of the liquor vitas. It is developed by the latter in the same sense as fire is produced out of wood, in which there is actually no fire, but out of which heat and fire may proceed. This emanation or separation takes place by a kind of digestion, and by means of an interior heat, which during the time of virility becomes produced in man by the proximity of woman, by his thoughts of her, or by his contact with her, in the same manner as a piece of wood exposed to the concentrated rays of the sun can be made to burn. All the organs of the human system, and all their powers and activities, contribute alike to the formation of semen; and the essences of all are contained in the liquor vitae, whose quintessence is the *aura seminalis*, and these organs and physiological activities are reproduced in the foetus out of this liquor. They are, therefore, germinally contained in the seminal fluid that is necessary for the reproduction of the human organism. The spiritual semen is, so to say, the essence of the human body, containing all the organs of the latter in an ideal form." Furthermore, Paracelsus makes a distinction between *Sperma cagastricum* and Sperma iliastricum, of which the former is the product of the imagination (thought), and the latter is attracted directly from the *Mysterium magnum*.[12]

"Woman, however, being nearer to Nature, furnishes the soil in which the seed of man finds the conditions required for its development. She nourishes, develops, and matures the seed without furnishing any seed herself. Man, although born of woman, is never derived from woman, but always from man. The cause of the mutual interaction of the two sexes is their mutual attraction. The tendencies of man cause him to think and to speculate; his speculation creates desire, his desire grows into passion, his passion acts upon his imagination, and his imagination creates semen. Therefore God has put semen into the imagination of man, and planted into women the desire to be attractive to man. The matrix contains a strong attractive power, to attract the semen, similar to that of the loadstone to attract iron."[13]

"The relationship existing between the Macrocosm and Microcosm finds its analogy in the relationship existing between the female body and the uterus. The latter may be regarded as a Microcosm in a Microcosm. As the semen of man contains potentially all the organs of the parent body, so there are contained potentially in the uterus all the attributes of the female body, the whole of man's body is potentially contained in the semen, and the whole of the body of the mother is, so to say, the soil in which the future man is made to ripen, because all the essences and forces of her body centre in the uterus, and there the power of her imagination is especially active. Thus is Man the product of a secondary fluid, while the Macrocosmos is the product of a primordial fluid, and as the Spirit of God in the beginning of creation moved upon the surface of the waters (the soul) likewise the human spirit, being diffused through the whole of man's organism, moves upon the (seminal) fluid, out of which the human form is developed. That Spirit of God is the vivifying and spiritualising element in the process of procreation. But the human foetus passes in the uterus through an animal-like existence, receiving the true spirit at a later period. It is then like a fish in the water, and brings an animal nature into the world."

The fact of the semen being formed of all parts of the body in equal proportion explains why persons are born in whom certain organs may be missing. If for some cause one part or another of the human organism does not participate in the formation of semen, its essence will be missing in the constitution of the seminal fluid, and cannot reproduce the corresponding part in the matrix.[14] If for some cause a part of the father's organism produces a double quantity of semen, a child will be born having supernumerary members.

"Whatever the mother imagines and obtains, the seed (spirit) of that thing is attracted to the matrix, and thereof grows the child; but the assertions of those astronomers who claim that the stars make a man are erroneous, and we will look upon such claims as a fable and joke to which one may listen during an idle hour. There are many fools in the world, and each one has his own hobby." (*Gebaerung des Menschen*).

As the imagination of man is productive of semen, likewise the imagination of the mother exerts a great constructive influence upon the development of the foetus, and upon this fact is based the similarity existing between children and parents.[15] Twins and other multiple births are caused if the uterus attracts the semen with more than one single draught. The power of attraction which the uterus exercises upon the seminal aura is so great that by coming into contact with the spermatic fluid of animals it may absorb it and bring forth monstrosities.[16]

It may therefore be said that the imagination of the father sets into activity the creative power necessary to generate a human being, and the imagination of the mother furnishes the material for its formation and development;[17] but neither the father nor the mother is the parent of the essential spiritual man, but the germ of the latter comes from the *Mysterium magnum*, and God is its father. Parents do not endow their children with reason, although they may furnish the child with a body, in which the principle of reason may or may not be able to act.[18] Reason is the natural birthright of every human being; it is eternal and perfect, and need not be educated in the child, but it may be overpowered and driven out by dogmatism and error. Intellectual acquisitions are perishable; memory is often lost much quicker in old age or on account of cerebral diseases than it is developed in youth.[19] Children may inherit from their parents the powers to employ their reason, but they do not inherit reason itself, because reason is an attribute of the Divine Spirit. Man cannot lose his reason, but he can become lost to it, because reason is an universal principle, and cannot be owned by any individual man, even if it is manifested in him.

"A man carrying seed in him (having a lewd imagination) uses no reason; he lives only within his lusts and morbid fancies. God has created man that he may live as a free being within the light of nature; therefore the philosopher should remain free in that light and not live in the seed of nature, which is called *Allara*. God has put the seed into the imagination; but He has given to man a free will, so that he may either allow himself to be carried away by his fancies, or rise superior to what nature desires in him" (*Gebaerung.*)

Woman and Marriage

Woman, in so far as she is a human being, contains, like man, the germs of all that exists in the Macrocosm, and can manifest the same mental characteristics as man. Moreover, there are males with preponderating female soul-qualities, and females in whom the male elements are preponderating; but woman, *as such*, represents the *will* (including love and desire), and man, as such, represents intellect (including the imagination); only in the *Lord*, within either of them, *i.e.*, in their own God, exists true wisdom. Therefore woman, as such, is more given to willing, and is led by her desires; while man, as such, is more given to arguing and calculating causes and effects. Woman represents the substance; man represents spirit. Man imagines, woman executes. Man creates images; the woman renders these images substantial. Man without woman is like a wandering spirit, a shadow without substance, seeking to embody itself in a corporeal form; woman is like a flower, a bud opening in the light of the sun, but sinking into darkness when man, her light, departs. The divine man (the angel) is male and female in one, such as Adam was before the woman became separated from him. He is like the sun, and his power may be reflected in men and women alike; but woman, as such, resembles the moon, receiving her light from the sun, and man without the woman (in him) is a consuming fire in want of fuel.

Originally, man and woman were one, and consequently their union could not have been more intimate than it actually was; but man, having become separated from the woman in him, lost his true substance. He now seeks for the woman outside of his true self, and wanders about among shadows, being misled by the illusions. Being fascinated by the charms of the terrestrial woman, he drinks of the cup of desires which she presents to him, and sinks into a still deeper sleep and forgetfulness of the true celestial Eve, the immaculate virgin, who once existed within himself. In this way woman is the enemy of man, and revenges herself for having been divorced from him and cast out from her true home within his heart; but, on the other hand, she is man's best friend and redeemer; for man, having lost the paradise in his soul, and having become unconscious of the true light which existed in him before he went to sleep in the spirit and awoke in the flesh, would sink into still lower degradation and descend to still lower hells, if woman did not stand upon the threshold to stop him, and for the true heaven which he lost offer him a terrestrial paradise, illuminated by the light of her love, whose origin is in heaven.

The Lord is the same in woman as He is in man; but males and females are not equals. They are constituted very differently from each other, not only according to their mental characteristics, but also in regard to the whole of their bodily substance. Male and female animals are made out of the same stuff; but woman was not originally created; she was formed out of a "rib" (a spiritual substance) of man, and is therefore of a nobler and more refined kind of matter, such as he possessed before the woman was formed from him. Woman is made of the best and substantial part of man, and is therefore the crown of creation.

"A common boor thinks that the blood of a woman is the same as that of a man; but a physician, unless he has been baptized with the blood of a boor, will see the difference between the two." (*De Morb. Matric.*)

Man represents the dark, fiery will, woman the light love-will; man the fire, woman the water. It is not the divine man who is attracted by any woman, but the *tincture* (nature) in him. The fiery element in man seeks for the watery element in woman, and carries the man along. Thus it is neither man nor woman who longs for sexual intercourse, but nature in them.

There is, perhaps, no doctrine which has done more mischief than the misconstrued teaching about affinities and soul-marriages; because such a doctrine is willingly accepted by the carnal mind. God did not create souls in halves, nor can Adam find his Eve again unless she grows within his heart. Man will never find his celestial bride unless he looks for her within his internal heaven, within "the Lord." Sexual cohabitation, whether authorised or unauthorised by Church or State, is merely an animal function. There is neither Absolute good nor absolute evil in marriage. It relates to the parties entering the contract, and is therefore relative. It may serve for their edification in one case, and for their degradation in another. To the semi-animal man it may be a school of education; but the regenerated man requires no sexual relationship. The procreation of children is an animal function, and he who is unable or unwilling to exercise it has no business to marry. If he, nevertheless, enters the connubial bonds, he commits a piece of stupidity, if not a fraud.[20]

It is also useless for a man to resist the claims of nature in him, if he cannot rise superior to that nature; and the power for that superiority does not depend on his human will, but comes from his higher and spiritual nature, in which he should seek his refuge.

"As long as the root is not, with all of its fibres, torn out of the earth (*i.e.*, as long as man has not become regenerated, and thereby free from sexual attractions), he will be blind and feeble; the spirit quick; the fancy strong; and the temptations so great that he cannot resist, unless he has been chosen for that purpose; for all things are ordained by God. If He wants you to be married, and to have children from you, then all your pledging yourself to chastity and your virginity will amount to nothing. If, in such a case, you refuse to marry, you will then fall into whoredom, or something still worse. Thus will God punish your disobedience, and your resistance to the will of God will be your eternal death." (*De Homunculis*)

In regard to the marriage obligations, Paracelsus says: "If a woman leaves her husband, she is then not free from him nor he from her; for a marriage union having once been formed, it remains a union for all eternity." This means that by entering willfully into sexual relationship with another being, we become attached to it in our will, and a partaker of its future Karma. A woman to whom a man is bound by promise and sexual intercourse becomes, as it were, a part of the man, and cannot be divorced from him by any ceremony or external separation. They constitute, so to say, one mind, and the component parts of the mind, which represent the carnal man, are not separated until the time of the second death.[21]

Sexual intercourse without love is merely a kind of onanism with a corporeal form substituted for the merely mental image; but if sanctioned (not "sanctified") by love, it is then a union, not merely of body, but also of soul; not of the spiritual soul, which needs no such union, it being already one with all other such souls in the substance of Christ, but a union of that which constitutes the lower mind of man.[22]

The Constitution of Man

According to Paracelsus, the constitution of man consists of seven principles, or, to express it more correctly, of seven modifications of one primordial essence, which are as follows, and to which we add their Eastern terms:[23]

1. The Elementary Body. (The Physical Body)—Sthula Sharira.
2. The Archaeus. (Vital force)—Prana.
3. The Sidereal Body. (The Astral body)—Linga Sharira.
4. Mumia. (The Animal Soul)—Kama rupa.
5. The Rational Soul. (The Human Soul)—Flesh of Adam. Manas.
6. The Spiritual Soul. (The Spiritual Soul)—Flesh of Christ. Buddhi.
7. The Man of the new Olympus. Atma Buddhi Manas.

In his "Philosophia Sagax" and his "Explanations of Astronomia," Paracelsus deals extensively with a description and explanation of these seven qualities. The most important points referring to the higher principles are as follows:

"The life of man is an astral effluvium or a balsamic impression, a heavenly and invisible fire, an enclosed essence or spirit. We have no better terms to describe it. The death of a man is nothing else but the end of his daily labour, or taking away the ether of life, a disappearance of the vital balsam, an extinction of the natural light, a re-entering into the matrix of the mother. The natural man possesses the elements of the Earth, and the Earth is his mother, and he re-enters into her and loses his natural flesh; but the real man will be re-born at the day of the resurrection in another spiritual and glorified body." (*De Natura Rerum*)[24]

In the study of anthropology the consideration of the divine part of man is of supreme importance; for the animal part of man is not the true man; neither is the elementary body the man; for that body without the true man within is merely a corpse. "Man has two spirits, a divine and a terrestrial spirit. The former is from the breath of God; the latter from the elements of the air and the fire. He ought to live according to the life of the divine spirit and not according to that of the animal." (*De Lunaticos*)

But the divine, immortal, and invisible man cannot be a subject for the investigation of any science, such as deals merely with external and visible things. He can be known to no one except to his own self; for the low cannot comprehend the high, and the finite mind cannot contain the infinite. The study of the divine man is the object of self-knowledge. "Physical science deals with the physical, and metaphysical science with the astral man; but these sciences are misleading and incomplete, if we lose out of our sight the existence of the divine and eternal man." (*De Fundamento Sapientiae*)

"Neither the external nor the astral man is the real man, but the real man is the spiritual soul in connection with the Divine Spirit. The astral soul is the shadow (ethereal counterpart) of the body, illumined by the spirit, and it therefore resembles man. It is neither material nor immaterial, but partakes of the nature of each. The inner (sidereal) man is formed out of the same Limbus as the Macrocosm, and he is therefore able to participate in all the wisdom and knowledge existing in the latter. He may obtain knowledge of all creatures, angels, and spirits, and learn to understand their attributes. He may learn from the Macrocosm the meaning of the symbols (the forms) by which he is surrounded, in the same manner as he acquires the language of his parents; because his own soul is the quintessence of everything in creation, and is connected sympathetically with the whole of Nature; and therefore every change that takes place in the Macrocosm can be sensed by the ethereal essence surrounding his spirit, and it may come to the consciousness and comprehension of man."[25]

Mortal man is a spirit, and has two bodies that are intimately connected together, an elementary and a sidereal body. These two bodies go to form one man. When a man dies, his elementary body returns to the elements of the Earth; the Earth absorbs the whole of his three lower principles, and nothing remains of the form of the body. The more material parts of the sidereal body undergo a similar decomposition. This body is formed of the astral elements, and is not dependent on physical substances. It is subject to planetary influences, and as the elementary body is dissolved into the elements from which it has been taken, likewise the astral form will in due time dissolve into the sidereal elements to which its substance belongs. The sidereal body remains near the decaying physical body until it is itself decomposed by the action of the astral influences. The two bodies were partners during life, and are only separated by death. Therefore they naturally remain near each other for a while after death, until they are consumed by their elements, the one in the grave, the other one in the air.[26] The decomposition of the elementary body requires a certain length of time according to its qualities and the qualities of its surroundings, and likewise the sidereal body may be decomposed slow or quick, according to the coherence of its particles, and according to the quality and strength of the astral influences acting upon it.

The elementary body is corporeal, but the sidereal body is ethereal. The elementary body is visible and tangible; the sidereal body is invisible and intangible for us, but visible and tangible for those beings that are of a nature similar to its own. The elementary body cannot move on its own account from the place where it has been deposited after death; but the sidereal body (Kama rupa) goes to that place to which it is mostly attracted by its own desires. If there are no particular places to attract it, it will remain near the elementary body;[27] but if it is attracted to other places it will visit them, and it is therefore especially liable to haunt the residence which the person occupied during his life, being attracted there by its acquired habits and instincts. Being devoid of reason and judgment, it has no choice in such matters, but follows blindly its attractions. The sidereal body will under certain (mediumistic) conditions become visible, and it therefore can be seen at places to which the reflex of its former passions, such as envy, avarice, repentance, revenge, selfishness, lust, etc., will attract it, and it may remain in such places until it is dissolved and decomposed. If a sensitive person asserts to have seen the spirit of a deceased person, we may believe that he has seen the sidereal body of such a person, but it is wrong to believe that such a ghost or apparition is the real man, because it is nothing else but the sidereal corpse that appears on such occasions. Such astral corpses may be seen like the reflection of a man in a mirror until they disappear, and the form of one may last longer than that of another.[28]

"The art called Nigromantia (Necromancy) teaches how to deal with such forms. It teaches their habits and instincts, their attributes and qualities, and how we may find out through them the secrets of the persons to whom those shadows belonged. As the image of a man in a large mirror shows the whole of his person and imitates all his movements and actions, so by observing the sidereal body of a deceased person, we can obtain information in regard to the former appearance and the acts and ways of that person, and find out who he was and where he lived."[29] (*Philosophia Sagax,* lib. i.: *Probatio in Scientiam Nigromanticam*)

Paracelsus ridicules the exorcists, and those who say prayers and read masses for the dead, "because," he says, "the former attempt to force a sidereal corpse to talk, while, in fact, no corpse can talk, and they can get from it at best a reflection of their own thoughts, and the latter attempt to fetch an inanimate body into a living heaven by their pious interposition."

In regard to the conjurers, he says: "They attempt to conjure sidereal bodies, and do not know that they are attempting an impossibility, because such bodies have no sense and cannot be conjured. The consequence is, that the devils (certain elementals) take possession of such sidereal bodies and play their pranks with the conjurers. Such devils will take possession of a living man, and make a weak man act as they please, and cause him to commit all sorts of foolishness and crimes. But if they can do this with a living soul, how much easier then will it be for them to take possession of a dead soul which has no spiritual power to resist! Therefore, such conjurers do not deal with the spirits of the dead, but with the powers of evil and the fathers of lies."[30]

The Elementals are also the beings which may produce so-called "physical manifestations," cause the appearance and disappearance of objects, throw stones, etc. In a fragment entitled "De Sagis et Earum Operibus" (On Witches and their Arts), cap. 3, he says: "In regard to such things, you ought to know that they are natural, and that no one can justly say otherwise but that Nature produces them, because, if, for instance, a blooming rose is brought in the midst of winter into a country where there are no roses, an ordinary man will think that such a thing took place in contravention to Nature's laws; but the *Magus* (the wise), who knows by what process such phenomena are produced, knows that they are produced according to the law of Nature, because such a flower is brought from a country where it has grown in a natural manner, and where there is no winter at that time. Thus, ice or snow may be brought with the same facility into a warm country in the midst of summer from another country in which it is winter. Ignorant persons should be informed that the Magus creates neither roses nor snow, but that he can receive them from places where they already exist."[31]

Intimately connected with the sidereal body is the Evestrum and the Trarames. In regard to these, Paracelsus says in his *Philosophia ad Athenienses,* "To speak of the Evestrum in its mortal and immortal aspects, we may say that everything has an Evestrum, and that it is like a shadow seen upon a wall. The Evestrum comes into existence, and grows with the body, and remains with it as long as a particle of the matter composing the latter exists. The Evestrum originates contemporaneously with the first birth of each form, and everything, whether it be visible or invisible, whether it belongs to the realm of matter or to the realm of the soul,[32] has its Evestrum; but Trarames means an invisible power that begins to be able to manifest itself at a time when the senses of the inner perception become developed. The Evestrum indicates future events by causing visions and apparitions, but Trarames causes an exaltation of the senses. Only those who are gifted with great wisdom may understand the true nature of Evestrum and Trarames. The Evestrum influences the sense of sight; Trarames the sense of hearing. The Evestrum causes dreams foreshadowing future events; Trarames communicates with man by causing voices to speak, music to sound that may be heard by the internal ear, invisible bells to ring, etc.[33] Whenever a child is born, there is born with him an Evestrum, which is so constituted as to be able to indicate in advance all the future acts and the events in the life of the individual to whom it belongs. If that individual is about to die, his Evestrum may indicate the approach of his death by raps or knocks, audible to all, or by some other unusual noise, by the movement of furniture, the stopping of clocks, the breaking of a picture, the fall of a mirror, or any other omen; but frequently such omens are neither recognised nor noticed, and not understood. The Trarames produces manifestations of a more subjective character, and may speak to a person in a way that is audible to him but inaudible to others."[34]

"The Evestrum of man is born with him, and after the death of the latter it remains in the earth-sphere,[35] and there is still some sympathetic connection between the Evestrum and the eternal and immortal part of man, and it will indicate the state of happiness or misery in which the soul of the person to whom it belongs exists. Such Evestra are not the souls of the dead walking upon the earth, but they are the ethereal duplicates of the persons to whom they belonged, remaining until the last particle of the matter composing the physical bodies of the latter has been consumed."

"All Evestra originate in the *Turba magna*, the collective activity of the universe.[36] The *Evestra prophetica* proceed directly from the *Turba magna*, the *Evestra obumbrata* come into existence at the time when the forms to which they belong appear. The *Evestra prophetica*[37] are the harbingers of great events that may concern the well-being of the world. If some such important event is to take place, they will be the forerunners to announce it to the world, so that the latter may be prepared for it, and a person who understands the true nature of such an Evestrum is a seer and prophet. Even the highest God has his *Evestrum mysteriales* by which his existence and his attributes may be recognised,[38] by which everything good may be known, and which may illuminate every mind. All the powers of evil, from the lowest to the highest, have their *Evestra mysteriales*, which may predict future evil, and which shed their bad influence over the world."

"*Necromantia* gives its signs through the *Astra*, which we also call '*Evestra*.' They mark the bodies of the sick and the dying with spots, showing that he will die on the third day; they mark the hands and fingers of men with yellow spots, foreshowing fortunate events. Through them the dead perform signs and wonders, such as the bleeding of a corpse in the presence of the murderer, and through their power voices are sometimes heard from out of the tombs. Noises and hauntings may thus take place in charnel-houses, and the dead appear in the clothing which they used to wear while living, and various visions be seen in mirrors, stones, water, etc. A great deal might be said about such things, but it would create fears and superstitions and other evils. This we wish to avoid, and we will therefore say no more about such things, which ought not to be publicly known." (*Signat. Rer.*, ix.)

"There are Evestra in all things,[39] and they are all prophesying spirits, whether the bodies to which they belong are rational or irrational, sensitive or without sensation. These Evestra teach Astronomia (natural science) to him who can understand what they say. The character of each thing may be known through its Evestrum, not by making astrological charts, calculating nativities, and composing prognostics, but by looking at it with the understanding, in the same manner as we may look at the image of an object in a mirror or at the shadow of a body on the surface of the water, or upon the earth. The *Ens* (the eternal cause and character of a thing) is reflected in its Evestrum. The form of the latter perishes, but the spirit remains. The number and variety of Evestra are as incalculable as that of the visible and invisible forms to which they belong. The Evestra of human beings know the thoughts of men, guide their instincts, watch over them in their sleep, warn them of dangers, and prophesy future events. The Sibyls of the past have read the future in the Evestra, and the Evestra have caused the ancient prophets to speak as it were in a dream." (*Philos. ad Athenienses*)

"The world of the Evestra is a world of its own,[40] although intimately interlaced and connected with ours. It has its own peculiar states of matter and objects that may be visible or invisible to its inhabitants, and yet corresponding to a certain extent to ours. Still, it is a world constituted differently from ours, and its inhabitants can know as little about our existence as we about theirs. The firmament of the universe[41] is fourfold in its essence, and divided into four planes. One belongs to Matter (Earth), one to Water, one to Air, and one to Fire, but the firmament in which rests the Evestrum is dispersed. The latter is not the firmament containing our visible stars, but the sphere in which the Nymphae, Undines, Salamanders, Flagae, etc., live. These beings are not dependent on our sphere of existence, but they have a firmament of their own; they have their own peculiar conditions, places of dwelling, localities, stars and planets. As there is in our world water and fire, harmonies and contrasts, visible bodies and invisible essences, likewise these beings are varied in their constitution and have their own peculiarities, for which human beings have no comprehension. But the two words intermingle and throw their shadows upon each other, and this circumstance causes delusive visions, apparitions, omens, and signs, mixing strangely with the two impressions coming from the *Evestra prophetica*, and only an intelligence illuminated by wisdom can distinguish the true from the false."[42]

"The first thing, however, which we ought to do is, as Christ says, to seek for the Kingdom of God and His justice. If we do this we will require no prophecies, because all that we need will be given to us."[43] (*De Arte Praesaga*)

Thus, the astral life is most active in man when his physical body is asleep. The sidereal man is then awake, and acts through the Evestrum, causing occasionally prophetic dreams, which the person after awakening to physical consciousness will remember, and to which he may pay attention. Such dreams may also be caused by other influences, and be delusive; and man ought therefore neither to reject nor to accept all dreams without discrimination, but always use his reason to distinguish the true from the false. "But, on the whole, there may be more reliance put into dreams than in the revelations received by the art of Necromancy; because the latter are usually false and deceptive, and although the Elementals, using the astral bodies of the dead on such occasions as masks, will give correct answers to questions, and often confirm their assertions with oaths, nevertheless no implicit confidence or reliance can be put into what they may say, because they do not wish to speak the truth, nor are they able to speak it."

"The patriarchs, prophets, and saints preferred, therefore, visions and dreams to any other mode of divination. Balaam was so well versed in the art of calling forth prophetic dreams that he could have them whenever he wanted. He was therefore falsely accused of being a sorcerer; for the Scriptures do not use any discrimination in such matters, but call every one a sorcerer who has such powers, and uses them to obtain information without being himself a saint. God wills that we shall be like the apostles in purity and simplicity of mind, and that we shall not speculate in hidden and secret things, such as are called supernatural[44] and which may be misused for the purpose of injuring one's neighbour in body and soul. The difference between a magus and a sorcerer is, that the former does not misuse his art. If magic (the power of the spiritual will) is misused, it is then sorcery." (*Philosophia Occulta*)

"There are two kinds of dreams—natural ones and such as come from the spirit. It is unnecessary to say much about the former, because they are known to all. They may be caused by joy or sadness, by impurities of the blood, by external or internal causes. A gambler may dream of cards, a soldier of battles, a drunkard of wine, a robber of theft. All such dreams are caused by the lower principles of such persons, which play with their imagination, heat their blood, and stimulate their phantasy."

"But there are supernatural dreams, and they are the messengers from God, that are sent to us at the approach of some great danger. Ananias, Cornelius, and many others had similar visions, and such supernatural dreams take place sometimes even among the present generation; but only the wise pay attention to them. Others treat them with contempt, although such dreams are true, and do not deceive."

"The dream in the *Gabal* plays with that which is in man, and that which the dream shows is the shadow of such wisdom as exists in the man, even if during his waking state he may know nothing about it; for we ought to know that God has given us all wisdom and knowledge, reason, and the power to perceive the past and the future; but we do not know it, because we are fooling away our time with outward and perishing things, and are asleep in regard to that which is real within our self. If one appears to have more talent than another man, it is not because he has been especially favoured by God, but because he has, more than the other, sought of that which God has given to each." (*Fragmenta Medico*)

"There are some persons whose nature is so spiritual, and their souls so exalted, that they can approach the highest spiritual sphere at a time when their bodies are asleep. Such persons have seen the glory of God, the happiness of the redeemed, and the torture of the wicked; and they did not forget their dreams on awakening, but remembered what they had seen unto the end of their days. Such things are possible, and the greatest mysteries are thus laid open to the perception of the spirit; and if we earnestly desire such gifts, and pray with an unrelenting faith to the power of the Supreme, that rests in ourselves, to grant them to us, we may be enabled to see the *Mysteria Dei,* and to understand them as well as Moses, Jesaiah, and John."

"It sometimes happens that the Evestra of persons who have died perhaps fifty or a hundred years ago appear to us in a dream, and if such an Evestrum comes to us in our dream and speaks with us, we should pay especial attention to what it says; for such a vision is not a hallucination or delusion, and it is possible that a man is as much able to use his reason during the sleep of his body as when the latter is awake, and if in such a case such an Evestrum appears to him, and he asks questions, he will then hear that which is true. A great deal could be said about such Evestra, but it is not proper to say more about them."[45]

"Through the Evestra we may obtain a great deal of knowledge in regard to good or to evil things, if we ask them to reveal them to us. Many persons have had such prayers granted to them. Some people that were sick have been informed during their sleep what remedies they should use, and after using such remedies they became cured. And such things have happened not only to Christians, but also to the heathens, to Jews, Saracenes, Mamelukes, Persians, and Egyptians; to good and to bad persons; and I cannot, therefore, believe that such revelations come directly from the Deity, because, there being only one God, all those peoples cannot have separate gods; but I believe that the universal light of Nature illuminated such disciples, and as that light has no organs of speech, it causes Evestra in the astral spheres of men during their sleep." (*De Caducis*)

"When men are asleep their bodies are like those of animals or plants, for animals and plants have also their elementary and their sidereal bodies; but the divine spirit can only become active in man. During sleep the sidereal body, by which man is connected with the inner nature of the Macrocosm, becomes free in its movements, and it can then rise up to the sphere of his ancestors, and converse with the stars (thoughts); that is to say, the processes taking place in the intellectual sphere of the Macrocosm will throw their reflections into his soul and come to his inner perception. Dreams, visions, and omens are gifts given to the sidereal man, and not to the elementary body."

"The day of the *corpora* is the night for the *spiritus*. When the bodies cease their labour, the spirits (in man) begin their work. When the body of man rests, his spirit begins to become active; and when the spirit rests, the body resumes its work. Therefore is the waking of the body the sleep of the spirit, and the spirit's sleep a waking for the body. They will not sleep or operate together; one acts, while the other reposes." (*Philosoph.*, v.)

"But dreams will be pure or impure, wise or foolish, rational or irrational, according to the position which man occupies in his relation to the light of Nature. Prophetic sights are caused by the circumstance that man has a sidereal body, related to the substance of the Universal Mind, and the former confabulates with the latter whenever the attention of the sidereal body is not needed by the requirements of the physical body. That is to say, all that takes place in the outer world is mirrored forth in the inner world, and appears as a dream. The elementary body has no spiritual gifts, but the sidereal body possesses them all. Whenever the elementary body is at rest, asleep or unconscious, the sidereal body is awake and active, because the latter needs neither rest nor sleep; but whenever the elementary body is fully awake and active, the activity of the sidereal body will then be restrained, and its free movements be impeded or prevented, like those of a man who is buried alive in a tomb."[46]

"The quality of the dreams will depend on the harmony that exists between the soul and the Astrum (Universal Mind). To those who are self-conceited and vain of their imaginary knowledge of exterior things, having no real wisdom, nothing can be shown to them, because the perverted action of their own minds opposes the harmonious action of the Universal Mind and repulses it. The spheres of their souls become narrow and contracted, and cannot expand towards the whole. They rest self-satisfied, buried in the shadow of their own ignorance, and are inaccessible to the light of Nature. Their attention is fully absorbed by the smoke of the candle-wick of their material reason, and they are blind to the light of the spiritual sun. The activity of the Universal Mind can only come to the consciousness of those whose spheres of mind are capable of receiving its impressions. Those who make room for such impressions will receive them. Such impressions are passing in and out of the sphere of the individual mind, and they cause visions and dreams, having an important meaning, and whose interpretation is an art that is known to the wise." (*Phil. Sagax*)

"Thus one spirit may teach another during the sleep of the body; for spirits deal with each other and teach each other their art. A foreign spirit cannot enter into a body which does not belong to him; it is bound to its own body. Therefore, the body of man must learn from its own spirit, and not from a foreign one; but his spirit must learn from other spirits, for it cannot always have everything out of its own self." (*Philos., v.*)

Death

The word "Death" implies two meanings: 1. Cessation of the activity of Life; 2. Annihilation of Form. Form is an illusion, and has no existence independent of Life; it is only an expression of life, and not productive of it. The form cannot cease to live, because it never lived before, and the death of a form is only the cessation of the eternal power of life in one form of manifestation of its activity preceding its manifestation in some other form. But Life itself cannot die or be annihilated, because it is not born of a form. It is an eternal power, that has always existed and always will exist. The annihilation of a particle of life would be a loss to the Universe that could not be replaced. Life is a function of God,[47] and will always exist as long as God is.

Before we can expect to die, we must first come to life. Life cannot cease to be active in a form as long as it has not become active therein. There are two kinds of life in man—the spiritual and the natural life. If the natural life ceases to be active in a man, the man dies, and he will then be conscious only of the life of his spirit; but if that life has not become active in him during his natural life, it will not become so by means of his death. No mortal man can become immortal by dying; he must have gained (become conscious of) eternal life during his terrestrial existence before he can expect to retain that life after the death of his body: become earth-bound spirits, until the time of their natural dissolution arrives. "What is death? It is that which takes the life away from us. It is the separation of the immortal from the mortal part. It is also that which awakens us and returns to us that which it has taken away." (*Paramirum*, ii.)

"Each form is an embodiment of certain principles or qualities. If there were, for instance, no heat, nothing could become hot. If there were no wisdom, no man could become wise; if there were no art, there would be no artists. If the principles from which men and animals derive their qualities did not exist, there could be no men or animals in whom such qualities are made manifest. These principles (forms of will) remain, although the forms in which they have been manifested for the time being decay. If a wise man dies, his wisdom still continues to be, and may be communicated to another person." (*De*

Fund. Sap.)

If a mill suddenly comes to a stop, it may be from two causes; either the miller who manipulated it has gone away, or there has been something wrong with the works, so that they could not operate any longer. In the same way the death of the body will occur, if for some reason the body is no longer capable to accomplish its work for the spirit by which it is inhabited, or it may be that the inhabitant (the soul) for some reason has left the house. The latter circumstance accounts for many cases of sudden death "from unknown causes", and therefore an apparently dead body should never be buried before the only certain sign, which shows that it is no longer inhabitable—namely, putrefaction—appears; for otherwise we are not sure that the inhabitant may only be temporarily absent, and find his house destroyed when he returns.

All forms are subject to annihilation; they are only illusions, and as such they will cease to exist when the cause that produced them ceases to act. The body of a king or a sage is as useless as that of an animal after the life whose product it was has ceased to act. A form can only maintain its existence as long as the action of life upon the substance of the form continues. But life is an eternal and perfect power; it can be brought into contact, but it cannot be united with physical matter. It can only be attracted to physical matter by the power of the spirit, and if the spirit ceases to attract it, life will depart from matter, and the form will be dissolved into its elements. Nothing can become united with eternal and perfect life except that which is eternal and perfect. That which is good and perfect can continue to live; that which is evil and imperfect will be transformed. If all the elements constituting a man were good, if his whole emotional and intellectual constitution were perfect, such a man would be wholly immortal. If there is nothing good in him, he will have to die and to be wholly transformed. If a part of him is good and another part evil, the good portion will live and the evil one will perish. "*Omne bonum perfectum a Deo; imperfectum a diablo.*"

"The divine man does not die; but the animals in him are subject to dissolution. Man will have to render account for his acts; not so the animals. An animal is only an animal and not a man; but the true man is an image of God. Animal man is that which the animal in him makes of him, and if a man is not really a *man* in regard to his wisdom, he is not a man but an animal." (*De Fund. Sap.*)

"The spirit of man comes from God, and when the body dies the spirit returns to God. The astral soul comes from the astral plane and returns to it. The body comes from Nature and returns to it. Thus everything returns to its own *prima materia*. If God is not conscious in us, how can we expect to be conscious in God? Who can see by a light which does not shine?" (*De Morb. Invis.*, iv.)

"No man becomes raised in the flesh of Adam and Eve (the lower *Manas*), but in the flesh of Christ (the *Atma-Buddhi Manas*); therefore that which is not in the flesh of Christ cannot be redeemed." (*De Fund. Sap.*, fragm.)

Everything that exists is a manifestation of life. Stones and metals have a life as well as plants, animals, or men; only the mode of the manifestation differs on account of the organic structure of the particles of which they are composed. A fly, for instance, has the same life as a stone, because there is only One Life; but in a fly it manifests itself otherwise than in a stone, and while the shape of the stone may exist for thousands of years, the fly lives only a few days.

The elements, which are used by the power of life for the purpose of manifesting itself, are as indestructible as life itself, but they continually change their states, they are continually undergoing transformations, they are continually calcinated, sublimated, dissolved, decomposed, distilled, coagulated, and tinctured in the alchemistical laboratory of Nature.

Each form has a certain period during which it may exist as a form, and the length of this period is predetermined by the number which is a constituent factor in the organisation of form, and which springs from life itself, because life is a conscious power, and does nothing at random, but everything according to its own inherent law; and if the form should be prematurely destroyed, life will nevertheless be active in the astral soul of the form, which cannot be destroyed until the time for its natural dissolution has arrived.[48] The outer form is only caused by the action of life upon the astral form, and if the exterior form is broken, the inner form still continues to exist, and can under certain conditions be brought again into contact with the remnants of the broken form, and thereby that form may be revived. If a thing dies a natural death, such a revival is impossible; but if the death has been premature, such a revival may take place, if the vital organs of the person or animal have not been irrevocably destroyed.[49]

But even in that case there still exists a very close sympathetic relationship between the remnants of the body and the living astral form, and this relationship continues to exist until the period of the natural life of the individual has expired, or until the substances composing his body have been entirely dissolved into their elements.[50] The remnants of such bodies, the corpses of persons that have committed suicide or died by the hands of an executioner, have therefore great occult powers. They do not contain life, but the balsam of life,[51] and it is very fortunate that this fact is not publicly known, because if evil-disposed persons knew these things and the use that can be made of the corpses, they might use them for sorceries and evil purposes, and inflict much suffering upon others.[52]

If we would burn a tree, and enclose the ashes and the smoke and the vapour, and all the elements that made up the tree, into a great bottle, and plant a living seed of that tree into the ashes, we might resurrect the same kind of a tree again out of its ashes, because there would be a centre of life, to which all the elements that were before necessary to form that tree could be again attracted to form another tree of the same kind, having all the characteristics of the former; but if there were no seed, there would be no tree, because the character of the tree is neither in the ashes nor in the vapour nor in the smoke, but in the *Mysterium magnum*, the eternal storehouse of life, from which it will be attracted again by the seed, and be made to live in a new form endowed with greater virtues and powers than the ones it possessed before.

All this goes to show not only the indestructibility of "matter" but also that of "mind." The *will-spirit* of a person retains its own qualities after the death of the person; but this will-spirit is not the person itself. The person's personality consists of that combination of personal qualities which are represented in his form, and if that form, be it on the physical or on the astral plane, is dissolved, there is then an end of that personality, and only the will-spirit remains. But the divine spirit of man, having attained self-consciousness in God and substance in the body of Christ, or, to express it in other words, that part of the

Manas which has become illumined by the light of the *Atma-Buddhi*, will continue as a self- conscious and self-luminous entity in the life of eternity.[53]

Thus there is something incorruptible and eternal, and something corruptible and temporal, in man, and he may use his free will to identify himself either with the one or the other. If he identifies himself with Nature, he will have to be transformed by her. If he identifies himself with the divine spirit, he will remain that which he is. "There is no death to be feared except that which results from becoming unconscious of the presence of God."

Chapter 5: Pneumatology

The orthodoxy of the Middle Ages looked upon angels and devils and departed human spirits as being personal invisible entities. They personified the powers of good and of evil, and made of them caricatures and monsters that flitted from place to place, attempting to subjugate the souls of men or to bring them within their power. The governmental institutions during those times were those of oligarchy, and the poor were dependent on the favours of the rich. The power of the Church was supreme, and the dictates of the clergy suffered no disobedience. Servility and the craving for personal favours were the order of the day, and this state of mind necessarily influenced and modified the religious conceptions of the people. The Supreme Spirit of the Universe became degraded in their eyes to a personal tyrant, into whose favour they attempted to wheedle themselves by penitences, supplications, and by means of the intercessions of priests, who were supposed to be his favourites. Everything that could not be reconciled with existing prejudices and opinions was attributed to the devil; and the horrors of the inquisitions, religious persecutions, and witch-trials are too well known to require to be recalled to the memory of the reader.

"*Pneuma*" or "soul," means a semi-material spirit, an essence or form which is neither "material," in the common acceptation of this term, nor pure spirit. It is (like everything else in the universe) a form of will, and may be with or without any intelligence. Usually it means the connecting link between spirit and body; but there are beings who belong entirely to the realm of the soul and have no such bodies as are commonly called "material."

It may be said that the soul is a certain state of activity of the will, and the same may be said of the physical body; for if we look at the universe as being a manifestation of will in motion, then all forms and objects that we know of, or which we can imagine, are certain vibrations of will. Thus we may look upon physical nature as being constituted of a low order of vibrations; upon the soul as a higher octave of the same, and of spirit as one higher still. If the physical body dies, the lower octave ceases to sound; but the higher one continues and will continue to vibrate as long as it is in contact with the highest; but if the spirit has become separated from it, it will sooner or later cease its activity. Thus if man dies the soul remains, and its higher essences go to form the substance of the body of the paradisiacal man, "the man of the new Olympus", and the lower essences of the soul, from which the spirit has departed, dissolve in the astral elements to which they belong, as the earthly body dissolves in the elements of the earth.

This dissolution, however, does not take place immediately at the time of the separation of the soul from the body, but may require a long time. That which constituted the mind of a man will still continue to exist after the death of the body, although it is not the man itself. "If a man has been true during his life, his spirit will be true after the man's death. If he has been a great astronomer, a magician, or alchemist, his spirit will still be the same, and we may learn a great many things from such spirits; they being the substance of the mind which once constituted the terrestrial Man." (*Philos.*, Tract v.)

There are two deaths or two separations—the separation of the spirit and soul from the body and the separation of the spirit from the astral soul, or, to express it more correctly, of the spiritual soul from the merely intellectual and animal soul. If a person dies a natural death (i.e., from old age), his passions having died out during his life, his selfish will having become weak and his mind like that of a child, putting its confidence in his father, his spirit and soul will, at the time of his death, become free from material bonds and be attracted to the body of Christ.[1]

"Such a soul is herself the flesh and blood of Christ, and Christ is her Master. She does not enter into communication with mortals, because she has no desire for anything earthly. She does not 'think' or speculate about terrestrial things, nor worry herself about her relatives or friends. She lives in a state of pure feeling, bliss, and enjoyment."[2]

Such is the fate of those who die a natural death in God; but the conditions of those who die prematurely without being regenerated, either by their own hands or in consequence of some accident, differ greatly; because, although their souls have become forcibly separated from their bodies, the spirit does not therefore necessarily leave the soul, but remains with it until another separation takes place. They remain in such cases human beings like any others; only with this difference, that they do not possess a physical body, and they remain in such a state until the time arrives when, according to the law of Nature and their own predestination (Karma), their physical death should have taken place. At that time the separation of their higher and lower principles takes place. Up to that time they possess their astral bodies. Such bodies are invisible to us, but they are visible to them, and have sensation and perceptive faculties,[3] and they perform in their thoughts that which they have been in the habit of performing during life, and believe that they are performing it physically. They still remain in the earth sphere, and Paracelsus calls them *Caballi, Lemures, etc.* They are still in full possession of their earthly desires and passions: they attempt to satisfy them, and are instinctively attracted to persons in whom they find corresponding desires and passions, and to such places where they may hope to satisfy them, by entering into sympathy with such persons (mediums), and they are therefore often inclined to instigate such mediumistic persons to the commission of crimes and immoralities; neither can they avoid doing so, because, by losing their physical bodies, they have lost the necessary amount of energy and will-power to exercise self-control and to employ their reasoning faculties. They often haunt the places where they used to spend their time during life,[4] thus attempting to find relief from their burning thirst after the gratification of their desires. Wherever their thoughts attract them, there they will go. If they have committed some crime, they will be bound by repentance to that place where it was perpetrated; if they have a treasure buried, care for their money will hold them there; hatred, or desire for revenge, will tie them to their enemies;[5] passion turns them into vampires, and connects them with the object of their passion, provided that there are some elements in these objects which will attract them; because the astral body of an evil person cannot influence the mind of a pure person, neither during life nor after death, unless they are mutually connected by some similarity in their psychic organisations.[6]

"Under certain circumstances, such human entities will become visible or manifest their presence in some manner. They may appear in bodily shape, or remain invisible and produce sounds and noises—such as knocks, laughing, whistling, sneezing, howling, groaning, sighing, walking, trampling, throwing stones, and moving articles of furniture or other objects, and all this may be done by them for the purpose of calling the attention of the living, so that they will obtain an opportunity to enter into communication with them."[7]

But not all the appearances of supermundane or submundane visitors are caused by the apparitions of the ghosts or astral bodies of suicides or victims of accidents, nor by the astral corpses and the Evestra of the dead; but there are other invisible entities sometimes haunting the houses of mortals, and becoming occasionally visible and tangible to the physical senses, if the conditions necessary for such a purpose exist.

"One of these classes is made up of beings called 'phantasmata.' These ghost-like beings are 'nocturnal spirits' having reasoning capacities similar to those of man. They seek to attach themselves to men, especially to such as have very little power of self-control, and over whom they can gain power. There are a great many kinds of such spirits, good as well as evil ones, and they love to be near man. In this they are comparable to dogs, who are also fond of the company of men. But man can profit nothing from their company. They are empty shadows (shells), and are only an encumbrance to him. They are afraid of red corals, as dogs are afraid of a whip; but the brown corals attract them."[8] (*Herbarius Theophrasti: De Corallis*)

"Some people believe that such spirits can be driven away with holy water and by the burning of incense; but a genuine holy water cannot be had so long as no man is found who is holy enough to be able to invest water with an occult holy power, and the odour of incense may sooner attract evil spirits than drive them away; because evil spirits are attracted by things that are attractive to the senses, and if we wish to drive them away it would be more reasonable to employ disagreeable odours for such a purpose. The true and effective power against all evil spirits is the spiritual will. If we love the source of all good with all our heart, mind, and desire, we may be sure never to fall into the power of evil; but priestly ceremonies—the sprinkling of water, the burning of incense, and the singing of incantations—are the inventions of clerical vanity, and they therefore take their origin from the source of all evil. Ceremonies have been instituted originally to give an external form to an internal act; but where the internal power to perform such acts does not exist, a ceremony will be of no avail except to attract such spirits as may love to mock at our foolishness." (*Philosophia Occulto*)

Another class consists of the Incubi and Succubi, of which rabbinical traditions speak in an allegorical manner as having been created by the spilling of the seed of Adam (the animal man) while engaged with Lilith, his first wife (meaning a morbid imagination). Paracelsus says in his book, *De Origine Morborum Invisibilium*, lib. iii: "Imagination[9] is the cause of Incubi and Succubi and fluidic Larvae. The Incubi are male and the Succubi female beings. They are the outgrowths of an intense and lewd imagination of men or women, and after they take form they are carried away. They are formed of the sperma found in the imagination of those who commit the unnatural sin of Onan in thought and desire. Coming as it does from the imagination alone, it is no true sperma, but only a corrupted salt (essence). Only a seed that enters the organs which Nature provided for its development can grow into a body.[10] If seed is not planted into the proper soil it will rot. If sperma does not come into the proper matrix it will not produce anything good, but something useless. Therefore the Incubi and Succubi grown out of corrupted seed, without the natural order of things, are evil and useless; and Thomas of Aquinas has made an error by mistaking such a useless thing for a complete one."

"This sperma, coming from the imagination, is born in *Amor Hereos*. This means a kind of love in which a man may imagine a woman, or a woman a man, to perform the connubial act with the image created in the sphere of the mind. From this act results the expulsion of an ethereal fluid, impotent to generate a child, but capable of bringing Larvae into existence. Such an imagination is the mother of a luxurious unchastity, which, if continued, renders man impotent and woman sterile, because much of the true creative and formative power is lost by the frequent exercise of such a morbid imagination. This is frequently the cause of moles, abortions, miscarriages, and malformations. Such corrupted sperma may be taken away by spirits that wander about at night, and who will carry it to a place where they may hatch it out. There are spirits that will perform an 'act' with it, as may also be done by witches, and, in consequence of that act, many curious monsters of horrible shapes come into existence" (*De Orig. Morb. Invis.*).

"If such monsters are born from a powerful, conscious imagination, consciousness will also be created in them. The spirits of night can use all that is born from such sperma according to their pleasure, but they can use nothing of a human character or possessing true spirit." "*Amor hereos* is a state of the invisible body, and is caused by an overheated imagination, stimulated to such an extent as to eject sperma, out of which Incubi and Succubi grow. In ordinary *pollutionibus nocturnalis*, the body loses sperma without any effort of the imagination, and the spirits of night can therefore not use it for their purposes."

"If women have passed beyond the age of fertility and are unchaste and of a vivid imagination, they often call such things into existence. If persons of either sex have lewd desires and an active imagination, or if they are passionately in love with another person of the opposite sex, and unable to obtain the object of their desire and fancy, then an Incubus or Succubus may take the place of the absent object, and in this way sorcerers call Succubi, and witches Incubi, into existence."[11] "To prevent such unfortunate occurrences, it is necessary to be chaste, honest, and pure, in thought and desire, and whoever is unable to remain so should not remain single.[12] Imagination is a great power, and if the world knew what strange things can be produced by the power of the imagination, the public authorities would cause all idle persons to go to work and to employ their time in some useful manner, and they would take care of those who are unable to control their own imagination, in order that such evil results should be avoided." (*Morb. Invis*, iv.)

"The so-called 'Dragon' is an invisible being, which may become visible and appear in a human form and cohabit with witches. This is accomplished by means of the sperma which is lost by masturbators, fornicators, and prostitutes in *acte venereo*[13] and which such spirits use as a corpus to obtain for themselves a human form, because the whole of the human form is typified in the sperma, and if such spirits use the sperma of a certain person, it is as if one man puts on the coat of another man; and then they have the form of that person and resemble him in all his parts and details."[14] (*De Fertilitate*, Tract, ii.)

"Another such hideous monster is the *Basilisc*, created by Sodomy, and also the *Aspis* and *Leo*. There are innumerable bastard forms, half man, half spiders or toads, etc., inhabiting the astral plane, belonging to the 'serpent which is to have his head crushed by the heel of Christ'."[15] (*Fragm.*)

"If such forms are sufficiently dense to become visible, they appear like a coloured shadow or mist, or black shadows. They have no life of their own, but they borrow it from the person who called them into existence, just as a shadow is cast by a body; and where there is no body, there can be no shadow. They are often generated by idiots, immoral, depraved, or diseased persons, who lead irregular and solitary lives, and who are addicted to bad habits. The coherence of the particles composing the bodies of such beings is not very strong, and they are afraid of draughts of air, light, fire, sticks, and weapons. They are a sort of airy appendix to the body of their creator, and there is sometimes such an intimate connection between them and the body of their progenitors, that if an injury is inflicted upon the former, it will be transmitted to the latter. They are parasites drawing vitality out of the persons to whom they are attracted, and they exhaust their vitality very soon, if such persons are not very strong."[16]

"Some such beings influence men according to their qualities; they watch them, increase and deepen their faults, find excuses for their mistakes, cause them to wish for the success of evil actions, and gradually absorb their vitality. They fortify and support the imagination in the operations of sorcery; they sometimes utter false prophecies and give out misleading oracles. If a man has a strong and evil imagination, and wishes to injure another, such beings are always ready to lend a helping hand for the accomplishment of his purpose." Such beings render their victims insane, if the latter are too weak to resist their influence. "A healthy and pure person cannot become obsessed by them, because such Larvae can only act upon men if they make room for them in their minds. A healthy mind is a castle that cannot be invaded without the will of its master; but if lusts are allowed to enter, they excite the passions of men and women, they create cravings in them, they produce bad thoughts which act injuriously upon the brain; they sharpen the animal intellect and suffocate the moral sense. Evil spirits obsess only those human beings in whom the animal nature is preponderating. Minds that are illumined by the spirit of truth cannot be possessed; only those who are habitually guided by their own lower impulses will become subjected to their influence. Exorcisms and ceremonies are useless in such cases. Praying[17] and abstinence from all thoughts that stimulate the imagination or excite the brain are the only true remedies" (*De Ente Spirituali*). "The cure of obsession is a purely psychical and moral act. The obsessed person should use true prayer and abstinence, and after that a strong-willed person should will such spirits to depart." (*Philosophia, Occulta*)[18]

The reason why we cannot see such astral entities is because they are transparent as air. We cannot see the air unless we produce a smoke in it, and even in that case we do not see the air itself, but the smoke that is carried by the air. But we can feel the air when it moves, and we may also occasionally feel the presence of such entities, if they are dense enough to be felt. Moreover, the purpose of our senses is to perceive the objects that exist on the plane for which those senses are adapted, and therefore the physical senses exist for the purpose of seeing physical things, and the senses of the inner man are made to see the things of the soul. When the outer senses are inactive, the inner senses awaken to life, and we may see the objects on the astral plane as we see things in a dream. There are also some poisons by which the organic activity of the body can be suppressed for a time, and the consciousness of the inner man be rendered more active, and which will therefore enable us to see the things on the astral plane. But such poisons are destructive of reason and very injurious to the health. In fevers, deliriums, etc., such things may also be seen. Some of them are the creations of the mind of the patient; others may have been created by the morbid imagination of another person, as described above.[19]

But if such entities are invisible under normal conditions to a human being, they will be well enough perceived by a human Elementary consciously existing on their plane, and, what is still more, depraved human characters after death take themselves the forms of animals and monsters, whom they were brought to resemble by their own evil thoughts. Form is nothing but an appearance representing a character, and the character shapes the form. If the character of a person is thoroughly evil, it will cause the astral form to assume a hideous form. Therefore the souls of the depraved appear in animal shapes.[20]

Pure spirit has no form: it is formless, like the sunshine. But as the sunshine causes the elements of matter to grow into plants, soul-substances are formed into beings having shapes, through the action of the spiritual rays. There are good spirits and spirits of evil; planetary spirits and angels. There are the spirits of the four elements, and there are many thousand different kinds.[21]

"Each child receives at the time of its birth a familiar spirit or genius, and such spirits sometimes instruct their pupils even while the latter are in their earliest youth. They often teach them to do very extraordinary things. There is an incalculable number of such genii in the universe, and we may learn through them all the mysteries of the Chaos in consequence of their connection with the *Mysterium magnum*. Such familiar spirits are called Flagae."[22]

"There are several kinds of Flagae, and there are two ways by which we may obtain knowledge through them. One way is by their becoming visible and able to talk with us; the other way is by their exercising an invisible influence upon our intuition. The art of Nectromancy[23] enables man to perceive interior things, and there is no mystery concerning any human being that may not be found out by that art, and the Flagae can be made to reveal it either by persuasion or by the strength of one's will, for the Flagae obey the will of man for the same reason that a soldier obeys the will of the commander, or an inferior obeys that of his superior, although the former may be physically stronger than the latter. The Flagae can be made to appear visibly in a mirror of *Beryl*, in a piece of coal or a crystal, etc.; and not only the Flagae themselves, but the persons to whom they belong, may be seen, and all their secrets be known. And if it is not practicable to cause them to become visible, such secrets can be found out by a communication of thought, or by signs, allegorical visions, etc. By the assistance of these Flagae hidden treasures may be found and closed letters be read, and everything secret be seen, no matter how much it is hidden from outward sight, for the opening of the interior sight removes the veil of matter. Things that have been buried will thus be found, stolen goods recovered, etc.[24]

The Flagae reveal their secrets to us in our dreams, the good as well as the evil. He who obtains knowledge from the spirit obtains it from his father; he who knows the Elementals knows himself; he who understands the nature of the elements understands how the Microcosm is constructed. The Flagae are the spirits that instructed mankind in arts and sciences in ancient times, and without them there would be no science or philosophy in the world."[25]

"In the practice of divination by sortilegium, etc., the Flagae guide the hand. Such arts are neither from God nor from the devil, but they are from the Flagae. The ceremonies that are customarily used on such occasions are mere superstition, and have been invented to give to such occasions an air of solemnity. Those who do practise that art are often themselves ignorant of the laws that control it, and they perhaps attribute the results obtained to the ceremonies, and mistake tomfooleries for the essential thing."[26]

In regard to the reliance to be put on the revelations of invisible beings, Paracelsus says: "Evil spirits love to lead men into error, and therefore their prophecies are usually unreliable and their predictions based upon trickery. God made spirits mute, so that they may not tell everything so plainly to man that man does not need to use his reason to avoid making mistakes. The spirits should not instruct man; but they do not always obey that command. Therefore they are often silent when their speech is mostly needed, and they frequently speak false when it is of the utmost importance to know the truth. This is the cause that so many things that have been told by spirits have been proved lies and illusions, and some spirits lie a great deal more than others. But it may happen that perhaps out of a dozen predictions made by such spirits one accidentally comes out true, and ignorant people will in such cases pay no attention to the fact that the other eleven predictions were false, but they will be ready to believe everything that such spirits say. Such spirits often teach those persons who deal with them to perform certain ceremonies, to speak certain words and names in which there is no meaning, and they do all such things for their own amusement, and to have some sport at the expense of credulous persons. They are seldom what they pretend to be; they accept names, and one will use the name of another, or they will assume the mask and the ways of acting of another. If a person has such a spirit, belonging to a better class, he may make a good fortuneteller; but one who has a lying spirit will hear nothing but lies; and, on the whole, all these spirits surpass each other in deception and lies." (*Philosophia Sagax*)[27]

"Man is an instrument through which all the three worlds—the spiritual, the astral, and the elementary world—are acting. In him are beings from all these worlds, reasonable and unreasonable, intelligent and unintelligent creatures. A person without any self-knowledge and self-control is made to act according to the will of these creatures; but the true philosopher acts according to the will of the Supreme, the Creator, in him. If the masters whom man obeys are foolish, their servants will also act foolishly. It is true that every one thinks that he is the master, and that he does what he pleases; but he does not see the fool within him, who is his master, and by whom he becomes a fool himself." (*De Meteoris*)

There is another class of spirits, the Saganae or Elemental Spirits of Nature. Paracelsus says about their bodies: "There are two kinds of flesh—one that comes from Adam and another that does not come from Adam. The former is gross material, visible and tangible for us; the other one is not tangible and not made from earth. If a man who is a descendant from Adam wants to pass through a wall, he will have first to make a hole through it; but a being who is not descended from Adam needs no hole or door, but may pass through matter that appears solid to us, without causing any damage to it. The beings not descended from Adam, as well as those descended from him, are organised and have substantial bodies; but there is as much difference between the substance composing their bodies as there is between Matter and Spirit. Yet the Elementals are not spirits, because they have flesh, blood, and bones; they live and propagate offspring; they eat and talk, act and sleep, etc., and consequently they cannot be properly called 'spirits.' They are beings occupying a place between men and spirits, resembling men and women in their organisation and form, and resembling spirits in the rapidity of their locomotion. They are intermediary compound beings, formed out of two parts joined into one; just as two colours mixed together will appear as one colour, resembling neither one nor the other of the two original ones. The Elementals have no higher principles; they are therefore not immortal, and when they die they perish like animals. Neither water nor fire can injure them, and they cannot be locked up in our material prisons. They are, however, subject to diseases. Their costumes, actions, forms, ways of speaking, etc., are not very unlike those of human beings; but there are a great many varieties. They have only animal intellects, and are incapable of spiritual development." (*Lib. Philos.*, ii.)

"These spirits of Nature are not animals; they have a reason and language like man; they have minds, but no spiritual soul. This may appear strange and incredible; but the possibilities of nature are not limited by man's knowledge of them, and the wisdom of God is unfathomable. They have children, and these children are like themselves. Man is made after the image of God, and they may be said to be made after the image of man; but man is not God, and the elemental spirits of Nature are not human beings, although they somewhat resemble man. They are liable to sickness, and they die like animals. Their habits resemble those of men; they work and sleep; they eat and drink and make their clothing; and as man is nearest to God, so are they nearest to man."[28] (*Lib. Philos.*, i.)

"They live in the four elements: the Nymphae in the element of water, the Sylphs in that of the air, the Pigmies in the earth, and the Salamanders in the fire. They are also called Undinae, Sylvestres, Gnomi, Vulcani, etc. Each species moves only in the element to which it belongs, and neither of them can go out of its appropriate element, which is to them as the air is to us, or the water to fishes; and none of them can live in the element belonging to another class. To each elemental being the element in which it lives is transparent, invisible, and respirable, as the atmosphere is to ourselves."

"The four classes of Nature-spirits do not mix with each other; the Gnomes have no intercourse with the Undines or Salamanders, nor the Sylvestres with either of these. As a fish lives in the water, it being its element, so each being lives in its own element. For instance, the element wherein man breathes and lives is the air; but to the Undines the water is what the air is to us, and if we are surprised that they are in the water, they may also be surprised because we are in the air. Thus the element of the Gnomes is the earth, and they pass through rocks and walls and stones like a thought; for such things are to them no greater obstacles than the air is to us. In the same sense the fire is the air wherein the Salamanders live; but the Sylvestres are the nearest related to us, for they live in the air like ourselves; they would be drowned if they were under water, and they would suffocate in the earth and be burned in the fire; for each being belongs to its own *Chaos* and dies if transported into another. If that Chaos is gross, the beings living in it are subtle; and if the Chaos is subtle, the beings are gross. Therefore we have gross bodies, so that we can pass through the air without being blown down, and the Gnomes have subtle forms, so as to be able to pass through the rocks. Men have their leaders and authorities; bees and ants their queens; geese and other animals have their leaders; and so also have the spirits of Nature their kings and queens. The animals receive their clothing from Nature; but the spirits of Nature prepare it themselves. The omnipotence of God is not limited to His taking care only of man, but is abundantly able to take care also of the spirits of Nature, and of many other things of which men know nothing. They see the sun and the sky the same as we, because each element is transparent to those who live therein. Thus the sun shines through the rocks for the Gnomes, and the water does not hinder the Undines to see the sun and the stars; they have their summers and winters, and their 'earth' bears them fruits; for each being lives on that element whereof it has grown." (*Lib. Philos.*, ii.)

"As far as the personalities of the Elementals are concerned, it may be said that those belonging to the element of water resemble human beings of either sex; those of the air are greater and stronger; the Salamanders are long, lean, and dry; the Pigmies are of the length of about two spans, but they can extend or elongate their forms until they appear like giants. The Elementals of air and water, the Sylphs and Nymphs, are kindly disposed towards man; the Salamanders cannot associate with him on account of the fiery nature of the element wherein they live, and the Pigmies are usually of a malicious nature. The Pigmies are building houses, vaults, and strange-looking edifices of some certain semi-material substances unknown to us. They have some kind of alabaster, marble, cement, etc.; but these substances are as different from ours as the web of a spider is different from our linen. Nymphs have their residences and palaces in the element of water; Sylphs and Salamanders have no fixed dwellings. On the whole, the Elementals have an aversion against self-conceited and opinionated persons, such as dogmatists, inquisitive sceptics, drunkards, and gluttons, and against vulgar and quarrelsome people of all kinds; but they love natural men, who are simple-minded and child-like, innocent and sincere, and the less there is vanity and hypocrisy in a man, the easier will it be for him to approach them; but otherwise they are as shy as wild animals."[29]

"Man lives in the exterior elements, and the Elementals live in the interior elements.[30] They have dwellings and clothing, manners and customs, languages and governments, of their own, in the same sense as the bees have their queens and herds of animals their leader. They are sometimes seen in various shapes. Salamanders have been seen in the shapes of fiery balls, or tongues of fire running over the fields or appearing in houses. Nymphs have been known to adopt the human shape, clothing, and manner, and to enter into a union with man. There are certain localities where large numbers of Elementals live together, and it has occurred that a man has been admitted into their communities and lived with them for a while, and that they have become visible and tangible to him."[31]

"The angels are invisible to us; but nevertheless an angel may appear to our spiritual sight, and likewise man is invisible to the spirits of nature, and what the Undines know of us is to them merely what fairy tales are to us. The Undines appear to man, but not man to them. Man is gross in the body and subtle in the Chaos; therefore they may enter his Chaos (*the physical plane*), and appear to him and remain with him, marry and have children with him. Thus an Undine may marry a man and keep house with him, and her children will be human beings and not Undines, because they receive a human soul from the man; and, moreover, the Undine herself thereby receives the germ of immortality. Man is bound to God by means of his spiritual soul, and if an Undine becomes united to man, she will thereby become bound to God. As an Undine without her union with man dies like an animal, likewise man is like an animal if he severs his union with God."

"Therefore the Nymphs are anxious to become united with man; they seek to become immortal through him. They have a mind and intellect like man, but not the immortal soul, such as we have obtained through the death of Christ. But the spirits of the earth, the air, and fire seldom marry a human being. They may, however, become attached to him and enter his service. It must not be supposed that they are airy nothings or merely ghosts or appearances; they are of flesh and blood, only subtler than man" (*i.e.,* of the substance of mind).

"The Nymphs sometimes come out of the water and may be seen sitting on the shore near their dwelling, and they as well as the Gnomes have a language like man; but the spirits of the woods are more rough and speak nothing, although they are able to speak and are clever. The Nymphs appear in human form and clothing; but the spirits of fire are of a fiery shape. They are usually not to be found in the company of men; but they come to cohabit with old women, such as are witches, and they are sometimes obsessed by the devil. If any man has a Nymph for a wife, let him take care not to offend her while she is near the water, as in such a case she might return to her own element;[32] and if any one has a Gnome for a servant, let him be faithful to him, for each has to be dutiful to the other; if you do your duty to him, he will do his duty to you. All this is in the divine order of things and will become manifest in due time; so that we will then be able to see that which seems now almost incredible." (*Lib. Philos.*, ii.)

In the legends of the saints the Elemental spirits of Nature are often alluded to as "devils," a name which they do not deserve, because there are good as well as bad Elementals; but, although some may be very selfish, they have not developed any love for absolute evil, because they have only mortal souls, but no spiritual essence to make them immortal.

Besides the astral spirits in man and the Elemental spirits of Nature, there are many other spirits born within the soul (the will and imagination of Nature); and as the mind of man may create monsters, and man paint their images on canvas, or sculpture them in stone or wood, so the universal power of Nature's mind creates monsters in the astral light, and they will throw their shadows forth in the physical world of appearances, by becoming objective in corporeal bodies upon the earth. Some of them are short-lived, and others will live unto the day of the dissolution of all things. "We all know that a man may change his character in the course of his life, so that he ultimately becomes a very different person from what he was before; and thus every creature having a will can change and become supernatural or unnatural; *i.e.*, different from that which normally belongs to its nature. Many of the head-lights of the Church, who now strut about with jewels and diamonds, will be dragons and worms when the human body in which they are now masquerading will have disappeared at the time of their death." (*Lib. Philos.*, iv.)

"There are the *Sirens*,[33] but they are merely a kind of monstrous fishes; but there are also two more kinds of spirits, related to the Nymphs and Pigmies, namely, the *Gigantes* (giants) and the *Dwarfs*. This may not be believed, but it ought to be remembered that the beginning of true knowledge is that the light of Nature illumines man, and that in this light he knows all things in Nature by means of the light of the inner man. The Giants and Dwarfs are monsters, being related to the Sylvestres and Gnomes in the same sense as the Sirens are related to the Undines. They have no (spiritual) souls, and are rather to be compared to monkeys than to human beings. Such spirits are often the guardians of hidden treasures."

"Such things will be denied and ridiculed by the worldly wise; but at the end of the world, when all things will be revealed, then will also come forward the so-called 'doctors' and 'professors,' who were great in their ignorance; then will it be seen who were those that were learned in the foundation of Nature, and the others learned in empty talk. Then we will know those who have written according to truth and those who taught according to their own fancy; and each one will receive what he deserves. There will then be no doctors and no magisters, and those who are now making a great deal of parade and noise will then be very silent; but those who have received the true understanding will be happy. Therefore I recommend my writings to be judged at that time when all things will become manifest, and when each one will see the light as it was revealed to him."

"The evil spirits are, so to say, the bailiffs and executioners of God (*Karma*). They have been called into existence by the influences of evil, and they work out their destiny. But the vulgar have a too high estimate of their powers, especially of the power of the devil. The devil has not enough power to mend a broken pot, much less to enrich a man. He—or it—is the poorest thing that can be thought of, and poorer than any being that can be found in the four elements.[34] There are a great many inventions, sciences, and arts that are ascribed to the agency of the (personal) devil; but before the world grows much older it will be found that the devil has nothing to do with such things, that the devil is nothing and knows nothing, and that such things are the results of natural causes. True science can accomplish a great deal; the Eternal Wisdom of the existence of all things is without a time, without a beginning, and without an end. Things that are considered now to be impossible will be accomplished; that which is unexpected will in future prove to be true, and that which is looked upon as superstition in one century will be the basis for the approved science of the next." (*Philosophia Occulta*)

Chapter 6: Magic and Sorcery

In proportion as an art or science is lost or forgotten, the very name by which it was called becomes misunderstood, misapplied, and finally forgotten. In proportion as men become unspiritual and material, they will grow incapable of comprehending the power of spirit. There are many persons even to-day who deny the existence of spirit, or of anything that transcends the power of perception of their physical senses. One example of the degradation of terms is the meaning which is at present commonly attributed to the word *magic*. The true significance of that term is the application of spiritual knowledge, or Wisdom, in contradistinction to that science which sees only the material aspect of Nature. But the vulgar have come to believe "magic" to mean only sleight-of-hand performances, or perhaps conjuring or dealings with the devil, or with the spirits of the dead. True magic is the greatest of all natural sciences, because it includes a true knowledge of visible and invisible Nature. It is not only a science, but also an *art*, because it cannot be learned out of books, but must be acquired by practical experience. To acquire that spiritual experience is to become spiritual; it is to perceive and know the true nature of the visible and invisible elements that compose the Macrocosm and the Microcosm, and to possess the art to direct and employ the invisible powers of Nature.[1] Divine knowledge and divine powers do not belong to the personal self. Therefore he who desires to know and to use the powers of magic must rise above the delusion of self, and become impersonal in the spirit. He must learn to distinguish between that which is divine and eternal and that which is animal and selfish in him. But there is also another art, called "black magic" or sorcery, which consists, not in acting in and through the power of God, which commands the elemental forces of Nature, but by propitiating the evil elementals, and in asking favours of them, becoming their slave. Paracelsus says:

"Magic and sorcery are two entirely different things, and there is as much difference between them as there is between light and darkness, and between white and black. Magic is the greatest wisdom and the knowledge of supernatural powers.[2] A knowledge of spiritual things cannot be obtained by merely reasoning logically from external appearances existing on the physical plane, but it will be acquired by obtaining more spirituality, and making one's self capable to feel and to see the things of the spirit. It would be well if our clergymen, who are called spiritual guides, would know more of spiritual things than what they have read in their books, and if they had some practical experience in divine wisdom, instead of merely repeating the opinions of the other people believed to have been divine."

"The wisdom which man ought to have does not come from the earth, nor from the astral spirit, but from the fifth essence—the Spirit of Wisdom. Therefore man is superior to the stars and the constellation, provided he lives in the power of that superior wisdom. Such a person, being the master over heaven and earth, by means of his free will,[3] is called a *Magus,* and therefore Magic is not sorcery, but supreme wisdom." (*De Peste*)

"Christ and the prophets and the apostles had magical powers, acquired less by their learning than by their holiness. They were able to heal the sick by the laying on of their hands, and to perform many other wonderful but natural things. Our clergymen talk a great deal about such things; but where is the priest of to-day who can do like Him? It has been said by Christ that His true followers would do the same things and still greater ones; but it would be difficult to find at present one Christian minister who can do anything as Christ did. But if any one who is not a man-made minister comes and cures the sick by the power of Christ acting through him, they call him a sorcerer and a child of the devil, and are willing to burn him upon a stake."

The first requirement for the study of Magic is a thorough knowledge of Nature. But there is a false and a true natural science. A science may be perfectly logical in all its deductions, but nevertheless false, if its fundamental doctrines are based upon a misunderstanding of spiritual truths, which a cold, unspiritual intellect is unable to grasp.[4] The true science of Nature draws its logical conclusions from fundamental truths, which it knows to be true, because it perceives them by the power of the mind illuminated by wisdom. False science bases its conclusions in regard to spiritual things upon external appearances caused by the illusion of the senses; true science rests in the faculty of the higher regions of the human soul to grasp spiritual truths which are beyond the power of perception of the semi-animal intellect.

Magic is a power which teaches the true nature of the inner man, as well as the organisation of his outward body. The superficial reasoner can comprehend nothing but what he can perceive by his external senses; but the inner man has perceptive faculties transcending those of his body. The spirit of man is not bound to any locality; it is as free as the wind which blows over the sea. If spiritual consciousness has once been attained, spiritual perception follows. During sleep the spirit is capable to move more freely, and to visit distant places. "You should know that man has the capability (latent or active) to foresee future events, and to read the future from the books of the past and from those of the present Man also possesses a power by which he may see his friends and the circumstances by which they are surrounded, although such persons may be a thousand miles away from him at that time. This art is taught by *Gabalis* (the spiritual perception of man). It is a power which may become especially active in dreams, and that which is seen in such dreams is the reflection of the light of wisdom and prophecy in man. If a man in his waking state knows nothing of such things, the cause of his ignorance is, that he does not understand how to search in himself for the powers that are given to him by God, and by which he can arrive at all the Wisdom, Reason, and Knowledge concerning everything that exists, whether it be near him or far away."

He who seeks the truth for his own purposes, or to adorn and glorify himself with it, will never find it. We should not seek to possess the truth, but to let it become manifested in us.

"There are those who imagine that man obtains his knowledge from his own self and from the stars, so that if one is born under a favourable star he will know every thing. But if man is to inherit the kingdom of God, how, then, can he be a child of the constellation, which is doomed to perish? Where, then, shall we seek for true wisdom, except in that which is higher than all the stars, namely, God?"[5] (*De Inventione Artium*)

Ignorance is the cause of imperfection. "Men do not know themselves, and therefore they do not understand the things of their inner world. Each man has the essence of God, and all the wisdom and power of the world (germinally) in himself; he possesses one kind of knowledge as much as another, and he who does not find that which is in him cannot truly say that he does not possess it, but only that he was not capable of successfully seeking for it."

The exercise of inner sight requires tranquility and peacefulness of the mind. "Sleeping is waking in regard to such arts, because it is the inner light of Nature that acts during sleep on the invisible man, who, notwithstanding his invisibility, is existing as truly as the visible one. The inner man is the natural man, and knows more than the one formed of flesh."[6]

"How can any one instruct others in regard to the works of God if he does not keep His laws? How can any one teach Christ if he does not know Him? How can that which is not eternal know the eternal? How can a fool teach divine wisdom? Verily, the nearer we approach the judgment-day the more will there be wiseacres and pretended instructors; but on that day those who were the first will be the last, and the last ones the first. Our sciences are worthless if they do not spring from the foundation of the true faith" (*Lib. Philos.*).

"Nature is the universal teacher. Whatever we cannot learn from the external appearance of Nature we can learn from her spirit. Both are one. Everything is taught by Nature to her disciple, if he asks for information in an appropriate manner. Nature is a light, and by looking at Nature in her own light we will understand her. Visible Nature can be seen in her visible light; invisible Nature will become visible if we acquire the power to perceive her inner light."[7] "The hidden things are there like a pillar of rock before a blind person. He can see it if he is able to open his eyes. The moon shines, but does not show things in their true colours; but if the sun arises, then will the true colours be seen. Thus the external light in Nature is like the moon, beyond which shines the internal light, and in this light that which has been invisible will appear visibly and comprehensibly." (*Morb. Invis.*) "There is a light in the spirit of man illuminating everything, and by which he may even perceive supernatural things. Those who seek in the light of external Nature know the things of Nature; those who seek knowledge in the light of man know the things above Nature, which belong to the kingdom of God."

"Man is an animal, a spirit, and an angel, for he has all three qualities. As long as he remains in Nature he serves Nature; if he moves in the spirit, he serves the spirit (in him); if he lives in the angel, he serves as an angel. The first quality belongs to the body, the two others to the soul, and they are its jewels. The body of man remains on the earth, but man, having a soul and the two additional qualities, is enabled to rise above Nature, and to know that which does not belong to Nature. He has the power to learn all that belongs to heaven and hell, to know God and His kingdom, the angels and spirits, and the origin of evil. If a man is to go to a certain place, it will be useful to him to know all about that place before he goes there; he will then after his arrival be enabled to move about freely, and to go wherever he pleases. The quality of each thing created by God, whether it be visible or invisible to the senses, may be perceived and known. If man knows the essence of things, their attributes, their attractions, and the elements of which they consist, he will be a master of Nature, of the elements, and of the spirits."[8] (*Philosophia Sagax*)

"The truth does not grow from your speculation and phantastry; but he who understands his own nature in the light of Nature possesses true knowledge. It is not sufficient that we should have a theory of the truth, but we should know the truth in ourselves." (*De Peste.*)

"There are two kinds of intelligence, that of the carnal man and that of the spirit; the former argues, the latter knows. Animals also have reasoning qualities; but their understanding is not from the (direct) light of the spirit."(*De Generat. Homin.*)

"The light of Nature teaches us that each form, reasonable and unreasonable, conscious ones and such as are without consciousness, has its natural spirit. The Nectromanticus (seer) must know these spirits, for without that knowledge he will not find their true character. By his art he can sense them, and having perceived them with his inner sense he will find their forms. Such spirits may be perceived in crystals; they guide the divining-rod and attract it as a magnet attracts iron; they turn the sieve and the key,[9] and draw the flame of a light away from the wick. By the art of Nectromancy we may look into the interior of rocks, closed letters may be read without being opened,[10] hidden things be found, and all the secrets of men be brought to light. Some people believe that such arts can best be practised by virgins and innocent children, because their minds are not clouded by false opinions nor darkened by memories of evil deeds; but any one can practise this art if he has the necessary qualifications." (*Philosophia Sagax*)

He who understands letters can read words, and he who knows words can read books. If we know that a certain cause may produce a certain effect, and if such an effect takes place, we will easily recognise the cause that produced it. "If the crowing of cocks announces a change of weather, and if we hear the cocks crow in an unusual manner, we may predict that the weather will change. Certain animals have inherited instincts that cause them to act in a certain manner, which will indicate other future events than a change in the weather. The peculiar cry of a peacock or the unusual howling of a dog indicates the approach of a death in the house to which they are attached; for every being is a product of the universal principle of life, and each contains the light of Nature. Animals possess that light, and men bring it with them into the world."[11]

The power of clairvoyance and prevision is especially active in dreams, when the activity of the physical body is subdued, and the disturbing influences coming through the avenues of the physical senses are excluded. "Artists and students have often received instructions in their dreams in regard to things which they desired to know. Their imagination was then free, and began to work its wonders. It attracted to it the Evestra of some philosophers, and they communicated to them their knowledge. Such things happen frequently, but it very often occurs that on awakening to consciousness in the outer world all or a part of what has been learned during the dream is forgotten. If this happens and we wish to remember such dreams, we should not leave the room after rising, and speak to nobody, but remain alone and undisturbed, and eat nothing until after a while we remember that dream."[12]

"It is often the case that dreams have an important meaning, but many dreams that are pleasant may signify sorrow, and disagreeable dreams often signify joy; and we should, therefore, not put too much confidence in dreams."[13]

Men's astral bodies may more easily be influenced during sleep than during the waking state. The power to influence persons during their sleep is sometimes used for evil purposes: "Some persons, being in love with others, and finding their love unrequited, have sometimes used this circumstance to influence those whose love they desired by appearing to them in their dreams. They wrote with their own blood their names upon pieces of new paper, and put the slips under their pillows or beds, so that these persons should see the intended lovers in their dreams and fall in love with them. Girls used to put their belts, ribbons, locks of hair, etc., under the pillows of young men for whose love they craved; but very seldom they found the desired result in this manner, because they forgot that faith is necessary to obtain success."[14]

A strong faith and a powerful imagination are the two pillars supporting the door to the temple of magic, and without which nothing can be accomplished. Imagination is the formative power of man; it often acts instinctively and without any conscious effort of the will. "Man has a visible and an invisible workshop. The visible one is his body, the invisible one his imagination (mind). The sun gives light, and this light is not tangible, but its heat may be felt, and if the rays are concentrated it may set a house on fire. The imagination is a sun in the soul of man, acting in its own sphere as the sun of the earth acts in that of the earth. Wherever the sun shines, germs planted in the soil grow and vegetation springs up, and the sun of the soul acts in a similar manner, and calls the forms of the soul into existence. Visible and tangible forms grow into existence from invisible elements by the power of the sunshine. Invisible vapours are attracted and collected together into visible mists by the power of the sun of the outer world, and the inner sun of man performs similar wonders. The great world is only a product of the imagination of the universal mind, and man is a little world of its own that imagines and creates by the power of imagination. If man's imagination is strong enough to penetrate into every corner of his interior world, it will be able to create things in those corners, and whatever man thinks will take form in his soul. But the imagination of Nature is like a monkey aping the actions of man. That which man does is imitated by the monkey, and the pictures formed in the imagination of man create corresponding images in the mirror of Nature."

"Imagination is like the sun. The sun has a light which is not tangible, but which, nevertheless, can set a house on fire; thus the imagination is like a sun in man acting in that place to which its light is directed."

"Man is mind; he is what he thinks. If he thinks fire, he is on fire; if he thinks war, then will he cause war; it all depends merely on that the whole of his imagination becomes an entire sun; *i.e.*, that he wholly imagines that which he wills." (*De Virtute Imaginativa*)

"The sun acts upon the visible soil of the earth, and upon invisible matter in the air; imagination acts upon the invisible substance of the soul, but the visible earth is formed from the invisible elements of the earth, and man's physical body is formed of his invisible astral soul. The soul of man is as intimately related to the soul of the earth as the physical body of the man is related to the physical body of the earth, and they continually act upon each other, and without the soul the vehicle could not exist. Visible matter becomes invisible, and is acted on by the soul, and invisible matter becomes organised and is made visible again through the influence of the soul. If a pregnant woman imagines something strongly, the effects of her imagination will become manifest in the child.[15] Imagination springs from desire, and as man may have good or evil desires, likewise he may have a good or an evil imagination. A strong desire of either kind will give rise to a strong imagination. Curses as well as blessings will be effective if they come from the heart." (*De Virtute Imaginativa*)[16]

"Nothing can come out of the sphere of the mind except what is drawn into it, and that which is drawn into it can come out. If a pregnant woman craves for strawberries, the image of strawberries will be drawn into her mind, and her imagination may impress a mark resembling a strawberry upon the child. Frogs do not grow in the sky, and if (as has happened) a multitude of frogs come down from it during a rain, these frogs must have been drawn up somewhere before they came down."

"The imagination of women is usually stronger than that of men. They are more passionate, stronger in love and stronger in hate, and their imagination may carry them during their sleep (in their astral forms) to other places, where they may be seen by others who are in the same state. They are then really at those places, and will remember what they have seen, although they were there without their physical bodies; for their minds were active at such places, and the mind is the real person, not the body that is asleep."[17]

If a pregnant woman forms an image in her mind and projects it by her desire, it will impress itself on the body of the child. "If, for instance, a woman in her imagination strongly conceives of a snail, and then puts her hand upon her knee, then will the image of the snail appear upon the knee of the child. Her will (although unconsciously) acts in this way like a master, bidding a painter to paint him a snail. Wherever the touch of the hand goes, there will be the image." (*De Virtute Imaginativa*)

"If a person dies, and seriously desires that another person should die with him, his imagination creates a force that will draw a vehicle from his dead body and give it shape, and this can be projected by the impulse given to it by the thought of the dying person towards that person, and cause him to die. Such is especially the case if a woman dies of puerperal fever,[18] and if such a woman wishes that the whole world should die with her, an epidemic may be the consequence of her poisoned imagination."

"Fear, terror, passion, desire, joy, and envy are six states of the mind which especially rule the imagination, and consequently the world of man; and as the mind of man is the microcosmic counterpart of the universal mind, the antitypes of these states are also active in the imagination of the world, and the thoughts of man act upon the latter as the latter acts upon him. It is therefore desirable that we should govern our imagination and not allow it to run wild. We should attempt to grasp the spirit by the power of the spirit, and not by speculative fancy."[19] (*De Virtute Imaginativa*)

"Man is a twofold being, having a divine and an animal nature. If he feels, and thinks, and acts as divine beings should act, he is a true man; if he feels and acts like an animal, he is then an animal, and the equal of those animals whose mental characteristics are manifested in him. An exalted imagination caused by a desire for the good raises him up; a low imagination caused by a desire for that which is low and vulgar drags him down and degrades him."

"The spirit is the master, imagination the tool, and the body the plastic material.

Imagination is the power by which the will forms sidereal entities out of thoughts. Imagination is not *fancy*, which latter is the cornerstone of superstition and foolishness. The imagination of man becomes pregnant through desire, and gives birth to deeds. Every one may regulate and educate his imagination so as to come thereby into contact with spirits, and be taught by them. Spirits desiring to act upon man act upon his imagination,[20] and they therefore make often use of his dreams for the purpose of acting upon him. During sleep the sidereal man may by the power of the imagination be sent out of the physical form, at a distance to act for some purpose. No place is too far for the imagination to go, and the imagination of one man can impress that of another, wherever it reaches." (*Philosophia Sagax*)

"Imagination is the beginning of the growth of a form, and it guides the process of its growth. The Will is a dissolving power, which enables the body to become impregnated by the 'tincture' of the imagination. He who wants to know how a man can unite his power of imagination with the power of the imagination of Heaven, must know by what process this may be done. A man comes into possession of creative power by uniting his own mind with the Universal Mind, and he who succeeds in doing so will be in possession of the highest possible wisdom; the lower realm of Nature will be subject to him, and the powers of Heaven will aid him, because Heaven is the servant of wisdom."[21]

"Before man is born, and afterwards, his soul is not perfect, but it may be perfected through the power of a holy Will. Spirits are essential, visible, tangible, and sensitive in relation to other spirits.[22] They stand in a similar relation to each other, as physical bodies to other physical bodies. Spirits speak with each other through spirit, but not by means of audible speech. While the body is asleep, the soul may go to a distant place, and act intelligently at such place.[23] If it meets another spirit, whether it be an incarnated or a disincarnated one, they will act in regard to each other as two human beings act, if they meet. One man communicates his thoughts to another with whom he is in sympathy, at any distance, however great it may be,[24] or he may act upon the spirit of another person in such a manner as to influence his actions after the body of the latter awakens from his sleep.[25] In this way he can even injure the health of that person, and upon this law of Nature is based the possibility of witchcraft and sorcery."

"The exercise of true magic does not require any ceremonies or conjurations, or the making of circles or signs; it requires neither benedictions nor maledictions in words, neither verbal blessings nor curses; it only requires a strong faith in the omnipotent power of all good, that can accomplish everything if it acts through a human mind being in harmony with it, and without which nothing useful can be accomplished. True magic power consists in true faith, but true faith rests in spiritual knowledge, and without that kind of knowledge there can be no faith. If I know that divine wisdom can accomplish a certain thing through me, I have the true holy faith; but if I merely fancy or suppose that a thing might be possible, or if I attempt to persuade myself that I believe in its possibility, such a belief is no knowledge, and confers no faith. No one can have a true faith in a thing which is not true, because such a 'faith' would be merely a belief or opinion based upon ignorance of the truth."

Nothing can be accomplished without the power of faith. If a loaf of bread were laid on a table before a hungry man, and the man did not believe that he could break a piece of it, he would starve to death in spite of the loaf. "It is the faith which gives us power, and through the power of faith we become spirits ourselves, and able to use spiritual power. Faith renders the spirit strong; doubt is the destroyer. All that is accomplished over and beyond our terrestrial nature is accomplished by us through the power of faith. That in which we have faith requires no proofs. He who asks for proofs departs from the faith. If God speaks in us, we require no proofs of the truth of what He says; for we recognise it in the power of truth. This power is taken from nobody, unless he throws it himself away. The good as well as the evil-disposed ones can only be strong through faith. There is only one power of faith, but its application may be for good or for evil." (*Morb. Invis.*)[26]

"How can there be any true faith in a man who has not in himself the power of God? The godless do not believe in faith because they have none of it, even if they continually talk about it. They cannot know what 'faith' is. Where can we find a theologian who drove out an evil spirit, or made a spirit come, or who healed the sick by the power of God's will; not to mention the fact that no clergyman ever removed a mountain by means of his faith, or threw it into the ocean? But if some one produces a sign, be it good or evil, they denounce him and call him a sorcerer; for they are not capable to distinguish between magic and sorcery." (*Philos. Occult.*, ii.)

"Faith is the cause of witchcraft and sorceries, by which means one person may injure another without running much risk of discovery; because he may kill or injure his enemy without going near him, and the latter cannot defend himself as he might if he were attacked by a visible foe. Great care should be taken that the powers of the faith are not misused, because in such a case it will be witchcraft. The witches[27] are the most dangerous persons in the world, if they use their evil will against anybody."

"It would be very easy to give instructions so that every one might convince himself of the truth of these statements, but such instructions might be misused by wicked persons who might employ such knowledge for evil purposes; and it is, moreover, not to be regretted if methods by which one man may injure another should not be publicly known.[28] But there are certain things that ought to be known to physicians, so that they may learn the cause of certain mysterious diseases, and know the means how to cure them, and to counteract evil influences by the power of good. There are, for instance, some sorcerers who make an image representing the person whom they desire to injure, and they drive a nail into the foot of that image, and evil will and malicious thought cause the person whom the image represents to experience a great pain in his foot, and to be unable to walk until the nail from the image is removed. Now, if a physician meets with such a case, and he does not know the cause of the pain in the foot of his patient, he will not be able to cure it; but if he knows the cause, he can employ the power of imagination to counteract the evil that has been caused by a similar power."[29]

"Thus, it has happened that nails and hair, needles, bristles, pieces of glass, and many other things have been cut or been pulled out of the bodies of certain patients, and were followed by other things of a similar character, and that such a state of affairs continued for many weeks or months, and the physicians stood there helpless, and did not know what to do. But if they had better understood their business, they would have known that these things had been brought into the body of a patient by the power of the evil imagination of a sorcerer, and they might have put one of the extracted articles into an elder or oak tree, on the side directed towards the rising sun, and that article would have acted like a magnet to attract the evil influence, and it would have cured the patient."

"A strong will subdues a weaker one, and therefore the first necessary condition for the purpose of producing magic effects is the development of the will. The power of the will acts more readily upon animals than upon man, because the soul of man, being supported by the divine spirit, has more power to defend itself against the influence of a foreign will than the sidereal body of animals. The will of a waking man will act upon another person, who may be awake or asleep; but it can also happen that one man acts spiritually upon another while both are asleep; the astral form of a sleeping person can visit another person in his dream, and influence the latter to love him; or it may injure that person, or perhaps cause him to perform something which he would not perform if left to himself."

In regard to the action of the will at a distance, Paracelsus says: "As to images of wax (which are made for the purpose of assisting the imagination and concentrating the will), I will tell you that, if a person desires to injure an enemy, he may do so through some medium; i.e., a vehicle. In this way it is possible that my spirit, without the assistance of my body and without a sword, can kill or wound another person simply by the action of my will. It is furthermore possible that I may bring the spirit of my enemy into an image, and afterwards injure or lame him in the image according to my will, and that the body of that enemy will be correspondingly injured or lamed thereby. The power of the will is the main point in medicine. A man who wishes every one well will produce good effects. One who begrudges everybody everything good, and is full of hate, will experience on his own person the effects of his evil thoughts. Images may be cursed, and diseases such as fevers, epilepsy, apoplexy, etc.—thereby be caused to the persons whom those images are made to represent. I am speaking seriously. Our physicians know only a very small part of the power of the will. The will creates spirits (forces) that have nothing to do with reasoning but obey blindly."[30] (*Paramirum*, tract, iv. cap. viii.)

"Faith stimulates and elevates the power of the spirit A person who has a strong faith feels as if he were lifted up, and were living independent of the body. By the power of faith the apostles and patriarchs accomplished great things that were above the ordinary run of Nature, and the saints performed their miracles[31] by the power of faith. Such miracles as were performed by them during their lifetime were performed by their own faith; other miracles that took place through their relics or near their tombs were caused by the power of faith of those who asked their help. All the wonders of Magic are performed by Imagination and Faith."

In producing magical cures, it is the power of faith in the patient himself, and not the dead saint or the relic, that cures the disease.

"A dead saint cannot cure anybody. A living saint may cure the sick by virtue of the divine power that acts through him. This divine power does not die with the body of the saint, and therefore true saints are still living, although their mortal bodies have died. The power which enabled the saints to work miracles is still alive, and accessible to all. It is the power of the Holy Ghost, and if you live in God He will overshadow you with that power, and it will teach you the laws of God, and you will be guided like other saints, even as the apostles Peter or Paul." (*De Sanctorum Beneficiis Vindictis*)

"Faith has a great deal more power than the physical body. You are visible and corporeal, but there is still an invisible man in you, and that invisible man is yourself too. Each act performed by your body is performed by the invisible man. The one acts in a visible, the other in an invisible, manner. If an injury is inflicted upon the invisible man, that injury will be reproduced on his visible body.[32] Such things can be done, but it is very wrong to attempt them. Whoever attempts them is tempting God, and he who succeeds will seriously injure his own soul. There have been people who have made images of wax representing certain persons of the opposite sex, and they melted such forms by the heat of a light, to assist their own evil imagination, and by using their faith they have succeeded in enticing those persons into an unlawful love. The Chaldaeans and Egyptians used to make images according to the constellations of the stars, and these images moved and talked, but they did not know the powers that acted in them. Such things are done by faith, but it is not the true faith in God, but a devilish faith, supported by the desire for evil; because a faith that kills and injures men is not good; a true faith can only come from the source of all good, in which there can be no evil, and that which is not good is not true. Evil belongs to the world, because without evil good could not be known or appreciated; but in the source of good there can be no evil."[33]

"True faith has wonderful powers, and this fact proves that we are spirits, and not merely visible bodies. Faith accomplishes that which the body would accomplish if it had the power. Man is created with great powers; he is greater than heaven and greater than the earth. He possesses faith, and when his faith has become a conscious power in him it will be a light more powerful and superior to natural light, and stronger than all mortal creatures. All magic processes are based upon that faith. By faith and imagination we can accomplish whatever we desire. The true power of faith overcomes all the spirits of Nature, because it is a spiritual power, and spirit is higher than Nature. Whatever is grown in the realm of Nature may be changed by the power of faith. Whatever we accomplish that surpasses Nature is accomplished by the power of faith, and by faith diseases may be cured."[34] (*Philosophia Sagax*)

"The sidereal man is of a magnetic nature, and for that reason he can attract the powers and effluvia of the astral-world. If, therefore, any inimical astral influences are circulating in the All of Nature, the man becomes sick, and if these currents change he will become well again. The same thing happens if a good or an evil thought, supported by a strong faith, changes or creates currents that act upon the sidereal man."[35]

The astral currents created by the imagination of the Macrocosmos act upon the Microcosmos, and produce certain states in the latter, and thus also the astral currents produced by the imagination and will of man produce certain states in external Nature, and these currents reach very far, because the power of the imagination reaches as far as thought can go. The physiological processes taking place in the body of living beings are caused by their life currents, and the physiological and meteorological processes taking place in the great organism of Nature are caused by the life currents of Nature as a whole. The astral currents of either act upon the other, either consciously or unconsciously, and if this fact is properly understood it will cease to appear incredible that the mind of man can produce changes in the universal mind, which will cause changes in the atmosphere, winds and rains, storms, hail, and lightning, or that evil may be changed into good by the power of faith. "Heaven (the mind) is a field into which the imagination of man throws the seeds. Nature is an artist that develops the seeds, and what is caused by Nature may be imitated by Art." (*De Sagis et eorum Operibus*)

"To conjure the spirit of a thing means to seek after the truth which that thing represents. To see the spirit of a thing means to recognise the character of that thing, with all its qualities and attributes.[36] To make the spirit of a thing subservient to one's power is to know how to use the powers that are hidden in such a thing for our own purposes. If I know the attributes of a thing, I know its spirit. If I can make use of the qualities of a thing, its spirit will be my servant. Nothing can be known of a thing unless we succeed in making its character appear plain to our understanding."

"The vehicle through which the will acts for effectuating good or evil is the living Mumia. Mumia[37] is a vehicle that contains the essence of life. If we eat the flesh of animals, it is not their flesh itself that forms again blood and bones in our bodies, but the invisible vehicle of life derived from the flesh of these animals is taken up into our bodies, and forms new tissues and organs. If an animal dies in consequence of some internal disease, we do not eat its flesh, because its Mumia has been poisoned by its disease; neither do we eat the flesh of animals that died of old age, nor the flesh of a rotten carcass, because its healthy Mumia has departed on account of the decomposition, and what is left of the Mumia has been poisoned by the process of putrefaction. The Mumia of a living being partakes of the characteristics of the being from which it is taken. For this reason we do not eat the flesh of ferocious animals, such as tigers, lions, wild-cats, etc. They contain a fiery Mumia which stimulates the astral essences of man, and causes in him such tendencies as were the characteristics of the animals from which they are taken.[38] We eat the flesh of domestic animals, because their character is more gentle and their Mumia less exciting, such as the stupid ox, the gentle sheep, etc.; but the healthiest animal food is the flesh of birds, because they live in the air, and the air is the noblest of the four elements."

The "Mumia" of a thing is its life-principle. "From the use of the Mumia have resulted the greatest and mysterious magnetic cures; for some persons who have learned to know and understand the action and power of their own Mumia, and that even a small dose of it attracts unto itself the powers of the whole body, like the magnet attracts iron, have in this way cured themselves of many ills. "(*Philosoph*., tract iii.)

"The Mumia of the dead body is useless, and the Mumia that is prepared by embalming a corpse is good for nothing but to serve as food for worms. The most efficacious Mumia is that of a person who died in an unnatural manner while his body was in good health; such a one, for instance, as has been hung or decapitated, or whose body has been broken on the wheel. A person who dies a slow death in consequence of some disease loses his powers before he dies, and putrefaction begins often in such cases even while the patient is still alive. His Mumia will then be worthless. But if our physicians knew the occult powers of the Mumia of persons that have died sudden deaths, they would not permit the body of an executed criminal to hang at the gallows for over three days, but they would take it away and use it for medical purposes. Such a Mumia is very powerful, especially after it has been exposed to the influence of the air, the sun, and the moon."

"The Mumia of a being who dies a violent death in the air returns to the air; the Mumia of a body is taken up by that element in which the body is decomposed. If a person is drowned, his Mumia will go to the element of water; if he is burnt, it will go to that of the fire."[39] (*Philosoph., tract iii*)

"These three kinds of Mumia have very wonderful occult powers, and many strange feats may be performed through their use by those who know how to employ them, especially by such as have taken the Mumia themselves from the persons for whose life it served as a vehicle. Such people are executioners, hangmen, and murderers, and the latter sometimes kill a man for the mere purpose of obtaining his Mumia to perform wicked things. But for such people it would have been better if a millstone had been hung about their necks and they had been thrown into the sea, because they will themselves end in a pitiful manner, and their souls will experience the evil which they themselves have created."[40]

On account of the great occult power contained in the Mumia, it is used in witchcraft and sorcery. "Witches and sorcerers may make a bargain with evil spirits, and cause them to carry the Mumia to certain places where it will come in contact with other people, without the knowledge of the latter, and cause them harm. They take earth from the graves of people who have died of the plague, and infect other people with it. They also infect the cattle, spoil the milk,[41] and cause a great deal of damage, and the injured people do not know the cause of the evils that afflict them. A great deal might be said in regard to this subject, but we will not write it down, because we do not desire to give instructions in sorcery, or enable the wicked to use the knowledge obtained for the purpose of injuring others" (*De Pestilitate*).

"It is very desirable that some good and wise men, well versed in the secret arts, should be appointed by the authorities to counteract and prevent the evils produced by the wicked who practise witchcraft and sorcery, and they should pay particular attention to convents, monasteries, and houses of prostitution, because in such places a lascivious and evil imagination is especially cultivated, and great quantities of sperma are there collected by evil spirits, and that sperma contains a powerful Mumia, which can be extracted, and transformed into evil things; or it may decompose and become a strong poison, furnishing life to innumerable invisible (microscopic) existences, by which epidemics and plagues will be caused. One witch may poison another by such means, and the familiar spirits of witches often steal sperma from persons who are addicted to bad habits and use it for evil purposes."

"An especially powerful poison that may be used in sorcery is the menstrual blood. If a woman exposes a cloth impregnated with the menstrual blood to the rays of the new moon at night, and to the rays of the sun during the day, a powerful basilisk is created, because it attracts the '*magnes salis.*' This invisible poison can give rise to many and various diseases, because the moon is the '*menstruum mundi*,' and exercises a very evil influence. Gold attracts mercury and amalgamates with it, and likewise the sun attracts the '*mercurium menstrui mulierum.*' The moon exerts a certain evil influence periodically every month, and the '*menstruum mulierum*' is renewed periodically every month, and during such periods there is an especially strong sympathy between them."

"Women should know such things and pay attention to them, else they may run great danger. It is a known fact that during the time of a plague many more women die than men. It is also known that women who, on account of their age, have lost the power to menstruate, are more powerful than others to effect evil spells and sorceries, and to injure men and animals."[42]

"If you take turpentine and distil it, the spirit of turpentine will go away and the rosin remain; and if you mix the rosin again with the spirit, you will have your turpentine again as it was before. In a similar way the human blood contains an airy, fiery spirit, and this spirit has its centre in the heart, where it is most condensed, and from which it radiates, and the radiating rays return to the heart. Thus the world has its fiery spirit pervading the atmosphere, and its centre is called the sun, and the influences radiating from the sun return to that centre. The sun radiates heat and attracts the vapours of the earth, and likewise the heart of man attracts the '*humidum menstrui,*' which is a poisonous planetary exhalation of the Microcosm of woman. The '*spiritus vitae cerebri*' of an insane person is attracted towards the moon in the same manner as the needle of the compass is attracted towards the Pole, and such a person will therefore—especially at the time of the new moon, when that attraction is the strongest—grow worse, and begin to rave; and likewise the sensitive spirit (aura) of a man who is weak and offers no resistance will be attracted towards the moon and be poisoned by its evil influence."

"The witches and evil spirits, moreover, use certain invisible and poisonous elements, taken from spiders, toads, and other villainous creatures, and use them in combination with the menstrual blood for evil purposes; but it is not advisable to publish the secret how this is done. We will, however, say that sometimes they make an image of a person in wax, and tie a rag, soiled with the menstrual blood, around it, and add the Mumia of the carcass of some animal—preferring one of an animal that has died of an ulcer and by using their evil imagination they throw the evil spell upon the person whom the image represents, and in this manner they poison his blood and cause him to die."[43]

"They sometimes take a mirror set in a wooden frame, and put it into a tub of water, so that it will swim on the top with its face directed towards the sky. On the top of the mirror, and encircling the glass, they lay a wreath of *Sinechrusmontes Behdem*, and thus they expose it to the influence of the new moon; and this evil influence is thrown towards the moon, and, radiating again from the moon, it will bring evil to those who love to look at the moon. The rays of the moon, passing through that ring upon the mirror, become poisoned, and poison the mirror; and the mirror throws back the poisoned ether into the atmosphere, and the moon and the mirror poison each other in the same manner as two malicious persons, by looking at each other, poison each other's souls with their eyes. If a mirror is strongly poisoned in this manner, the witch takes good care of it; and if she desires to injure some one, she takes a waxen image made in his name, she surrounds it with a cloth spotted with the menstrual blood, and throws the reflex of the mirror through the opening in the middle of the head of the figure, or upon some other part of his body, using at the same time her evil imagination and curses; and the man whom the image represents will then have his vitality dried up and his blood poisoned by that evil influence, and become diseased, and his body covered with boils. Such is the '*pestis particularis,*' which may be known if it affects a man who has not been near any other persons or places from which he might have caught the disease."

"But if a witch desires to poison a man with her eyes, she will go to a place where she expects to meet him. When he approaches she will look into the poisoned mirror, and then, after hiding the mirror, look into his eyes, and the influence of the poison passes from the mirror into her eyes, and from her eyes into the eyes of that person; but the witch cures her own eyes by making a fire and staring into it, and then taking the menstrual cloth, and, after tying it around a stone, throwing it into the fire. After the cloth is burned she extinguishes the fire with her urine, and her eyes will be cured; but her enemy will become blind." (*De Pestilitate*)

"There are, furthermore, certain substances used by witches and sorcerers which they give to other persons in their food or drink, and by which they render those persons insane, and such an insanity manifests itself in various ways. Sometimes it renders men or women amorous, or it makes them quarrelsome; it causes them to be very courageous and daring, or turns them into cowards. Some will fall deeply in love with the person who administered to them such philtres; and it has happened that in this way masters and mistresses have fallen deeply in love with the servants who administered to them such things, and thus they became themselves the servants of their own servants. Even horses, dogs, and other animals have thus been brought under the influence of such spells. If women administer such things to men, the latter may fall so deeply in love with the former as to be unable to think of anything else but of them; and if men administer such things to women, they will continually think of them." (*De Morbis Amentium*)

"But the things which such persons use for such purposes are nothing else but substances that have long been in contact with their own bodies, and which contain a part of their own vitality. Women are more successful in such experiments, because they are more impulsive, more implacable in their revenge, and more inclined to envy and hate. If they are fully absorbed by their own imagination, they call into existence an active spirit that moves their imagination wherever they may desire it to go. A wood-carver takes a piece of wood and carves out of it whatever he has in his mind, and likewise the imagination can create something out of the essence of life. The Mumia is the vehicle of which the imagination makes use for the purpose of taking some form.[44] It is lifted up and expanded by the power of faith, and it contracts and penetrates the mind by being impressed by the will. Women have a greater power of imagination during their dreams and when they are alone; and they ought, therefore, not to be left alone a great deal, but ought to be amused, because if they are ill-disposed and harbouring evil thoughts, they may, by the power of their imagination, poison the food which they cook, or make it impure, without being themselves aware of it. Women who are occupied a great deal with an evil imagination, and who are unable to control it, should not be permitted to nurse and educate infants, because the impressions which their imagination creates unconsciously impresses itself and acts injuriously upon the minds of the children. The imagination is the cause that beings have been created out of the 'Mumia spiritualis' which possesses great powers."[45] (Fragment: *De Virtute Imaginationae*)

"By the power of the imagination foreign bodies are transferred invisibly into the bodies of human beings, in the same manner as if I take a stone in my hand and put it into a tub of water, and, withdrawing my hand, I leave the stone in the water. Menstruating witches especially may dissolve (dematerialise) bodies by the power of their imagination. They make a figure of wax representing the person whom they wish to injure, and they tie a cloth spotted with menstrual blood around the neck of that figure, and attach it there by means of a string drawn through the pulpy mass of a crushed spider.

They then take a bow and an arrow made of a certain kind of wood; they tie pieces of glass, or nails, or bristles, or anything else, to that arrow, and shoot it into the waxen image; and in this way the articles dissolved by their imagination are by the power of the Mumia transmitted into the body of the sensitive person, and there they will be found in a corporeal form." (*De Sagis*)

"The power of the imagination is a great factor in medicine. It produces diseases in man and in animals, and it cures them. But this is not done by the powers of symbols or characters made in wax or being written on paper, but by an imagination which perfects the will. All the imagination of man comes from the heart. The heart is the 'seed' of the Microcosm, and from that seed the imagination proceeds into the Macrocosm. Thus the imagination of man is a seed that becomes materialised or corporeal. A thought is an act having an object in view. I need not turn my eye with my hand in the direction in which I desire to see, but my imagination turns it wherever I want it. An imagination coming from a pure and intense desire of the heart acts instinctively and without any conscious effort. The power of a strong imagination directed upon another can kill or cure him according to the nature of the desire that impels the force, and which may be good or evil. Therefore a curse will become productive of evil, and a blessing productive of good, if it comes from the heart."[46]

"The curse of the oppressed poor is nothing but an imagination; but that imagination is firm, and not a wavering and uncertain thing. It is penetrated by and followed with an earnest desire that the object of their wish shall be accomplished, and that which men desire in cursing enters into their imagination, and from the imagination results the act. The evil elements in the soul of him who acted evil attract unto themselves the evil will set free by the curse of him who has been injured; for the soul is like a magnet, attracting unconsciously that which corresponds to its nature." (*Fragm.*)

"Magic is great hidden wisdom, just as that which is commonly called human wisdom is great folly. To use wisdom, no external ceremonies and conjurations are required. The making of circles and the burning of incense are all tomfoolery and temptation, by which only evil spirits are attracted. The human heart is a great thing, so great that no one can fully express its greatness. It is imperishable and eternal, like God. If we only knew all the powers of the human heart, nothing would be impossible for us. The imagination is fortified and perfected through faith, and each doubt destroys the effect of its labour. Faith must confirm the imagination, because it perfects the will. The reason why men have not a perfect imagination is because they are still uncertain about their power, but they might be perfectly certain if they only possessed true knowledge."

"If the imagination of a man acting upon another cannot always accomplish what he desires, it is because it is too weak to penetrate the armour of the soul of that other person, and a weak imagination has no effect upon another person, if the latter is protected by a strong and resisting faith; and each one may strengthen his own faith and make his soul invulnerable by believing in the supreme power of Good."[47] (*De Peste.*, lib. i.)

"Those who are strong in their faith, and full of confidence that the divine power in man can protect him against all evil influences, whether they come from an incarnated or a disincarnated entity, cannot be harmed by either. But if a weak person is obsessed by such an evil influence and is unable to drive it out, then it is necessary that some other person who possesses that spiritual power should drive it out in his place. A worm may grow in a hazel-nut although the shell of the nut is whole, and there is no place where the worm could have entered. Thus an evil spirit enters into the body of a man and produces some disease without making a hole into him. If the mind is weak and the soul not protected by faith and confidence, it will enter; and therefore the best remedy is a strong mind, illuminated by the interior light of wisdom coming from God."

"Ills of the body may be cured by physical remedies or by the power of the spirit acting through the soul. Ills of the soul are cured by the power of the spirit, but to do this requires more than mere lip prayer and gibberish and idle ceremonies; it needs the consciousness of the spirit that it can accomplish that which it desires to do. A paternoster is useless if the lips speak it while the heart desires evil. He who is dressed up like a clergyman is therefore not necessarily a spiritual person, although he may have been ordained by the Church. To be ordained by man does not imply the possession of spiritual power, because such a power can only be given by the spirit; he who possesses the power to cure diseases and to drive out evil influences by the power of the spirit is ordained by God. The others are quacks and maleficants, in spite of their superstitious beliefs, their illusory science, diplomas, and manmade authority." (*De Sanctorum Beneficiis*)

"God looks at the heart and not at the ceremony. All fasting and praying done by hypocrites for the purpose of showing off their piety is the work of the devil in them. All blessings and benedictions with 'holy water,' etc., are things which the devil has invented to make men believe that they could dispense with God and find their salvation in ceremonies. St. Peter is not superior to God, neither can the spirits in man do anything but what the Lord in him permits them to do. All good things should be sought for in God, and not in the spirits or saints; neither in angels nor devils. If we give the true faith out of our hand we will be without it; if God departs from the soul, then will the evil spirits therein have free play." (*Morb. Invis.*)

If the followers of the Christian Church or the modern "theosophists" were to realise these truths, they would cease to kneel before external Christs or run after strange "Mahatmas," and every one would try to know the Christ or "Mahatma" within himself.

Chapter 7: Medicine

"Those who imagine that the medicine of Paracelsus is a system of superstitions which we have fortunately outgrown, will, if they once learn to know its principles, be surprised to find that it is based on a superior kind of knowledge which we have not yet attained, but into which we may hope to grow."— LESSING, *Paracelsus*.

The practice of medicine is the art of restoring the sick to health. Modern medicine is, to a great extent, looked upon and employed as if it were a system by which man by his cunning and cleverness may cheat Nature out of her dues and act against the laws of God with impunity, while, to many persons calling themselves physicians, it is merely a method of making money and gratifying their vanity.[1] Instead of seeking to know the divine laws in Nature, and to help to restore the divine order of things, the highest aim of medical science is at present to find means to so poison the body of man and make it pestiferous by inoculation as to render it immune, which means, to make it incapable of reacting upon the introduction of a similar poison. This system corresponds in religion to that which succeeds in quieting the voice of conscience by never paying any attention to it.

Four hundred years ago Paracelsus spoke the following words to the physicians of his times, and we leave it to the reader to judge whether or not his words may find just application today. He says:

"You have entirely deserted the path indicated by Nature, and built up an artificial system, which is fit for nothing but to swindle the public and to prey upon the pockets of the sick. Your safety is due to the fact that your gibberish is unintelligible to the public, who fancy that it must have a meaning, and the consequence is that no one can come near you without being cheated. Your art does not consist in curing the sick, but in worming yourself into the favour of the rich, in swindling the poor, and in gaining admittance to the kitchens of the noblemen of the country. You live upon imposture, and the aid and abetment of the legal profession enables you to carry on your impostures, and to evade punishment by the law. You poison the people and ruin their health; you are sworn to use diligence in your art, but how could you do so, as you possess no art, and all your boasted science is nothing but an invention to cheat and deceive? You denounce me because I do not follow your schools; but your schools can teach me nothing which would be worth knowing. You belong to the tribe of snakes, and I expect nothing but poison from you. You do not spare the sick: how could I expect that you would respect me, while I am cutting down your income by exposing your pretensions and ignorance to the public?"

This is not applicable to the medical profession of our day as a whole; not because that profession has of itself risen to a higher standard, but because physicians are human beings, and humanity as a whole has been somewhat improving in morals. There are, however, numerous well-intentioned fools in the medical profession, knowing nothing whatever about the real nature of man, and their mistakes are not less injurious if committed in ignorance than if they were intentional. Moreover, their folly is the more dangerous as it is protected by the authorities of the State.[2]

There are three kingdoms acting in the constitution of man, an outer, an inner, and an innermost principle; namely, the external physical body, the inner (astral) man, and the innermost centre or soul. Ordinary (regular) physicians know hardly anything about the external body, nothing about the inner man, the cause of the emotions, and less than nothing about the soul. Nevertheless, it is the divine spark in the soul which created and supports the inner man, and the outer form is the vehicle in which the inner man is outwardly manifesting himself. Man's natural body is produced by Nature; but the power in Nature is God, and God is superior to Nature. Man's divine spirit is therefore able to change his nature, and to restore the health of his physical form through the instrumentality of the soul.

The medicine of Paracelsus deals not merely with the external body of man, which belongs to the world of effects, but more especially with the inner man and with the world of causes, never leaving out of sight the universal presence of the divine cause of all things. His medicine is therefore a holy science, and its practice a sacred mission, such as cannot be understood by those who are godless; neither can divine power be conferred by diplomas and academical degrees. A physician who has no faith, and consequently no spiritual power in him, can be nothing else but an ignoramus and quack, even if he had graduated in all the medical colleges in the world and knew the contents of all the medical books that were ever written by man.

The Virtues of a Physician

The object of medical instruction should be to educate the natural talents of those who are born physicians, so that they may make use of the experiences gained by their elders. It is useless and dangerous to make a medical practitioner out of a person who is not a physician at heart.

"The greatest and highest of all qualifications which a physician should possess is *Sapientia*—i.e., *Wisdom*—and without this qualification all his learning will amount to little or nothing as far as any benefit or usefulness to humanity is concerned. He alone is in possession of wisdom who is in possession of reason and knows how to use it without error or doubt. The book of wisdom is the recognition of the truth, and the truth is God; for He who has caused all things to come into existence, and who is Himself the eternal fountain of all things, is also the source of all wisdom and the book in which the truth is to be found without any interpolation or error. In and through Him alone shall we be able to find wisdom and to act wisely, and without Him all our learning will be mere foolishness. As the sun shines upon us from above and causes plants to grow, so the talents necessary for the exercise of this art, whose germs exist in the human heart, must be developed in the rays of the sun of divine wisdom. We cannot find wisdom in books, nor in any external thing; we can only find it within ourselves. Man cannot create day, nor can he create night; and he cannot create wisdom, but it must come to him from above. He who seeks wisdom in the fountain of wisdom is the true disciple, but he who seeks it where it does not exist will seek for it in vain."

Wisdom is not created, manufactured, or "developed" by man, but it becomes manifest in him by its own power, whenever the conditions are favourable. Intellectual learning is an artificial thing, and may be accumulated by man's selfish efforts to learn and possess knowledge; but wisdom is the realisation of truth within the soul, that comes from an awakening to its realisation.

"It is said that we should seek first the kingdom of heaven which is within us, and that everything else would be added; it has also been said that if we only knock strongly enough the door will be opened, and we will never ask in vain, provided we ask with a sincere heart and not with an adulterous object in view. A physician must seek for his knowledge and power within the divine spirit; if he seeks it in external things he will be a pseudo-medicus and an ignoramus. God is the Great First Cause in and from which all things came into existence, and all our knowledge should therefore come from God and not from man-made authorities." (*Labyrinthus Medicorum*)

"A physician should exercise his art, not for his own benefit, but for the sake of the patient. If he practises merely for his own benefit, such a physician resembles a wolf, and is even worse than an ordinary murderer; for, while a man may defend himself against a murderous attack made upon him on the high-road, he has no means of defence against the murderer who, under the guise of a benefactor and protected by law, comes to steal his goods and destroy his life."

"A physician should be above all honest and true. Let his speech be 'yes' and 'no,' and let him avoid using subterfuges and prevarications; God acts through him who is upright, honest, and pure, but not through him who is wicked and false. God is absolute Truth, and His power does not become manifest in those who are not true. The power of the physician should be resting in the truth; if it rests upon lies, it will be useless and belongs to the devil."

"If man were made only out of one kingdom, the kingdom of heaven, then would it be sufficient for him to lead a holy life, to enable him to cure all diseases in himself and in others; but as he is made of three worlds, it is necessary that the physician should also have a knowledge of the conditions existing in the two other worlds, the world of mind and external Nature."[3]

"He should also be well experienced; for there are many kinds of disease, and they cannot be known without experience and learning. No one ever knows so much that he could not learn more. Every art requires experience. You cannot become a good painter, sculptor, or shoemaker by the mere reading of books, much less can you be a good physician without being experienced. He should know the laws of Nature, but above all the constitution of man, the invisible no less than the visible one. His knowledge will strengthen his faith, and his faith will endow him with power, so that he will be like an apostle, healing the sick, the blind, and the halt."

The medicine of Paracelsus therefore rests upon four pillars, which are: 1. *Philosophy*, i.e. a knowledge of physical nature; 2. *Astronomy*, i.e., a knowledge of the powers of the mind; 3. *Alchemy*, i.e., a knowledge of the divine powers in man; and 4. *The personal virtue (holiness) of the physician.*

The Four Pillars of Medicine

1. A physician should be a *philosopher*; i.e., acquainted with the laws of external Nature.

"The knowledge of Nature is the foundation of the science of medicine, and it is taught by the four great departments of science: *Philosophy, Astronomy, Alchemy,* and *Physical Science.* These four sciences cover a large field, and require a great deal of study. A common proverb says, 'Life is short, art is long.' Ever since the beginning of the world men have sought for the art to destroy disease, and they have not found it yet; but to the patient it appears that the medical art is very short and the acquisition of science very slow, while his disease is quick, and does not wait until the doctor has found his art. If a physician is in possession of true knowledge, then will his art make short work with the disease, and the life of the patient will be comparatively long. Art is short, for it requires little time to apply it when it is once in our possession; but error is long, and many die before finding the art." (*Commentaria in Aphorismas Hippocratis*)

"A physician must be a *Philosopher*; that is to say, he must dare to use his own reason and not cling to opinions and book-authorities, be they old or new. He must above all be in possession of that faculty which is called Intuition, and which cannot be acquired by blindly following the footsteps of another; he must be able to see his own way. There are natural philosophers and there are artificial philosophers. The former have a knowledge of their own; the latter have borrowed knowledge from their books. If you wish to be a true physician, you must be able to do your own thinking, and not merely employ the thoughts of others. What others may teach you may be good enough to assist you in your search for knowledge, but you should be able to think for yourself and not cling to the coat-tail of any authority, no matter how big-sounding the title of the latter may be." (*De Modo Pharmacandi*)

"The wisdom of our sophists and medicasters does not consist in a knowledge of Nature, but in a knowledge of what Aristoteles, Galen, Avicenna, and other accepted authorities have supposed Nature to be; they only know the dead body of man, but not the living image presented by Nature; they have become untruthful and unnatural, and therefore their art is based upon their own fancies and speculations, which they imagine to be science. The true physician is a product of Nature, not a product of speculation and imagination. If you are not able to see a thing, it will be useless to try to imagine how it may look; perception enables you to see, but speculation is blind. Wisdom is not given by Nature, nor does man inherit it from the latter; it is planted in him by his eternal parent, and grows and increases in him by practice."

It is not true, as has been asserted by certain modern writers, that Paracelsus has objected to the dissecting of dead bodies and called it useless; what he said is, that such a practice was unnecessary for those who had developed the true inner sight; just as it is useless for a man to walk on crutches when he is in perfect health. He says:

"The anatomy of man is twofold. One aspect of it may be known by dissecting the body, so as to find out the position of its bones, muscles, and veins, etc.; but this is the least important. The other is more important, and means to introduce a new life into the organism, to see the transmutations taking place therein, to know what the blood is, and what kind of *sulphur, salt,* and *mercury* (energy, substance, and mind) it contains." (*Paramir.*, i. cap. c.)

"By the power of wisdom man is enabled to recognise the unity of the All, and to perceive that the microcosm of man is the counterpart of the macrocosm of Nature. There is nothing in heaven or upon the earth which may not be found in man, and there is nothing in man but what exists in the macrocosm of Nature. The two are the same, and differ from each other in nothing but their forms. This is a truth which will be perceived by every true philosopher, but a merely animal intellect will not be able to see it, nor would man's fancy enable him to understand it. That philosophy which is based upon wisdom—*i.e.*, upon the recognition of the truth of a thing—is true philosophy; but that which is based upon fancy and the idle speculation is uncertain. The former is the true gold; the latter is merely an imitation which if put into the fire will leave nothing but sulphur and ashes."

"He who wants to know man must look upon him as a whole and not as a patched-up piece of work. If he finds a part of the human body diseased, he must look for the causes which produce the disease, and not merely treat the external effects. Philosophy—*i.e.*, the true perception and understanding of cause and effect—is the mother of the physician, and explains the origin of all his diseases. In this understanding rests the indication of the true remedy, and he who is not able to understand will accomplish nothing; he will go on in the future laming, crippling, and killing his patients in *Nomine Domini* as he did in the past."

"A physician who knows nothing more about his patient than what the latter will tell him knows very little indeed. He must be able to judge from the external appearance of the patient about his internal condition. He must be able to see the internal in the external man; for if he wanted to experiment merely according to his own fancy, the world could not furnish him enough patients to arrive at the end of his experiments. He must have the normal constitution of man present before his mind and know its abnormal conditions; he must know the relations existing between the microcosm of man and the macrocosm of Nature, and know the little by the power of his knowledge of the great. We should rise up to a true realisation of the nature of man and his position in the universe, and then apply our knowledge according to the teaching of wisdom, and this kind of study will injure no man; but those who experiment with their patients, without knowing the real constitution of man, are murderers, and may God protect the sick from them!"

"Nature—not man—is the physician. Man has lost the true light of reason, and the animal intellect with its speculations and theories has usurped the place. Try to enable yourself to follow Nature again, and she will be your instructor. Learn to know the storehouse of Nature and the boxes in which her virtues are stored up. The ways of Nature are simple, and she does not require any complicated prescriptions."

2. A physician should be an *Astronomer*; this means that he should know the heaven (the mental sphere) wherein man lives, with all its stars (ideas) and constellations.

"A physician must be an *Astronomer*, for he ought to know the influences of the seasons, of heat and cold, of dryness and moisture, of light and darkness, etc., upon the organism of man. There is a time for everything, and what may be good at one time may be evil at another. There is a time for rain and a time when the roses are blooming, and it is not sufficient that a physician should be able to judge about today, he should also know what tomorrow will bring. Time is man's master, and plays with him as the cat with a mouse, and no one knows the future but God. A physician should, therefore, not depend too much on the accomplishments of the animal intellect in his brain, but he should listen to the divine voice which speaks in his heart, and learn to understand it. He should have that knowledge which cannot be acquired by reading in books, but which is a gift of divine wisdom. He should be married to his art as a man is married to his wife, and he should love her with all his heart and mind for her own sake, and not for the purpose of making money or to satisfy his ambition. If he loves his art, his art will be true to him; but if he sticks to it only for mercenary purposes, or if he merely imitates the art of another, it will be an adulterous alliance, and no good will be the result. True marriage is not a mere binding together of two forms, but it is an union of the soul. The physician who is not married to his art with his soul is a quack, an adulterer, and an impostor. (*Comm. in Aphor. Hippocr.*)

Man's body is itself a product of mind, and its condition depends to a great extent on the state of his mind. All his diseases, in so far as they are not directly due to external mechanical causes, are due to mental conditions.

"Philosophy (anatomy) deals with the visible material part of man's constitution; but there is a vastly greater part of man which is ethereal and invisible. As the terrestrial body of man is intimately related to his terrestrial surroundings, likewise his astral body is in relation with all the influences of the astral world; and that part of philosophy dealing with these astral influences is called astronomy."

"Astronomy is the upper part of philosophy by which the whole of the microcosm may become known. Philosophy deals with the elements of earth and water, belonging to man's constitution. Astronomy deals with his air and fire (the mind). There is a heaven and earth in man as there is in the macrocosm, and in that heaven there are all the celestial influences, whose visible representations we see in the sky, such as the planets and stars, the *Milky Way*, the Zodiac, etc., neither more nor less; for the microcosm is an exact counterpart of the macrocosm in every respect except its external form."

"The terrestrial part of man is a child of the earth, and the astral man is a child of the astral world, and as the two worlds are intimately connected with each other, the physician should be acquainted with the influences of the astral as well as with those of the terrestrial world. Man's diseases do not originate in himself; they originate from the influences which act upon him and enter his constitution. The astral influences are invisible, but they act upon man, unless he knows how to protect himself against them. Heat and light are intangible and incorporeal; nevertheless, they act upon man, and the same takes place with other invisible influences. If the air becomes vitiated, it will poison man's body; if the astral influences are in a state of corruption, they will do likewise. The elements themselves are invisible; that which is visible belongs merely to the external form. The Arcanum of Man—i.e., the real inner man—is invisible; that which we see of him is not an essential part of his constitution, but merely his external corporeal form."[4]

"The things which we see are not the active principles, but merely the *corpus* containing them; the visible forms are merely external expressions of invisible principles. Forms are, so to say, the vehicles of powers, and they may be visible or invisible. The invisible air and the ether of space, or a perfectly clear and, therefore, invisible crystal, are just as much corporeal as the solid earth, a piece of wood, or a rock. Each of these corporeal things has its own particular life and inhabitants (micro-organisms); we walk about in the air, although the air is corporeal; fishes swim about in the water, and the yolk of an egg rests in the albumen without sinking to the bottom of the shell. The yolk represents the Earth, and the white represents the invisible surroundings of the Earth, and the invisible part acts upon the visible one, but only the philosopher perceives the way in which that action takes place."

"All the influences of the terrestrial and the astral world converge upon man, but how can a physician recognise the manner in which they act and prevent or cure the diseases which are caused by that action, if he is not acquainted with the influences existing in the astral plane? The star-gazer knows only the external visible heaven; but the true astronomer knows two heavens, the external visible and the internal invisible one. There is not a single invisible power in heaven which does not find its corresponding principle in the inner heaven of man; the above acts upon the below, and the latter reacts upon the former."

3. The physician ought to be an *Alchemist*; that is to say, he ought to be regenerated in the spirit of Jesus Christ and know his own divine powers.

"He should be an *Alchemist*; that is to say, he should understand the *Chemistry of Life*. Medicine is not merely a science, but an art; it does not consist merely in compounding pills and plasters and drugs of all kinds, but it deals with the processes of life, which must be understood before they can be guided. All art, all wisdom, all power, acts from one centre towards the periphery of the circle, and whatever is enclosed within that circle may be regarded as medicine. A powerful will can cure where doubt will end in failure. The character of the physician acts more powerfully upon the patient than all the drugs employed. A carpenter or a mason will fail to make perfect work without compass and square, and a physician without religion and firmness will be a failure. Alchemy—*i.e.*, the employment of a strong will, benevolence, charity, patience, etc.—is, therefore, the principal corner-stone in the practice of medicine."

"The psychical surroundings of the patient have a great influence upon the course of his disease. If he is waited upon by persons who are in sympathy with him, it will be far better for him than if his wife or his attendants wish for his death. In a case of sickness, the patient, the physician, and the attendants should be, so to say, all one heart and one soul, and they should always keep in mind the doctrine of Christ, which says: Thou shalt love thy neighbour as thyself."[5] (*Comm. in Aph. Hippocr.*)

"The physician should be well versed in physical science. He should know the action of medicines, and learn by his own experience and by the experience of others. He should know how to regulate the diet of the patient, and neither overfeed nor starve him. He should know the ordinary course of disease, and the premonitory symptoms; for a disease is like a plant, which may grow to a big tree if it is not rooted out while it is young. A child can cut down an old oak when it first comes out of an acorn, but in time it will require a strong man and an axe to cut it down."

"A physician should be learned, and profit by the experience of others, but blessed is he who knows the living medicine and how to obtain it. He knows that there are innumerable remedies in Nature, which are the *Magnalia Dei*—*i.e.*, the mysteries of God, hidden from the eyes of the vulgar, but opened to the spiritual perception of the wise."[6] (*Comm.*)

4. The physician must have a *natural qualification* for his occupation.

"He who can cure disease is a physician. To cure diseases is an art which cannot be acquired by the mere reading of books, but which must be learned by experience. Neither emperors nor popes, neither colleges nor high schools, can create physicians. They can confer privileges and cause a person who is not a physician to appear as if he were one, but they cannot cause him to be what he is not; they can give him permission to kill, but they cannot enable him to cure the sick, if he has not already been ordained by God. Theory should precede practice; but if it consists in mere suppositions and assumptions, and is not confirmed by practical works, such a theory is worthless and ought to be abandoned. The pseudo-physician bases his art on his books—i.e., on that which he believes the authors of those books to have known; the art of the true physician is based on his own knowledge and ability, and is supported by the four pillars of medicine—Philosophy, Astronomy, Alchemy, and Virtue." (*Paragranum*)

"A physician who is true to his own higher self will also have faith in himself, and he who has that faith will easily command the faith of the people. A preacher who utters moral sermons, but does not observe his own doctrines, will not command respect; he will rightly be despised and bring his doctrines—even if they are true—into discredit; likewise a physician who is seen to be untruthful, wavering, and ignorant will lose the confidence of the public. The art of medicine should be based on truth; it is a divine art which should not be prostituted for base purposes. A physician who deserves the confidence of the people will be trusted by God, for it is the Spirit of God that guides the hearts of mankind."

"I praise the spagyric physicians (the alchemists), for they do not go about idling and putting on airs, being dressed in velvets and silks, having golden rings on their fingers and their hands in white gloves; but they are daily and nightly patiently engaged in their work with the fire and seeking their pastime within their own laboratory (the mind). They do not talk much or praise their medicines; for they know that the work must praise the master, and not the master the work." (*De Separat. Rer.*)

"All arts originate in divine wisdom, and no man ever invented anything through his own power. Man cannot accomplish even the most trifling thing without the power of the Will; but the will of man is not his product and does not belong to him; it belongs to God, and has merely been lent to man; he is permitted to use it, and he abuses it on account of his ignorance. All things come from God, the good as well as the evil ones; but while the former are His direct products, and in harmony with the Law, the latter are, so to say, His grandchildren which have become degenerated; for evil is good perverted. Those who put their trust in God—that is to say, in the power of Goodness, Wisdom, Justice, and Truth—will surely succeed; but those who, while they pretend to serve God, serve merely themselves, are the children of evil, and will perish with it."

"One of the most necessary requirements for a physician is perfect purity and singleness of purpose. He should be free of ambition, vanity, envy, unchastity, pomposity, and self-conceit, because these vices are the outcome of ignorance and incompatible with the light of divine wisdom which should illumine the mind of the true physician; but our practitioners of medicine will not believe me when I say that it is necessary that a physician to be successful should be virtuous; because they imagine that success is due only to learning, and they cannot realise that all true wisdom and power is derived from God."

"There is a knowledge which is derived from man, and another one which is derived from God through the light of Nature. There are artificially made physicians and there are born physicians. The latter possess their talent from birth, and it may be unfolded and grow like a tree if it is properly nursed. He who has no natural talent to be a physician will never succeed. He who is not a physician in the spring of his life will not be one in the fall."

"A physician should be faithful and charitable; he should have full and perfect faith, a faith which is not divided. Faith and Charity are essentially identical; they both spring from God, and God is one and cannot be divided. The faith of a physician is not manifested by making many visits to his patient, but by his ability to recognise and treat the disease. He should give to his patient his utmost attention, he should identify himself heart and soul with him, and this cannot be done without charity and benevolence. He who loves only himself and his own profit will be of little benefit to the sick, for he will neglect the patient. To recognise the disease of the latter and to be able to benefit him, entire harmony should exist between the physician and the patient; a physician who loves his art for its own sake will also be charitable towards the sick." (*Origin of Diseases*)

The Archaeus

All organic functions are caused by the activity of one universal principle of Life. This principle acts in all the members of the body, either slow or quick, perceptible or imperceptible, consciously or unconsciously, normal or abnormal, according to the constitution of the organs in which it is active. As long as the character (the spirit) of an entity is preserved, it acts in that entity as a whole; if the form is broken up and loses its character, it manifests itself in other forms; the life which is active in a man during his lifetime in causing the organic functions of his body, will manifest its activity in creating worms in his body after the spirit has left the form. The spirit is the centre which attracts the principle of life; if the spirit has left the form, life will be attracted to other centres.

If the activity of the life-principle takes place in a form in an harmonious and regular manner, unimpeded by any obstacles, such a state is called health. If its activity is impeded by some cause, and if it acts abnormally or irregularly, such a state is called "disease."

This principle of life is called by Paracelsus, Archaeus. It is not a material substance, in the usual acceptation of that term, but a spiritual essence, everywhere present and invisible. It causes or cures disease according to the conditions under which it acts, as it may be pure or impure, healthy or poisoned, by other influences. The animal organism attracts it from its surroundings and from the nutriments which enter into its form; it assimilates it, and loses it again. "The Archaeus, or Liquor Vitae, constitutes the invisible man. The invisible man is hidden in the visible one, and is formed in the shape of the outer one as long as it remains in that outer one. The inner man is, so to say, the shadow or the counterpart of the material body. It is ethereal in its nature, still it is substance; it directs the growth and the formation and dissolution of the form in which it is contained; it is the noblest part in physical man. As a man's picture is reflected in a mirror, so the form of the physical man is reflected in the invisible body."[7] (*De Generatione Hominis*)

"The Archaeus is an essence that is equally distributed in all parts of the human body, if the latter is in a healthy condition; it is the invisible nutriment from which the visible body draws its strength, and the qualities of each of its parts correspond to the nature of the physical parts that contain it. The Spiritus Vitas takes its origin from the Spiritus Mundi. Being an emanation of the latter, it contains the elements of all cosmic influences, and is therefore the cause by which the action of the stars (cosmic forces) upon the invisible body of man may be explained." (*De Viribus Membrorum*)

"The Archaeus is of a magnetic nature, and attracts or repels other sympathetic or antipathetic forces belonging to the same plane. The less power of resistance for astral influences a person possesses, the more will he be subject to such influences. The vital force is not enclosed in man, but radiates around him like a luminous sphere, and it can be made to act at a distance. In those semi-material rays the imagination of man produces healthy or morbid effects. It will poison the essence of life and cause diseases, or strengthen and purify it after it has been made impure, and restore the health."

"All diseases, except such as come from mechanical causes, have an invisible origin, and of such sources popular medicine knows very little. Men who are devoid of the power of spiritual perception are unable to recognise the existence of anything that cannot be seen externally. Popular medicine knows, therefore, next to nothing about any diseases that are not caused by mechanical means,[8] and the science of curing internal diseases consists almost entirely in the removal of causes that have produced some mechanical obstruction. But the number of diseases that originate from some unknown causes is far greater than those that come from mechanical causes, and for such diseases our physicians know no cure, because, not knowing such causes, they cannot remove them. All they can prudently do is to observe the patient and make their guesses about his condition; and the patient may rest satisfied if the medicines administered to him do him no serious harm, and do not prevent his recovery. The best of our popular physicians are the ones that do the least harm. But, unfortunately, some poison their patients with mercury; others purge them or bleed them to death. There are some who have learned so much that their learning has driven out all their common sense, and there are others who care a great deal more for their own profit than for the health of their patients. A disease does not change its state to accommodate itself to the knowledge of the physician, but the physician should understand the causes of the disease. A physician should be a servant of Nature, and not her enemy; he should be able to guide and direct her in her struggle for life, and not throw, by his unreasonable interference, fresh obstacles in the way of recovery." (*Paragranum*)

"Medicine is much more an art than a science; to know the experience of others may be useful to a physician, but all the learning in the world could not make a man a physician, unless he has the necessary talents, and is destined by Nature to be a physician. If we want to learn to know the inner man by studying only the appearance of the exterior man, we will never come to an end, because each man's constitution differs in some respect from that of another. If a physician knows nothing more about his patient than what the latter tells him, he knows very little indeed, because the patient usually knows only that he suffers pain. Nature causes and cures disease, and it is therefore necessary that the physician should know the processes of Nature, the invisible as well as the visible man. He will then be able to recognise the cause and the course of a disease, and he will know much more by using his own reason than by all that the books or the patient may tell him. Medical science may be acquired by learning, but medical wisdom is given by God."[9] (*Paragranum*)

"Natural man has no wisdom, but the wisdom of God may act through him as an instrument. God is greater than Nature, for Nature is His product; and the beginning of wisdom in man is therefore the beginning of his supernatural power. The kind of knowledge that man ought to possess is not derived from the earth, nor does it come from the stars; but it is derived from the Highest; and therefore the man who possesses the Highest may rule over the things of the earth, and over the stars. There is a great difference between the power that removes the invisible causes of disease, and which is Magic, and that which causes merely external effects to disappear, and which is Physic, Sorcery, and Quackery."[10]

The Mumia

"The Archaeus is the essence of life, but the principle in which this essence is contained, and which serves as its vehicle, is called Mumia. In the Mumia is great power, and the cures that have been performed by the use of the Mumia are natural, although they are very little understood by the vulgar, because they are the results of the action of invisible things, and that which is invisible does not exist for the comprehension of the ignorant. They therefore look upon such cures as having been produced by the 'black art,' or by the help of the devil, while in fact they are but natural, and have a natural cause; and even if the devil had caused them, the devil can have no power except that which is given to him by God, and so it would be the power of God after all."[11]

"There is a twofold power active in man—an invisibly acting or vital power, and a visibly acting mechanical force. The visible body has its natural forces, and the invisible body has its natural forces, and the remedy of all diseases or injuries that may affect the visible form are contained in the invisible body, because the latter is the seat of the power that infuses life into the former, and without which the former would be dead and decaying. If we separate the vital force from the physical form, the body dies and putrefies; and by impregnating a dying body with vitality it can be made to live again. The invisible forces acting in the visible body are often very powerful, and may be guided by the imagination and be propelled by the will. As the odour of a lily passes from the flower into the surrounding air, so the vital force contained in the invisible body passes into the visible form and beyond it. The physical body has the capacity to produce visible organs—such as the eyes and the ears, the tongue and the nose—but they all take their origin from the invisible body, of which the external visible form is only the outward representation."

"But if the germs and the essences of all the organs of the physical body are contained in the invisible vehicle of life, it follows that this invisible microcosmic body contains certain definite qualities, which, if they are properly understood, may be used for some purpose; and the cures that have been performed by the use of this Mumia prove that this assertion is true. The pinks are beautiful flowers so long as they are not separated from the plant upon which they grow, and the chelidonium grows as long as it can draw its nutriment from the earth; but if the pinks are separated from the parent stem, and if the roots of the chelidonium are dead, these plants, being separated from the source out of which they drew their vitality, will decay. The life that made them live is not dead, but it is departed from the dead form; and if it could be restituted, the form could be made to live again. The Mumia, or vehicle of life, is invisible, and no one sees it depart; but nevertheless it is a spiritual substance containing the essence of life, and it can be brought again by art into contact with dying forms, and revive them, if the vital organs of the body are not destroyed. That which constitutes life is contained in the Mumia, and by imparting the Mumia we impart life. The visible body seems to see and to talk, and yet we do not see the powers that see and talk through it. Likewise the action of the Mumia upon the visible body cannot be perceived by the senses—only its effects can be seen. A visible form without vitality has no other power but its own weight; but if it contains the Mumia, it may perform a great deal. The Mumia is the arcanum, the 'flower of man,' and the true elixir of life. The Mumia acts from one living being directly upon another, or it may be connected with some material and visible vehicle, and be employed in that shape."[12] (*De Origine Morbor. Invisibilium*)

Sympathetic Cures

"Man possesses a magnetic power by which he can attract certain effluvia of a good or evil quality in the same manner as a magnet will attract particles of iron. A magnet may be prepared from iron that will attract iron, and a magnet may be prepared out of some vital substance that will attract vitality. Such a magnet is called the '*magnes microcosmi*,' and it is prepared out of substances that have remained for a time in the human body, and are penetrated by its vitality. Such substances are the hair, the excrements, urine, blood, etc. If it is desirable to use the excrements, they are to be dried in a shadowy, dry, and moderately warm place until they have lost their humidity and odour. By this process all the Mumia has gone out of them, and they are, so to say, hungry to attract vitality again. If such a magnet is applied to a part of the patient's body, it attracts and absorbs vitality from that part in the same manner as a sponge absorbs water, and it will thereby allay the inflammation existing in such a part, because it attracts the superabundance of magnetism carried to that place by the rush of the blood. The Mumia coming from the body of a person continues to remain for a while in sympathetic relationship (magnetic *rapport*) with the Mumia contained in such a person, and they act magnetically upon each other. If, therefore, the Mumia is extracted from a diseased part of a person by a microcosmic magnet, and the magnet mixed with earth, and an herb is planted into it, the Mumia in the magnet will be extracted by that plant, and lose its diseased matter, and react in a beneficial manner upon the Mumia contained in the body of the patient; but it is necessary that the selected plant should be one which bears the signature of the disease with which the patient is affected, so that it will attract the specific influence from the stars. In this way diseased elements may be magnetically extracted out of a person and inoculated into a plant. This is called the transplantation of diseases; and diseases may, in a similar manner, be transplanted into animals that are healthy and strong, or the virus be transferred upon other persons; and many practices of sorcery are based upon that fact.[13] In this way diseases can be cured in one person and caused to appear in another; love between two persons of the opposite sex may thus be created, and magnetic links be established between persons living at distant places, because there is only one universal principle of life, and by it all beings are sympathetically connected together."

The plants used for the transplantation of diseases bear the signatures of the diseases whose names are added. In cases of ulcers and wounds the Mumia may be planted with *Polygonum persicaria, Symphytum officinal, Botanus europeus*, etc. The plant is to be brought for a while in contact with the ulcer, and then to be buried in manure. As it rots, the ulcer heals.[14] In toothache the gums should be rubbed with the root of *Senecio vulgaris* until they bleed, and the root is then to be replaced into the earth; or a splinter may be cut out of a blackthorn or willow after the bark has been lifted up. Pick the gums with that splinter until they bleed, and replace the splinter into the tree and tie the cut in the bark up so that it will heal. In *menorrhagia uterina*, the Mumia should be taken from the groins and planted with *Polygonum persicaria*. In *menorrhoea difficilis, Mentha pulegium* is used. In *phthisis pulmonalis* the Mumia may be planted with an *orchis* in the vicinity of an oak or cherry tree, or the Mumia be planted directly into such trees. The (fresh) urine of a patient should be heated in a new pot over a fire, and an egg boiled in it. When the egg is hard boiled, some holes should be made into the egg, and the urine boiled down until the pot is dry. The egg is then to be put into an ant-hill; the ants will eat it, and the patient recovers. In atrophy of the limbs the Mumia is taken from the upper and lower joints of the diseased limb, and planted with an oak or cherry tree. Diseases can also be cured by transplantation, if the diseased part is covered for a while with a piece of fresh beef, until the sweat enters into it, and the beef is then given to a cat to eat.[15]

Occult Properties of Plants

An especially favourite remedy of Paracelsus is the *Hypericum perforatum*, which is used especially against elementals, spirits, and larvae inimical to man. The veins upon its leaves are a signatum, and being perforated, they signify that this plant drives away all phantasmata existing in the sphere of man. The phantasmata produce spectra, in consequence of which a man will see and hear ghosts and spooks, and from these are induced diseases by which men are induced to kill themselves, or to fall into epilepsy, madness, insanity, etc. The hypericum is almost an universal medicine.[16] (*De Naturalibus*)

Another plant of great occult power is the Rosemary (*Rosmarinus officinalis*), which also has the quality of keeping away evil influences, and is therefore a protection against witchcraft, obsession, vampirism, and the influence of evil thoughts.

The *Herbarium* of Paracelsus describes the occult properties of thirty-six plants, and also of minerals and precious stones; but it would make this book too voluminous to enter into details.

The Magnet

Paracelsus was better acquainted than our modern physicians with the therapeutic powers of the magnet, and used it in various diseases. He knew the powers of mineral, human, and astral magnetism, and his doctrines in regard to human magnetism have been confirmed to a great extent since the time of his death. More than a hundred years ago Mesmer created a sensation in the medical world by his discovery of animal magnetism and by his magnetic cures. His discovery was then believed to refer to something new and unheard of, but Lessing proved already in 1769 that the real discoverer of animal magnetism was Paracelsus.

In regard to the powers of the magnetism Paracelsus says:

"That which constitutes a magnet is an attractive power, which is beyond our understanding, but which, nevertheless, causes the attraction of iron and other things. Our physicians have always had magnets at their disposal, but they did not pay much attention to them, because they did not know that they may be used for any other thing than to attract nails. Our doctors have ceased to learn anything from experience, and they make use of idle talk; and it is a pity and a shame that the representatives of our science should know so little. They have every day occasion to see magnets publicly and privately, and yet they continue to act as if no magnets were in existence."[17]

"They complain of me because I do not follow the methods prescribed by the ancients; but why should I follow the ancients in things in which I know they were wrong? They could not know things of which they had no experience, and it would be foolish to follow them in things in which they were mistaken. Whatever I know I have learned by my experience, and I therefore depend upon my own knowledge, and not upon the ignorance of another."

"Our doctors say that the magnet attracts iron, and verily it does not require a great deal of learning to be able to perceive a fact that may be seen by every ignorant boor; but there are qualities in a magnet not known to every ignoramus, and one of these qualities is that the magnet also attracts all martial humours that are in the human system."

"Martial diseases are such as are caused by auras coming and expanding from a centre outwards, and at the same time holding on to their centres; in other words, such as originate from a certain place, and extend their influence without leaving the place from where they originate. In such cases the magnet should be laid upon the centre, and it will then attract the diseased aura towards the centre, and circumscribe and localise the disease, until the latter disease becomes reabsorbed into its centre.[18] It is useless to try to suppress the external symptoms that are caused by a disease, if we at the same time allow the disease to spread. A poisonous tree cannot be kept from growing if we simply cut off some of its branches or leaves; but if we could cause the vital essence which it draws by its roots from the earth to descend again into the roots and re-enter the earth, the poisonous tree would die on its own account. By the attractive power of a magnet acting upon the diseased aura of the blood in an affected part, that aura may be made to return into the centre from which it originated, and be absorbed therein; and thereby we destroy the herd of the virus and cure the patient, and we need not wait idly to see what Nature will do. The magnet is therefore especially useful in all inflammations, in fluxes and ulcerations, in diseases of the bowels and uterus, in internal as well as in external disease."

"The magnet has a front (north pole) and a back (south pole); the former attracts and the latter repulses. In a case of hysteria the attracting part of the magnet is applied above the uterus, and the repulsing part of another magnet below. In this way the nervous force controlling the movements of the uterus will be propelled towards its proper place. In cases of epilepsy, where there is a great determination of nervous fluid towards the brain, the repulsing (negative) pole of a magnet is applied to the spine and to the head, and the attracting (positive) pole of other magnets upon the abdominal region. There are a great many other diseases that may be cured by the proper use of the magnet, but for those who are able to understand such things the hints already given will be sufficient, while those who have little understanding would not comprehend this system even if we were to write a book about it. It should, however, be remembered that the manner of employing a magnet changes according as to whether we wish to draw the diseased aura out of the body, or to cause it to be reabsorbed into its centre."

The forces composing the Microcosm of man are identical with the forces composing the Macrocosm of the world. In the organism of man these forces may act in an abnormal manner, and diseases will be thereby created; in the great organism of the Cosmos they may act in an abnormal manner, and thereby abnormal conditions, or diseases in the earth and atmosphere, in the water and in the elements of fire (electricity), may be created. Man may be affected with spasms, or dropsy, or colic, or fevers, etc., and the Macrocosm of the earth may be affected with earthquakes, rainspouts, storms, and lightnings. The elements that constitute the life of the heart of man constitute the life of the sun; the quality of life found in the elements constituting his blood corresponds to the quality of the invisible influences radiating from Mars; if the soul-essences that characterise the influences of Venus did not exist, the instincts which cause men and animals to propagate their species would not exist, and thus every planet and every star contains certain magnetic elements that correspond with the identical magnetic elements existing in the constitution of Man. A physician who wishes to be rational must know the constitution of the universe as well as the constitution of man; he must be an anatomist, a physiologist, and an astronomer; and it will avail him little to learn these sciences from the books, but he should have an understanding of them by the power of interior perception, which cannot be taught in books, but must be acquired by practice.

Anatomy

Paracelsus regarded man as being not merely a compound of muscles and bones, tissues and nerves, but as representing on a smaller scale all that is contained in the great world. Therefore his soul and mind are as much parts of his true constitution as are the earthly elements of which his elementary body is made up. Thus the anatomy of Paracelsus takes in all the parts of man's constitution, which has already been described in a previous chapter.

There are two kinds of Anatomy of the Microcosm, one teaching the constitution of the external form of man, the other one that of the internal living man. To seek for the internal man by dissecting the external form is useless, for in doing so we do not find life, but we destroy the form in which it manifested itself.

"The Anatomy of the Microcosm is twofold: (1) The *local anatomy*, which teaches the constitution of the physical body, its bones, muscles, blood-vessels, etc.; and (2) The more important *essential* anatomy—i.e., the anatomy of the living inner man. The latter is the kind of anatomy which is most important for the physician to know, but it will be difficult to bring it to the understanding of those who merely judge by external appearances and refuse to follow the way of the truth. If we know the anatomy of the inner man, we know the *Prima materia*, and may see the nature of the disease as well as the remedy. That which we see with our external eyes is the *Ultima materia*. By dividing and dissecting the external body, we can learn nothing about the inner (astral) man; we merely destroy the unity of the whole." (*Paramir.*, i. 6)

The life of a thing, being latent in the form, is set free when the form is destroyed; its entering into a new form is regeneration.

"The rose is beautiful and has a sweet odour as long as it remains in the form; but to manifest its medicinal qualities in the constitution of man, its form must be destroyed and its spirit enter the body of man. Only that which enters into regeneration is useful; the rest is useless. In this regeneration enters the true *Sulphur, Mercury, and Salt* (the ethereal essences contained within the gross particles)."

Physiology

"As each of the component parts has its own life, so it has its own death; there is a continual process of death and regeneration going on in man. As a tree or a plant grows out of its seed, so the new life grows out of the old one, and that which was heretofore invisible becomes visible. The physician should be able to see that which is not visible to everybody. He should see it in the light of Nature, and if this light is to be called a light, it must be visible and not dark."

"The physical body of man is grown from a physical germ, and requires physical nutriment for its support. There is something like a fire (energy) within ourselves which continually consumes our form, and if we were to add nothing to our body to supply the waste caused by that combustion, our form would soon die. We continually eat our own selves; we eat our fingers, our heart, our brain, etc.; but in each morsel of food which we eat, there is contained the material required to replace that which has been consumed by that internal fire. Each part of our organism selects what it needs, and that which is superfluous or useless is rejected. The Master in man, who superintends the building up of the organism, supplies every organ with that which it needs. We need not eat bones to cause our bones to grow, nor veins, ligaments, and brain, to have those things formed within us. Bread will produce blood, although there is no blood in the bread." (*Paramir.*, i. 7)

"Besides the visible body, man has an invisible one. The former comes from the Limbus, the latter is made from the breath of God. As a breath is like nothing in our estimation, likewise this spiritual body is like nothing to our external senses. This invisible body is the one which is spoken of as constituting our corporeal form on the day of the resurrection." (*Paramir.*, i. 8)

"Heaven and Earth, air and water, are scientifically considered *a Man*, and man is a world containing a heaven and an earth, air and water, and all the various principles which constitute the mineral, vegetable, and animal kingdoms, and the higher acts upon the lower. Thus the principle constituting *Saturn* in the Macrocosm acts upon the *Saturn* in man; the *Melissa* of the Macrocosm acts upon the *Melissa* in the Microcosm, etc. There are innumerable principles in the Macrocosm and in the Microcosm; they are not differing from each other in the number of things of which they are composed, but in the way they are composed; for they all consist only of three things—*i.e., Sulphur, Mercury, and Salt*. As a million of figures are (potentially) contained in a rough piece of wood from which a woodcutter may cut one or many images or forms; so many hundred different diseases may be produced from the *Corpus* of man, and yet it is but a single Corpus; and as all the wooden images may be consumed by one fire, so there is one *Fire* in the universal storehouse of Nature which consumes that which is impure and separates it from that which is pure."

"A painter paints a picture upon a piece of wood, and you will then see the picture, but not the wood; but a wet rag may wipe out all that the painter has made. Thus we have been cut out by the hand of God, and He formed us in the three Substances and painted us all over with Life, but death wipes out the picture. Therefore we should not allow ourselves to be seduced by the temptations of life, seeing that they are nothing but illusions, resembling colours which in themselves are neither red, nor yellow, nor green, but merely appear to be so to the eye. Death too has its colours, and if the colour of death takes the place of the colour of life, death gets the mastery over life; these two colours the physician should know, but they do not explain the disease; they are merely outward signs, and as such they are illusive." (*Paramir.*, i. 5)

"It is erroneous to speak of *Fever* as if this were disease. The name 'fever' refers to the heat of the disease, and this heat is merely a symptom; it is neither the cause nor the substance of the disease; it would be more appropriate to call it *Morbus Nitri* or *Morbus Sulphuris incensi*. '*Apoplexy*' is a misnomer; because it is caused by a sublimation of Mercury, and ought to be more properly called *Mercurius Cachinialis Sublimatus*.[19] The same may be said in regard to many other diseases and their misnomers. Names ought to indicate the true nature and not merely the external effects of the diseases. If a physician cannot see deeper than a boor, then he is a boor and not a physician. What is there in the ocean, in the earth, in the air, or in the *firmament*—i.e., the 'fire'—which should not be known to a physician? Why is professional ignorance so great and success so little, but because the practitioners study only external effects and the anatomy of the external form, and are not able to look with the eye of the spirit into the mysterious part of Nature? We cannot see the life in things that are dead; the eyes of the soul must open, and we must become able to see not only the house of life, but its living inhabitant."

Therapeutics

"If we wish to restore health, we should be able to use the virtues contained in all the four elements of the celestial and terrestrial realm. Man's organism is composed of many parts; if one part is diseased, all the other parts suffer, and one disease may be the death of the whole. Man has in him the whole *firmament*, the upper and lower spheres; if his organism is sick it calls for help to heaven and to the earth. As the soul must fight against the devil with all her strength, and call God to her aid with her whole heart, her whole mind, and all her powers; so the diseased physical organism calls to its aid all the celestial and terrestrial powers with which it has been invested by God to resist the cruel and bitter death." (*Paramir.*, i. 2)

Paramirum; or, The Book of the Causes and the Beginning of Diseases—The Five Causes

"There is only one eternal and universal Cause of everything, which is God, and if we were to write in a true Christian spirit, we should not make any divisions; but for the sake of helping our finite understanding, which is not able to grasp the power of the Infinite, we are forced to accept the theory of a variety of causes, hoping thereby to sharpen our intellect for the comprehension of finite things, until by the illumination of Divine

Wisdom we shall become able to behold with the eye of Faith the eternal Unity of the All."

"We have therefore divided the cause of all diseases into five classes, which are as follows:—*Ens Astrale, Ens Venenale, Ens Naturale, Ens Spirituale,* and *Ens Deale*;[20] but the latter is the fundamental cause of everything that exists."

"As there are five causes of disease, there are also five different methods of treating diseases, and five classes of faculties or sects of physicians which follow these methods. Each method is alone sufficient to treat all the five classes of diseases, and each physician should be well experienced in the methods of the sect to which he belongs, and he should not change from one system to another, but confine himself to the one he has chosen to adopt.[21] He should not be wavering and uncertain, but he should be firm and full of faith, and be able to know more by his own internal power of recognition than by external observation or by what the patient may tell him; for the patient, being only conscious of suffering, is not in a condition to judge his own case correctly, and the physician must be able to see things which are not seen by every one."

But the origin of some particular disease may be not in only one of these causes, but in two or more of them, and unless a person is able to recognise all the causes of such a disease he will be unable to prognosticate the time of its duration. An astrologer may calculate your horoscope correctly, and tell you by what diseases you are threatened and when they will end; but he takes only one of the five causes into consideration, and the chances are four to one that his predictions will prove to be wrong, and that he will be laughed at by those who have only a superficial knowledge, and who do not know the cause of his failure.

1. *Diseases caused by Astral Causes*

"The world is the Macrocosm and man the Microcosm, and the elements of all that exists in the former exist in the latter. All the influences that come from the sun, the planets, and stars act, therefore, invisibly upon man, and if these influences are evil they will produce evil effects. No vegetables would grow without the influence of the sun, but if that influence is too strong they will wither and perish. The world is surrounded by a vaporous sphere, like an egg surrounded by a shell. Through that shell the cosmic influences pass towards the centre, and on that occasion they may become poisoned by the miasmas in the air, and create epidemic diseases. An evil astral influence does not poison the whole world, but only those places where causes for infection exist. If no germs of disease exist in our atmosphere, the astral influences coming from the outside will cause no harm. If evil elements exist in the sphere of our soul, they attract such astral influences as may develop diseases. If the water in a lake freezes to the bottom the fish will die, and they will likewise die if the water gets too warm; and if certain evil elements exist in the water which attract certain correspondingly evil planetary influences,[22] a great many fish may die, and no one may know the cause." (*Paramirum*)

"The astral influences are the servants of man and not his ruler. A seed which is planted in the ground contains in itself all that is necessary for developing into a tree, if the conditions necessary for such a development are furnished. It has the *Ens Seminis* in itself; but if the sun did not exist, it would never grow. The seed needs a *Digest*, and this is furnished by the soil, but the soil would be useless without being warmed by the sunshine. A child in the womb of its mother contains in its *Ens Seminis* the power to grow, its *Digest* is the womb in which it lives, it requires neither planets nor stars; its planet and star is its mother. A child may be conceived or born during the best constellation of planets, and nevertheless have very bad qualities. In such a case the planets are not to blame; it is the *Ens Seminis*, which it has inherited in its blood."

"Man lives within the invisible world comparable to the yolk in an egg. The chicken grows from the white of the egg, which constitutes its *chaos*, and man is nourished by his *chaos*. Within man are the sun and moon, the planets and all the rest of the stars, and also the *chaos*." (*Paragran.*, ii.)

The outward influence of the stars on the sky avails nothing, if there is not a corresponding power in the organism of man upon which it can act; but if the germ of disease is present, the corresponding influence of the stars acts upon it. For instance, a man in whom ♀ or ♂ are the ruling powers may be rendered very passionate during a conjunction of Venice and Mars. Another born under the influence of ♆ may be troubled with rheumatic pains whenever Neptune stands prominent on the sky. An observation of the contents of the astronomical almanac might often aid our physicians in making a correct prognosis.

"The moon exercises a very bad influence, especially at the time of the new moon, which may be very injurious for persons whose sidereal bodies possess magnetic elements that will attract that influence, and the conjunction of the moon with certain other planets will make her influence still more injurious.[23] For instance, a conjunction of the moon, Venus, and Mars may give rise to the plague; a conjunction with Saturn to certain acute diseases, etc.; but no evil influence can develop a disease where the germ of that disease does not already exist. The seat of the sun in the Microcosm is in the heart, that of the moon is in the brain. The moon's influence is cold; and insane people have been called 'lunatics' because they are often injuriously affected by the moon, whose influence acts upon the brain and stimulates the sexual passions, and causes injurious dreams and hallucinations."[24]

"There are certain stars whose influence corresponds to the medical qualities of certain metals, and others that correspond to those of certain plants, and they will act for good or for evil if they are attracted by corresponding elements in the sidereal body of man. A physician should know the physiology and anatomy of heaven as well as that of man to understand the cause and cure of astralic diseases, because he will vainly try his remedies as long as his patient is under the ascending influence of an evil star; but after that evil influence ceases, the disease will also be changed or disappear. Every metal and every plant possesses certain qualities that can attract corresponding planetary influences, and if we know the influence of the star, the conjunctions of the planets, and the qualities of our drugs, we will know what remedy to give to attract such influences as will act beneficially upon the patient."[25]

"If, for instance, a woman is deficient in the element of Mars, and consequently suffers from poverty of the blood and want of nervous strength (anaemia), we may give her iron, because the astral elements of iron correspond to the astral elements represented by Mars, and will attract them as a magnet attracts iron. But we should choose a plant which contains iron in an etherealised state, which is preferable to that of metallic iron.[26] In a case of dropsy it would be exceedingly injurious to give any remedy that would help to attract the evil influence of the moon; but the sun is opposed to the moon, and those remedies which attract the astral essences of the sun will counteract those of the moon, and thereby the cause of dropsy can be removed. The same mode of reasoning may be applied in all other astralic diseases.

2. *Diseases caused by Poisonous Substances and Impurities.*

"Everything is perfect in itself and nothing is impure if it is what it ought to be; but if two things come together, then one may be a poison to the other." (*De Ente Veneni*)

"Impurities and injurious elements enter the human organism in various ways. They may be taken in the food or drink, inhaled with the air, or be absorbed by the skin. There are visible and invisible poisonous substances that are not injurious if they enter the organism alone, but will become poisonous if they come into contact with others. There are poisons and impurities of various kinds, and what is healthy food for one organism may be injurious if taken into another, and each thing contains hidden virtues that will be useful for some beings while they are evil for others. The salamander eats fire, the ox eats grass, the peacock can swallow snakes and the ostrich stones; but man requires a different kind of food."

Philosophy informs us that the world is made out of the will of God. If, then, all things are made out of will, it logically follows that the causes of all internal diseases are also originating within the will. All diseases, such as are not caused by any action coming from the outside, are due to a perverted action of the will in man, such as is not in harmony with the laws of Nature or God. If his will begins to move in disharmony with these laws, then will a state of disharmony be created, which ultimately finds its expression on the external visible plane, and it is not necessary that the diseased person should be intellectually aware of the cause of such an inharmonious action, for the will in man produces the harmonious and inharmonious performances of his internal organs without man being aware of it and without the consent of his intellect. A mere thought, an idea, a mental impression, may produce such an inharmonious action of will, and as the name Tartarus expresses that which is perverted, impure, or opposed to good, diseases of such an origin are called by Paracelsus "*Tartaric Diseases.*"

"First of all should the physician know that there are three invisible substances which by their coagulation form the physical body of man, and which are symbolised as '*sulphur, mercury,* and *salt.*' The '*sulphur*' represents the auras and energies, the '*mercury*' the fluids, and the '*salt*' the material and substantial parts of the body; and in each organ these three substances are combined in certain proportions, differing from each other. These three substances are contained in all things, and the digestive power is the great solvent for these substances, of which each part of the body assimilates whatever it will require. Dew falls from the invisible air, corals grow in the water, and seeds draw their nutriment out of the soil; the earth is a great stomach, in which everything is dissolved, digested, and transformed, and each being draws its nutriment from the earth; and each living being is a stomach that serves as a tomb for other forms, and from which new forms spring into existence." (*Paramir.*, i.)

Each organism requires that kind of food which is adapted to its own nature. The body cannot be nourished with theories, nor the mind with potatoes. The body requires material food, the mind mental knowledge; but the soul needs the nutriment that comes from the holy spirit of truth.

"Every living being requires that particular kind of food which is adapted to its species and to its individual organism, and Life, the great alchemist, transforms the food taken. In the alembic of the animal organism it extracts from it those substances which the various organs need. The lower class of animals are even better alchemists than man, because they can extract the essence of life out of things which he is forced to reject. Man extracts the more refined essences from food; but a hog, for instance, will extract nutriment out of substances that would act as poisons in the organism of man, but there is no animal known that will eat the excrements of a hog. Animals refuse to eat or drink things which are injurious to them, and they select by their natural instincts those things which they require; it is only given to intellectual man to disobey his natural instincts, and to eat or drink things which are injurious to him, but which may gratify some artificially acquired taste. Man is much more subject to diseases than animals in a state of liberty, because animals live in accordance with the laws of their nature, and man acts continually against the laws of his nature, especially in regard to his eating and drinking. As long as his body is strong it can expel or overcome the injurious influences which are continually caused in it by intemperance, gluttony, and morbid tastes; but such a continuous effort at resistance will imply a serious loss of vitality, and a time will come when disease will be the result, because the organism requires a period of rest and a renewal of strength to expel the accumulated poisonous elements. If the physician attempts to prevent such an expulsion of poisonous elements, he attempts a crime against Nature, and may cause the death of his patient. If he weakens in such cases the strength of his patient by abstracting blood, he will become his murderer. Rheumatism and gout, dropsy, and many other diseases are often caused by such accumulations of impure or superfluous elements, and Nature cannot recover until such elements are expelled and the vital power of the organs restored. While the organism is weakened and its vitality on the wane, the germs of other diseases may become developed by attracting injurious astral influences, because its power of resistance is enfeebled, and thus one kind of a disease grows out of another." (*De Ente Veneni*)

3. Ens Naturae—Diseases arising from the Condition of Man's Nature; i.e., from Psychological Causes.

The world of corporeal forms is an external expression of the world of mind. Each thing represents an idea; each star in the sky is a visible symbol of a universal power or principle. A diseased state of the body is often caused by a diseased state of the mind. The majority of diseases are due to moral causes, and the treatment ought to be of a moral kind, and consist in giving instruction and in applying such remedies as correspond to those states of mind which we wish to induce in the patient.

Modern science knows almost nothing about the cause of the action of medicines, and for this reason the use of herbs and roots has been almost entirely abandoned. She has her purgatives, her *suporifica, diaphoretica*; she says that *Aloes* increases the peristaltic movements of the bowels, and that strychnine paralyses the nerves, etc.; but why these remedies act thus and not otherwise, this she does not explain.

Modern medicine requires, so to say, a sledge-hammer for killing a fly; but the finer natural remedies, such as have not a merely mechanical, gross, immediate, and destructive action, have almost entirely disappeared from the pharmacopoeia, and, as harmless and useless, been remitted to the care of old women. Their action is not understood, because it is not so violent as that of the poisons used by the orthodox regular physician, and therefore the effects produced are not at once apparent to the eye; but while the finer forces of Nature silently and noiselessly act upon the body of the patient, the violent drugs administered by the modern practitioner usually serve only to drive away effects by shifting the seat of the disease to a still more interior and more dangerous place.

The doctrines of Paracelsus go to show that the same power which exists in the mind of the universe, and which produced a star on the sky, is also capable to become manifest as a plant; that the whole world consists of various states of spirit, having become embodied or corporified in forms in Nature, in which the qualities of the will, which produced them, is represented and made manifest; and that, all things originating primarily out of one will-spirit, they are all related together and may be made to act upon each other by the law of induction. Each thing, from the sun down to a tumour in the body of an animal, constitutes a certain state of vibration of the one original essence, and by applying a remedy which is in a near relation to a diseased organ (according to the quality of its spirit) we can induce a healthy action in that organ, and thus restore its normal condition.

"Many diseases are caused especially by the abuse of physiological powers, in consequence of which the organs lose their strength and vitality. Thus the stomach may be overloaded with food and irritated by stimulating drinks, which force it to perform more than its natural and legitimate amount of work; the kidneys may be inflamed by stimulating and poisonous drinks, and become weak, or enlarged, on account of their overwork; the same may be said of the liver; the sexual powers may become prematurely exhausted by excesses, and the health of women be destroyed by the unnatural frequency by which connubial acts are performed. Animals live according to their nature, and it is only given to reasoning man to act against his instincts, to neglect to listen to the warning voice of his nature, and to misuse the organism with which he has been entrusted by the creative power of God. In many cases of lost vitality the weakened organs will recover their strength after a time of rest and cessation of abuse. Nature is a patient mother that often forgives the sins committed against her, although she cannot forget them. We may therefore often trust to her recuperative powers, and Nature will be able to restore that which has not been irrevocably lost; for Nature is a great physician, and the dabblers in medicine and apothecaries are her enemies, and while the latter fill the graveyards of the country with corpses, Nature distributes the balsam of life."

"Every organ in the human body is formed by the action of certain principles that exist in the universe, and the former attract the corresponding activity in the latter. Thus the heart is in sympathy with the elements of the sun, the brain with the moon, the gall-bladder with Mars, the kidneys with Venus, the lungs with Mercury, the liver with Jupiter, the spleen with Saturn, etc. There are many stars in the great firmament of the universe, and there are many germs hidden in the little world of man, and the high influences the low; and in the Microcosm and Macrocosm all things stand in intimate sympathetic relationship with each other, for all are the children of one universal father."[27]

Not only is Man a compendium of invisible forces, having grown into corporeal shape; every animal, plant, and mineral is a corporified principle, a materialised power, or a combination of such; and the *Astronomy* of Paracelsus includes, therefore, not merely a knowledge of the stars, but also a knowledge of Zoology, Botany, and Mineralogy. "What is *Mars* but the principle of Iron, which is found universally distributed in Nature and in the constitution of man? What is Venus but the power which excites the *Vasa Spermatica* in men and in animals? What is *Melissa* but a power which exists in the astral light and finds its material expression in the herb *Melissa*, which grows in our gardens? What are the animals but the personifications of those characters which they represent? Everything is an expression of the principle of life in a material form, and the life is the real thing; the external form is merely the house or *Corpus* in which it resides (*De Pestilitate*).

Signatures

"All natural forms bear their signatures, which indicate their true nature. Minerals, vegetables, and animals remain true to their nature, and their forms indicate their character. Man, who has become unnatural, is the only being whose character often belies his form, because, while his character may have changed into that of an animal, his form has retained the human shape. If such men could re-enter the *Limbus* of Nature and be born again in forms which correspond to their true nature, and if this should take place, many of our Pharisees, strutting about in scarlet coats and pretending to be benefactors of mankind, while they in reality care for nothing but for the gratification of their ambition and lusts, would be born in the shape of monkeys, camels, and buffaloes." (*De Philosophia*)

"He is not a physician who can see only that which is visible to every boor. The experienced gardener can tell by looking at a seed what kind of a plant will grow from it, and likewise the physician should be able to perceive how a disease originates, and in what way it will develop. He who knows how the rain originates will also know the origin of dysentery; he who knows the origin of the winds knows how colic originates; he who knows the periodical changes of the seasons may know the origin of intermittent fevers; he who knows the ebbs and tides in the Macrocosm will know the cause of menorrhagias of the Microcosm, etc. The quack studies diseases in the affected organs, where he finds nothing else but effects which have already taken place, and he will never arrive at an end; for if he were to kill a thousand people for the purpose of studying those effects, he would still be ignorant in regard to the causes. The true physician studies the causes of diseases by studying man as a whole. In him exist all the diseases that did exist in the past or will exist in the future. The destroyer is not a physician, but an executioner and murderer. Let the honest man ask his own conscience whether God meant that we should acquire wisdom by murder."[28] (*Paragran.*, i)

"As the sunshine penetrates through a glass window into a room, so the influences of the astral light enter into the body of man, and as the rain is absorbed by the soil, while stones and rocks are impenetrable to it, so there are certain elements in man's organisation which absorb these influences, while other elements resist their action. To obtain a correct idea of the construction of the Microcosm, we should know how the Macrocosm is constructed; we mast look upon man as an integral part of universal Nature, and not as something separate or different from the latter. The earth nourishes the physical body, and the astral body is nourished by the astral light, and as the former hungers and thirsts for the elements of the earth, so the latter longs for the influences which come from the astral plane. There are many thousands of 'magnets' in the constitution of man; good attracts good, evil attracts evil; good improves the good, and causes it to be better; evil attracts evil, and is rendered worse thereby. Innumerable are the *Egos* in man; in him are angels and devils, heaven and hell, the whole of the animal creation, the vegetable and mineral kingdom; and as the individual little man may be diseased, so the great universal man has his diseases, which manifest themselves as the ills that affect humanity as a whole. Upon this fact is based the prediction of future events." (*Paragran.*)

"Those who merely study and treat the effects of disease are like persons who imagine that they can drive the winter away by brushing the snow from the door. It is not the snow which causes the winter, but the winter is the cause of the snow. Those people have departed from the light of reason and lost themselves in idle vagaries, to the great detriment of the welfare of humanity. Consider how great and how noble man is, and that his visible form is merely the outgrowth of invisible powers. As it is outside of man, so is it inside, and *vice versa*, for the outside and inside are essentially one thing, one constellation, one influence. It is the *Limbus* in which the whole of creation is hidden. He who knows only the external form of man, and not the power by which it is produced, knows nothing but an illusion; his science is illusive, only fit to impose upon the ignorant." (*De Astronomia*)

"Good or evil influence comes down from the sun, the moon, or the stars; the action of the macrocosmic influences stimulates the corresponding elements (the *Corpora Microcosmi Astralia*) existing in man into action. The same element which produces *Mars, Venus,* or *Jupiter* in the sky exists also in the body of man; because the latter is the son of the astral body of the Macrocosm in the same sense as the physical body of man is a son of the earth. To be a physician, it is not sufficient to know the anatomy of the physical body; you should also know that of the astral body; you should know not merely a part, but the whole constitution of the Macrocosm and the Microcosm of man. Adam is not the father of man, nor is Eve his mother; they were both human beings themselves. The first man was a product of creation, and all created things constitute together the *Limbus* (Nature). Man is born from the *Limbus*, and still remains in it; the two, *i.e.*, Man and Nature, are one, and he who knows the anatomy of Nature knows also the constitution of man. If a man gets sick, it is not the eternal part in him which suffers, but it is his *Limbus*, which is composed of many hundreds of different elements, which are all related to their corresponding elements in the great *Limbus* of Nature."

"Nature (Heaven) is Man, and Man is Nature; all men are one universal Heaven, and Heaven is only one universal Man. Individual man is the individualised universal Man, and has his own individual heaven, which is a part of the universal Heaven. If all children were born at once and upon one point, they would all be constituted alike, and be sick or well at the same time; but at the time of conception a differentiation takes place, and each child receives his own individual nature, which, however, still remains an integral part of the universal nature of mankind. Thus, there are many points in a circle, and each point constitutes a circle of its own, and yet they all belong to the great circle, and as each little circle may expand so as to encompass the whole, so the heaven in man may grow so as to expand towards the whole, or contract into his own centre and disappear."

"Why does man want to eat, to drink, and to breathe but because he is related to the elements of earth, water, and air, and must attract these things to his constitution? Why does he need warmth but because he is related to the element of the fire and cannot do without it? And all these elements may produce diseases. There is no disease in the elements, but the disease starts from the centres. The origin of diseases is in man, and not outside of man; but outside influences act upon the inside and cause diseases to grow. Man is himself a cosmos. A physician who knows nothing about Cosmology will know little about disease. He should know what exists in heaven and upon the earth, what lives in the four elements and how they act upon man; in short, he should know what man is, his origin and his constitution; he should know the whole man, and not merely his external body. If man were in possession of a perfect knowledge of self he would not need to be sick at all."

"Diseases serve to teach man that he is made out of the universal *Limbus* and that he is like the animals and by no means better than they. He should study himself and the rest of creation, so that he may attain self-knowledge; and this self-knowledge should be above all obtained by the physician. Man is the highest of all animals, and the whole of the animal creation is contained in him, and, moreover, he has the power to attain self-knowledge, a faculty which the animals do not possess."

"Every star (faculty) in the nature of man is of a double nature, and he who knows the stars also knows the nature of the disease; but the *Arcana* of Nature are single.[29] If the two opposites in the constitution of man (heat and cold, love and hatred, etc.) are at war with each other, each of them asks for help from their common mother (Nature), and the physician should, therefore, be well acquainted with the astronomy of the inner heaven of man, so as to know how to assist Nature in her work."

True love and true knowledge are inseparable.

"To understand the laws of Nature we must love Nature. He who does not know Maria does not love her; he who does not know God does not love Him; his belly (his greed) is his god. He who does not understand the poor does not love them. The more knowledge we obtain, the stronger will be our love and the greater our power. He who knows God has faith in God; he who does not know Him can have no true faith. He who knows Nature will love her, and obtain the power to employ her forces. No one can be made into an artist or inventor if he has not the natural love and capacity for it; no one can be a good physician unless he is born to be one. The art to invent is a species of Magic, which cannot be taught, but which must be acquired. All Wisdom comes from the East; from the West we can expect nothing good; therefore, you who desire to be useful physicians, act according to the sun of true Wisdom, and not for the aggrandisement of the moonshine of self." (*Labyrinthus Medicorum*)

"It must not be supposed that a certain material element coming from the planets enters the organism of man and adds something to it which it does not already possess.

The light of the sun does not contribute any corporeal substance to the organisms existing upon the earth, and a man does not become heavier if he stands in the sun; but the natural forces acting in the various organs are intimately related to similar forces acting in the organism of the world, and as the liver, the spleen, the heart, etc., are the bodily representatives of certain organic activities, likewise the sun and the moon, Venus, Mars, etc., are the visible representatives of the corresponding activities of the Cosmos. If a man gets angry, it is not because he has too much bile, but because the 'Mars,' the combative element in his body (the invisible power that guides the production of bile), is in a state of exaltation. If a man is amorous, it is not because his spermatic vessels are overloaded, but because the 'Venus' (the amorous element) in his body is in a state of exaltation. If in such cases a conjunction of the combative and amorous elements takes place in his body, an ebullition of jealousy will follow; and if such an internal conjunction should take place at a time when conjunction of the planets Mars and Venus takes place in the sky, the sympathetic relationship existing between the elements representing these planets in the Microcosm and the elements represented by those of the Macrocosm may lead to serious consequences unless counteracted by the superior power of reason and will."[30]

There are a great many stars in the universe; there are a great many forces active in the organism of man. There are a great many giants which are the earthly representations of astral influences corresponding to the qualities of the stars, and which will attract the influences of the stars to which they are sympathetically related. By using such plants as medicine we attract the planetary life-influences needed to restore the vitality in diseased parts.

We give below a list of some principally useful herbs, the names of the planets to which they are sympathetically related, and the names of the principal diseases in which they may be used with advantage. It will, however, appear reasonable that it makes a vast difference whether such plants are fresh or whether they have been dried, and their occult properties are, moreover, to a great extent modified by the time of the day or night, and under what planetary conjunctions they have been gathered, and at what time they are used. Each plant should be gathered at a time when the planet to which it is related rules the hour, and its essence should be extracted as long as it is fresh.[31]

Sun.—Rosmarinus officinalis, Lavandula officinalis, Salvia officinalis, Satureja officinalis, Melissa officinalis. (Acute inflammations, diseases of the heart, rheumatism, etc.)

Moon.—Thymus majorana, Helleborus niger, Ruta graveolens. (To be used in insanity, hysteria, nervous diseases, etc.)

Mercury.—Pulmonaria off., Althaea off., Plantago laureola. (Pneumonia, catarrh, phthisis pulmonalis, inflammations of mucous membranes.)

Venus.—Ononis spinosa, Verbascum thapsus, Apium petroselinum. (Dropsical swellings, diseases of kidneys or bladder, etc.)

Mars.—Carduus benedictus, Urticaria diocia, Erythraea centaurium. (Fevers, diseases of an acute and violent character; eruptive fevers, etc.)

Jupiter.—Ruta graveolens, Hepatica nobilis, Adianthum veneris, Chelidonium magus, Linum usitatissimum, Cannabis sativa. (Jaundice, liver diseases.)

Saturn.—Chrysosplenium alternifolium, Scrophula nodosa, Teucrium

Chamaedrys. (Hypochondria, piles, melancholia, etc.)[32]

There are a great many other plants whose essences correspond to the ethers radiating from other planets and stars, and if we knew all the qualities of the stars, we would find that the quality of each of them is represented on the earth by some plant. By the judicious use of plants beneficial astral activities may be attracted and evil influences neutralised; but to know what plants are required in each case it is necessary to know not only the anatomy of the human body and the functions of its organs, but also the constitution of the starry heavens, the qualities of the stars, and the time of the appearance and conjunctions of planets. The impossibility to grasp at once all these things intellectually shows that the power of spiritual perception is a most necessary qualification for the true physician.

It is not within the scope of this work to enter into a detailed account of the treatment of special diseases adopted by Paracelsus. It may suffice to say that the difference between the system of medicine of the present day and that of Paracelsus is a difference growing out of an entirely different apprehension of fundamental truths. Modern science looks upon the universe as being a conglomeration of dead matter out of which, by some unexplainable process, life may become evolved in forms. The science of Paracelsus looks upon the whole of the universe as the manifestation of a universal principle of life, acting through the instrumentality of forms. Modern science seems to regard the forms as the sources of life; the science of Paracelsus looks upon the forms as being the products of life. Forms are, so to say, condensed forces or crystallised space; but space itself is an aspect of the one life, and there is no dead matter in the universe, for that which dies returns again into the matrix of Nature, to be reborn into other forms, and to serve again as an instrument for the manifestation of life.

In the universe of Paracelsus there is life everywhere, and all beings are connected together by a common link. Some forms are in a close mutual sympathy, while between others an antipathy is prevailing. Some attract and others repel each other. During the ascendency of a planet[33] its essence will be especially attracted by plants and by animal organs that are in harmony with it; but what else is this radiating planetary essence but the *elixir of life*, the invisible vehicle of a quality peculiar to that power? And therefore a patient may grow better or worse without any visible cause. A medicine that will do good at one time will be useless at another, and a system of medicine without understanding and without true knowledge of natural laws will remain a system of mere suppositions and superstitions, of passive observation and inactivity, and if it attempts to interfere with the cause of a disease, the probability is that it will do serious harm. Paracelsus says: "Our physicians pay no attention to the position of the planets,[34] and therefore they kill more patients than they cure, because a medicine that may do good at one time may be injurious at another, according to the prevailing influence. That which is active in medicines is their astral elements acting upon the astral man, and they are produced by astral influences, and it makes the greatest difference whether a medicine is pervaded by one influence or by another." (*De Caducis*)

It should always be remembered that astral influences do not act directly upon the physical bodies of men and animals, but upon their vital essence, in which all elements are contained. Love for a certain person may be created by a word or a touch, by a breath or a kiss, but only if the person who is touched or breathed upon has in his soul the elements that are capable to manifest that particular kind of love. The vehicle of life that contains the life-essence in the body of man (the Mumia) is the same as that which contains the universal life and forms the astral body of the world; but each energy may exist in various states and modifications, differing from each other. "Even the ignorant knows that man has a heart and lungs, a brain and a liver and stomach; but he thinks that these organs are independent things, that have nothing to do with each other; and even our most learned doctors are not aware of the fact that these organs are only the material and bodily representatives of invisible energies that pervade and circulate in the whole system; so that, for instance, the real 'liver' is to be found in all parts of the body, and has its herd in that organ which we call the liver. All the members of the body are potentially contained in the centre of the vital fluid, which has its seat in the brain, while the activity which propels it comes from the heart."[35] (*De Viribus Membrorum*)

Mind is not created by the brain, neither is love nor hate created by the heart; but mind acts through the brain, and love and hate have their origin in the heart. "A man who is angry is not only angry in his head or in his fist, but all over; a person who loves does not only love with his eye, but with his whole being; in short, all the organs of the body, and the body itself, are only form-manifestations of previously and universally existing mental states."

"The body of a man is his house; the architect who builds it is the astral world. The carpenters are at one time Jupiter, at another Venus; at one time Taurus, at another Orion. Man is a sun and a moon and a heaven filled with stars; the world is a man, and the light of the sun and the stars is his body; the ethereal body cannot be grasped, and yet it is substantial, because substance (from *sub*, under, and *sto*, standing) means existence, and without substance nothing exists. If the life of the sun did not act in the world, nothing would grow. The human body is vapour materialised by sunshine mixed with the life of the stars. Four elements are in the world, and man consists out of four, and that which exists visibly in man exists invisibly in the ether pervading the world. Where is the workman that cuts out the forms of lilies and roses that grow in the field? and where is his workshop and tools? The characters of the lilies and roses exist in the astral light, and in the workshop of Nature they are made into forms. A blooming flower cannot be made out of mud, nor a man out of material clay; and he who denies the formative power of Nature, and believes that ready-made forms grow out of the earth, believes that something can be taken out of a body in which it does not exist." (*De Caducis*)

"The power of sight does not come from the eye, the power to hear does not come from the ear, nor the power to feel from the nerves; it is the spirit of man that sees through the eye, and hears with the ear, and feels by means of the nerves. Wisdom and reason and thought are not contained in the brain, but they belong to the invisible spirit which feels through the heart and thinks by means of the brain. All these powers are contained in the invisible universe, and become manifest through material organs, and the material organs are their representatives, and determine their mode of manifestation according to their material construction, because a perfect manifestation of power can only take place in a perfectly constructed organism, and if the organism is faulty the manifestation will be imperfect, but not the original power defective." (*De Viribus Membrorum*)

The animal intellect differs from the human intellect especially in that the animal can see only the vehicle, but the human intellect discovers the principle manifested therein. For this reason those of our would-be scientists who only see external effects, and cannot see the principles therein, have only an animal intellect, however well trained it may be.

4. Diseases originating from Spiritual Causes.[36]

This class of diseases includes all evils that are caused by an evil will, resulting from passions, evil desires, disordered thoughts, and a morbid imagination. Such psychological states produce physiological changes in the physical body. Shame produces a blush in the face, and terror produces a paleness. Fear causes diarrhoea; melancholy, obstructions; anger or envy gives rise to jaundice. Gaiety may cure, and grief may kill. Violent emotions produce miscarriages, apoplexy, spasms, hysterics, and cause malformations of the foetus, etc., etc. Such things are known to all who have investigated such matters; but it is less generally known that the evil imagination of one person can affect the mind of another, poison his vitality, and injure or kill his body.

The reason why this is not generally known is that the imagination of the majority of men and women in our present state of civilisation is too weak, their will too feeble, and their faith too much pervaded by doubt to produce the desired effects; and it is fortunate that their imagination, however evil it may be, has not much power as long as the state of morality is not higher advanced than it is at present.[37] Nevertheless, there have been persons whose evil will was so strong as to project the products of their imagination instinctively or consciously upon a person whom they desired to injure, and such persons are still in existence, although they may not deem it prudent to boast of their gifts or to exhibit their powers in public. Envy and hate produce an evil imagination, and create forces that are more active during sleep than during waking. The evil thoughts of a malicious person can affect another (sensitive) person, not only while the former is awake, but also during his sleep; because when the physical body is asleep, the sidereal body is free to go wherever it pleases or wherever it may be attracted.

"The life that is active in the organs is the *anima vegetiva* (the animal soul). It is an invisible fire (*sulphur*), that can easily be blown into a flame by the power of the imagination. Imagination creates hunger and thirst, produces abnormal secretions, and causes diseases; but a person who has no evil desires will have no evil imagination, and no diseases will spring from his thoughts."

"A person who has evil desires will have an evil imagination, and the forces created in the sphere of his mind can be projected by powerful will into the mental sphere of another. Thoughts are not empty nothings, but they are formed out of the substance that forms the element of the mind, in the same sense as a piece of ice is made out of the substance of water. The will is the power that concentrates the image formed in the mind, in the same way as the power of cold will cause a body of water to freeze into solid ice; and as an icicle may be thrown from one place to another, likewise an evil thought, formed into substantial shape by an intense will, may be hurled into the mental sphere of another, and enter his soul if it be not sufficiently protected."

"Imagination is the cause of many diseases; faith is the cure for all. If we cannot cure a disease by faith, it is because our faith is too weak; but our faith is weak on account of our want of knowledge; if we were conscious of the power of God in ourselves, we could never fail. The power of amulets does not rest so much in the material of which they are made as in the faith with which they are worn; the curative power of medicines often consists, not so much in the spirit that is hidden in them, as in the spirit in which they are taken. Faith will make them efficacious; doubt will destroy their virtues."

The *Ens Spirituale* is the *Will*. The power of the true spiritual Will is known very little, because it is attained by very few. In our present civilisation, men of strong, determined, and enlightened Will are few and far between; men and women are ruled to a great extent by their instincts and desires, and have not sufficient will power to rise above and control them.

"The *Ens Spirituale* is a power which may affect the whole body and produce or cure all kinds of diseases; it is neither an angel nor a devil, but it is a spiritual power which in the living body is born from our thoughts."

"There are two principles active in man; one in the principle of Matter, which constitutes the corporeal visible body; the other one is the Spirit, intangible and invisible, and the spiritual principle may be vitiated and diseased as well as the body, and transmit its diseases to the body. The *Ens astrale, veneni,* and *naturale* act upon the body, but the *Ens spirituale* and *deale* belong to the spirit; if the body suffers, the spirit need not suffer; but if the spirit suffers the body suffers; the body cannot live without the spirit but the spirit is not confined by the body, and therefore is independent of it. The spirit in man sustains the body as the air supplies him with life; it is substantial, visible, tangible, and perceptible to other spiritual entities, and spiritual beings stand to each other in the same relationship as one corporeal being to another. I have a spirit and you have one, and our spirits communicate with each other in the same sense as our bodies; but while we need language to understand each other, our spirits understand each other without using words. If one spirit is angry at another it may injure him, and the injury received be transmitted upon his body. Spirits harmonise and associate with each other, or they repel or injure one another. Spirits are not born from the intellect, but from the soul, for the soul is the substance of life. Thought alone produces no spirit, but it determines the qualities of the will."

"There is no spiritual power in children, because they have no perfect will-power; he whose will is perfected gives birth to a spirit, as a pebble produces a spark, and this spiritual power partakes of the nature of his will. He who lives in the will, possesses the spirit—*i.e.*, the *Ens spirituale*. There is a corporeal world and a spiritual world, and the two are one, and the spiritual beings live in their own spiritual world as we live in ours. They have their likes and dislikes, their sympathies and antipathies, like ourselves, and they do not always correspond to the likes and dislikes of the bodily forms. Men may quarrel and fight with each other and their spirits nevertheless be in harmony, but if a spirit injures another spirit, the material body of the latter will become also affected."

"The spirits of a man may act upon another without the other man's consent or intention, unconsciously and involuntarily to him; but if man's will is in unity with his thought and desire, a spirit (force) will be produced which can be employed for good or for evil. If two such spiritual forces battle with each other, the weaker one, or the one which does not defend itself sufficiently, will be overcome, and bodily diseases may be the result. An evil-disposed person may throw the force of his will upon another person and injure him, even if the latter is stronger than the former, because the latter does not expect and is not prepared for the attack; but if the other is stronger and resists successfully, then a force will be kindled in him which will overcome his enemy and which may destroy him."[38] (*Repercussio*)

"Waxen images, figures, etc., may be used to assist the imagination and to strengthen the will. Thus a necromancer will make a waxen image of a person and bury it, covering it with heavy stones, and if his will and imagination are powerful enough, the person whom it represents feels very miserable until that weight is removed. Likewise, if he breaks a limb of that figure, a limb will be broken in the person whom the figure represents, or he thus inflicts cuts, stabs, or other injuries upon an enemy. It is all done through the spirit acting upon the spirit. No necromancer can by his will act directly upon the body of a person, but he can act upon his astral spirit, and the spirit of the injured person reproduces the injury upon his own body. Thus a necromancer plants a tree, and he who cuts the tree cuts himself; that is to say, he does not cut his body, but the spirit, which has the same limbs as the body, and the cuts made upon the spirit are reproduced upon the body."

"Thus the spirit of a person may, without the assistance of his body and without a knife or sword, cut or stab or injure another person by the mere force of the imagination and will, and images can be cursed effectually, and fever, apoplexy, epilepsy, etc., be caused thereby; but our scientists have no conception of what a power the will is, because they have no strong will, and they do not believe in such things, because they are beyond their comprehension. The will produces such spirits, and they can also act upon animals, and it is even easier to affect animals than to affect men, because the spirit of man is better able to defend itself than that of an animal."[39]

"Not only may a necromancer thus consciously injure another person by his evil will and imagination, but the spirit of envious, jealous, revengeful, and wicked persons can, even if they are ignorant of the practices of sorcery, injure those who are the objects of their evil will while the body is asleep; for dreams which come from the spirit are actually enacted, but dreams which do not come from the spirit are only plays of fancy."

"One poison will render another poison harmless, and thus the effect of the imagination of one person neutralises the effects of the imagination of another. If any one can make an image of wax to injure my body, I may make another image to attract the evil spell. His image obtains its power by the force of his faith, and my image obtains its virtue by the power of my faith; and the injuries inflicted by my enemy upon the image will leave me unharmed, and the curses that he heaps upon me will return to him and leave me unhurt."

"If a person is gloomy and despondent, he ought not to be left alone, but he ought to have some one to cheer him up and to explain to him that he must free himself of his own morbid thoughts. There are some who believe that it is possible for witches to pass through doors and to vampirise people; but no witch can bodily (physically) pass through a closed door in the way in which this is done by sylphs and pigmies; they do such things in their astral forms."

"O you doubtful man, you Peter of little faith, who are moved by each wind and sink easily! You are yourself the cause of all such diseases, because your faith is so little and feeble, and your own evil thoughts are your enemies. Moreover, you have hidden within yourself a magnet which attracts those influences which correspond to your will, and this celestial magnet is of such power that for more than a hundred or even thousands of miles, it attracts that which your spirit desires out of the four elements." (*Philos. Occulta*)

5. Diseases originating from the Divine Cause (Karma).[40]

All diseases are the effects of previously existing causes. Some originate from natural and others from spiritual causes. Spiritual causes may have been created by a man during a former existence. For such cases there is no remedy but to wait patiently until the evil force is exhausted and the law of universal justice satisfied; for even if the just retribution for our sins can be evaded at one time, it will only be postponed, and the evil returns at another time with an accumulation of interest and with increased force.

"All diseases originating from the above-mentioned four causes may be cured by the power of the true Faith. All health and all disease come from God, and in God is the cure. Some diseases, however, do not directly come from God, but are natural (although they, too, come from God indirectly, because Nature is a manifestation of the power of God), but other diseases are directly sent by God as a punishment for our sins. Each disease is a purgatory, and no physician can know exactly when or how it will end; the physician is only a servant of God, who works to accomplish His will. If it is the will of Providence (*Karma*) that the patient should still remain in his purgatory, then will the physician not be able to help him out of it; but if his time for redemption has come, then will the patient find the physician through whom God will send him relief. The physician may cure the sick by using remedies, but it is God who makes the physician and the remedy. God does not perform miracles without man; He acts through the instrumentality of man, and restores the sick to health through the instrumentality of the physician, and therefore the physician should be in possession of faith (in harmony with God), so as to be a perfect instrument through which the will of God can be accomplished."

"He who expects help from medicine or from a physician is not a Christian, but he is a Christian who hopes to receive aid from God through the instrumentality of man. God is the first and most potent physician; human physicians are only His deputies. Call not for help to the personal self of any man, but ask it from God acting through man, and He will cause you to find the physician, if it is well for you that you should receive aid; or He may aid you through the power within yourself, provided you are holy or a physician yourself."

"Two kinds of punishment (*Karma*) are waiting for the sinner. One takes place during his life, the other one after his death. Those sins which are not expiated after death will produce certain effects in our next life. God is the master of Nature, and the physician is her servant, and let no physician fancy that he can be a master of Nature unless he is a servant of God."

"There are two ways of practising the medical art: the first is to employ art; the second is to employ fancy. The former means the employment of observation, reason, knowledge, experience, and wisdom; the latter is the product of speculation, self-conceit, preconceived opinions, and ignorance. Those who are wise will know which way to choose." (*De Ente Dei*)

"No physician should presume to know the hour of recovery in such cases, because it is not given to man to judge of the offence of another, and the inner temple contains mysteries in which no uninitiated stranger is permitted to pry. If the trial is over, God will send the physician. If a patient recovers by following the advice of a physician, it is a sign that the physician has been sent by God; but if no recovery takes place, God did not send the physician. Nothing in the world happens without a cause. The ignorant physicians are the servants of hell, sent by the devil to torment the sick; but the true physician is God. God does nothing in an unnatural manner, and if He produces wonders, He produces them through human agencies. God does not go about practising medicine or come to see a patient; if He comes to him, He comes in the shape of a man. If a town possesses a good physician, people may look upon him as a blessing from God; but the presence of an ignorant or greedy doctor is a public calamity and a curse to all. But all bodily diseases will be cured at the legitimate hour, when the battle of life is ended and the angel of death opens the portal to the eternal[41] kingdom of rest."[42]

The Practice of Medicine

As there are five causes of diseases, so there are five different ways of removing them, and therefore five classes of physicians:

"1. *Naturales*—i.e., those who treat diseased conditions with opposite remedies; for instance, cold by warmth, dryness by moisture, etc., according to the principle, *Contraria contrariis curantur*. To this class belonged *Avicenna, Galen*, etc." (Allopathy, Hydrotherapie, etc.)

"2. *Specifici*.—Such as employ specific remedies, of which it is known that they have certain affinities for certain morbid conditions. To this class belong the *Empirics*." (*Homoeopathy*)

"3. *Characterales*.—The physicians of this class have the power to cure diseases by employing their willpower." (*Magnetism, Suggestion, Mind-Cure*)

"4. *Spirituales*.—The followers of this system have the power to employ spiritual forces, in the same sense as a judge has power over a prisoner in the stocks, because he is in possession of the keys. Such a physician was *Hippocrates*." (*Hypnotism, etc.*)

"5. *Fideles*.—i.e., those who cure by the power of Faith, such as Christ and the apostles." (*Magic*)

"Among these five classes, the first one is usually the most orthodox and narrow-minded, and rejects the other four for not being able to understand them."

"From each of the five causes of diseases all kinds of diseases may spring, and each kind of disease can therefore be divided into five classes, according to its cause. There are consequently five kinds of plague and five kinds of cholera, five kinds of dropsy or cancer, etc."

"If, for instance, a plague appears, the *Naturales* will say it is caused by a disorganisation of the bodily structures, while the *Astrologer* will say it is caused by a certain constellation of planetary influences; but there may be three more causes which produced that epidemic, and which will determine its character. Moreover, each disease may manifest itself in two ways, one of which belongs to the department of Medicine, the other one to the department of Surgery. That which radiates from the centre (constitutional diseases) belongs to Medicine; that which is localised—*i.e.*, circumscribed or confined to a certain locality—belongs to Surgery."[43]

"Each physician, no matter to which sect he belongs, should know the five causes of diseases and the five methods of treatment; but each method is in itself sufficient to cure all diseases, no matter from what cause they originate." (*De Entibus Morbosom*)

"No knowledge is perfect unless it includes an understanding of the origin—*i.e.*, the beginning; and as all of man's diseases originate in his constitution, it is necessary that his constitution should be known, if we wish to know his diseases."

The Three Substances

"The Bible tells us that Man is made out of nothing; that is to say, his spirit, the real man, is from God, who is not *a thing*, but the eternal reality; but he is made into three somethings or 'substances,' and these three constitute the whole of Man: they are himself, and he is they, and from them he receives all that is good or evil for him. Every state in which man can possibly enter is determined by *number, measure,* and *weight*."

The "Three Substances" are the three forms or modes of action in which the universal primordial Will is manifesting itself throughout Nature, for all things are a Trinity in a Unity. The "*Salt*" represents the principle of corporification, the astringent or contractive and solidifying quality, or, in other words, the *body*; the "*Sulphur*" represents the expansive power the centrifugal force, in contradistinction to the centripetal motion of the first quality—it is that which burns, *i.e.*, the *soul* or light in all things; and the "*Mercury*" is the *Life*, *i.e.*, that principle or form of will which manifests itself as life, or consciousness and sensation. Each of these forms of will is an individual power;[44] nevertheless they are substantial, for "matter" and "force" are one, and originate from the same cause. The three substances, held together in harmonious proportions, constitute health; their disharmony constitutes disease, and their disruption death.

"These three substances should be *practically* known to the physician, for his usefulness does not consist in merely possessing theoretical knowledge, but in his ability to restore health. He must learn to know these substances by studying the light of Nature, not by seeking them in his own imagination; he should become able to see Nature as she is, and not as he or others may imagine her to be. His art should be baptized in the fire; he must have himself been born from the fire, and tested in it seven times and more. No one is born a physician out of himself, but out of the light of Nature, and this light is the great world. He should pass through the examination of Nature and know her laws. He should not seek for wisdom in his own fancy, but in the light of Nature, and from the ability to recognise this light springs the true science. Not in the books, but in the light of Nature is to be found true wisdom and art, theory and practice; but those who cannot find wisdom in that light, and seek for it in their own fancy, will continually err."[45]

"There is nothing in man which would naturally cause him to be a physician. He has the capacity to collect ideas intellectually, but this alone does not constitute art. This faculty is like an empty box, useful only to store up useful things. Let us look at two examples the glass-maker and the carpenter. The glass-maker did not learn his art from himself, he found it in the light of Nature, for Nature showed him how to melt the materials by means of the fire, and discovered the glass for him; but a carpenter who builds a house constructs it according to his own ideas, provided he has the necessary materials. A physician may have the necessary materials—*i.e.*, the patient and the remedies—but he is not a true physician as long as he has not the true knowledge as to how and when and why they must be applied. The glass-maker is taught by Nature, the carpenter follows his own fancy; the former is taught by the fire, and the true physician receives from the fire of Nature his wisdom and his art—*i.e.*, his experience. This is his true *approbation*."[46]

"The ignorant refuse to follow Nature, and they follow their own fancies. Understanding is twofold. One understanding comes from experience, the other from aptitude; the former, again, is twofold, and is based either upon the understanding of the law or merely upon haphazard experiment. The former is the one upon which true medicine rests, and implies the knowledge of the three *substances*; the other is merely supposition and error, for a haphazard experiment may succeed once and fail at another time."

"We should not follow in the footsteps of persons, but in the footsteps of Nature; we should not act on account of hearsay, but on account of our own understanding. The first man who learned anything useful was taught by Nature; let Nature teach us as she taught him. If my art is to be based upon a firm foundation, it must be based upon my own understanding, not upon that of another man. A physician should have God before his eyes, visibly and tangible; he should see the truth, not shadowy or as in a dream, but tangible and without any doubt. Our science should be based upon our own perception of truth, not upon mere belief or opinion. Information received from men can only assist us in forming opinions, but it constitutes no knowledge. True knowledge consists in a direct recognition of the real, and is taught by Nature herself."

"As far as the patient is concerned, there are three things required of him to effect a cure: his disease should be a natural one,[47] he should have a certain amount of will, and a certain amount of vital energy. If these conditions are not present, no cure can be effected; for even Christ could not benefit those who were not receptive of His power. This power is Faith, and it should be present in the patient as well as in the physician. Christ did not say to the sick, 'I cured thee,' but He said, 'Thy faith made thee whole.' It is not the physician who heals the sick, but it is God who heals him through Nature, and the physician is merely the instrument through which God acts upon the nature of the patient. The patient should therefore have faith in God and confidence in his physician. God acts according to universal law, and makes no exceptions in special cases; but all power comes from God, and may be guided properly or its action impeded by the physician. God kills no one; it is Nature which causes people to die. God is Life, and the physician in whom the power of God is manifest will be a fountain of life and health to the sick. To God belongs the praise, and to man the blame. Those who attempt to cure diseases by their own power, without recognising the eternal source of all power, will never know the deeper mysteries of Nature. They deal with lies, and do not perform the will of God; and if they murder their patients, it is they themselves who are responsible for it."

"Those who attempt to cure the sick by means of what they learn in books, and without using their own judgment, are like the foolish virgins mentioned in the Bible, who wasted the oil from their lamps, and tried to borrow light from others. Those whose minds are open for the reception of the truth, who are charitable to all, who love their art for its own sake, and seek to do the will of God, without any thought of self, they belong to my school, and are my disciples. They will be taught by the light of wisdom, and God will perform His miracles through their instrumentality." (*De Virtute Medici*)

Arcana (Mysteries)

Why is the practice of medicine of Theophrastus Paracelsus almost incomprehensible to the modern practitioner? It is because the latter seeks to treat the diseased organs themselves, which are as such merely the external effects of internal causes, and he knows of no other way to act upon them except by mechanical or chemical means; while the method of treatment of Paracelsus, by means of which he made the most wonderful cures, is to change the interior spiritual causes from which the outward effects grow; to treat the very essences out of which corporeal organs become crystallised, and to supply them with the power of vitality of the quality which they require. To accomplish this, deep insight into the causes of disease, spiritual perception, spiritual knowledge, and spiritual power are needed, and these qualities belong not to that which is human in man, but to the light of the spirit which shines into him. For this reason the *Arcana* of Paracelsus have been universally misunderstood, and it is believed even to this day that his "secret remedies" were certain compounds which he concocted, and which might be prepared by any apothecary, if he were put in possession of the prescriptions for them. This is, however, not the case. A prescription that might be learned from books is not an *Arcanum*;[48] a secret that might be communicated intellectually from one person to another is not a *divine* or spiritual mystery. A cow can give birth to nothing else but a calf, a monkey cannot produce a man; neither can he who has not himself been reborn in the spirit produce or endow things with spiritual power. Man must himself be that which he desires to produce.

We do not blame those who, not being spiritual, are unable to grasp spiritual truths; we only reject the conceit of those who, not being capable to see the true light, dogmatically deny its existence.

Even of the direct disciples of Paracelsus, few only were able to see the truth clearly. He says: "Twenty-one of my servants have become victims of the executioner (the illusions of this world, false reasoning). May God help them! Only a few have remained with me." (*Denfensio*, vi.)

"The first *Arcanum* is the *Mercurius vivus*; the second, the *Prima Materia*; the third is the *Lapis Philosophorum*; and the fourth, the *Tinctura*. These remedies are rather of an angelic than of a human character." (*Archidoxes*, iv.)

If the will of God acting within Nature could create a world, surely the same divine will, acting within man, can cure all diseases; but only that will which is active in man, not that which is outside of him, can act within his organisation; and before a man becomes able to send his soul within the soul of another person, his own will must become godlike and free. A *"hypnotiser"* merely paralyses the will of a weak-minded person and induces a kind of dream; but the magic power of the true Adept is the power of God acting through him. Such powers do not belong to that which is mortal in man, but to that which is divine, and therefore those who wish to graduate in the school of Paracelsus and follow his example will have to outgrow their self-conceit and become regenerated in the spirit of divine wisdom, which is the realisation of truth.

"We are not intent upon showing our feelings and thoughts, mind and heart, to idiots and fools, and we protect ourselves, therefore, by a good wall, to whose door only the wise ones possess the key. If you have the proper understanding, you will comprehend it and act accordingly; but if you are deficient in your knowledge or in its practical application, you will also be without all the planets,stars, and signs." (*Coelum Philos.*)

NOTE.—The above-named Arcana may, although imperfectly, be described as follows:

Mercurius vivus.—Spiritual Intelligence, Divine Self-consciousness, Wisdom.

Prima Materia.—The Logos in its aspect as the substance and essence of all things, the Word (Akasha).

Lapis Philosophorum.—The spiritual man himself, having attained self-knowledge.

Tinctura.—The power of divine love, it being identical with divine wisdom.

Chapter 8: Alchemy and Astrology

Alchemy and Astrology are sciences which are at the present time very little understood, because they deal with spiritual things, which cannot be known to persons who are not in the possession of spirituality. Chemistry deals with physical matter; alchemy deals with their astral principles. Astronomy deals with the physical aspect of the bodies of planets and stars; astrology deals with the omnipresent psychic influences which their souls exert upon each other, and upon the Microcosm of man.

Chemistry is a science that may be learned by any one who has ordinary intellectual capacities, and a certain amount of skill required for its practical application. Astronomy may be studied by anyone who is able to comprehend mathematics and possesses logic and physical sight. Alchemy is an art which cannot be understood without spiritual or soul knowledge. Astrology is incomprehensible to those who cannot realise the true character of the stars. The books treating of alchemy and astrology will easily be understood by persons who know the things of which they treat, but to those who are not in possession of such knowledge they will be incomprehensible.

Everything in Nature has a threefold aspect. The highest aspect of alchemy is the regeneration of man in the spirit of God out of the material elements of his physical body. The physical body itself is the greatest of mysteries, because in it are contained in a condensed, solidified, and corporeal state the very essences which go to make up the substance of the spiritual man, and this is the secret of the "*Philosopher's Stone.*" The sign in which the true alchemist works is the Cross, because man roots with his material elements in the earth, penetrates with his soul through the animal forces of Nature, while his higher nature reaches above the animal creation into the realm of immortality.

The next aspect of alchemy is the knowledge of the nature of the invisible elements, constituting the astral bodies of things. Each thing is a trinity having a body and a spirit held together by the soul,[1] which is the cause and the law. Physical bodies are acted upon by physical matter; the elements of the soul are acted upon by the soul, and the conscious spirit of the enlightened guides and controls the action of matter and soul. By the power of the spirit material elements may be sublimated into invisible elements, or invisible substances be coagulated and become visible. Instances of this may be occasionally seen in "spiritualistic séances," although in such cases the alchemist who produces them is invisible.

The lowest aspect of alchemy is the preparation, purification, and combination of physical substances, and from this science has grown the science of modern chemistry, which in its present state is a great advancement over the lower aspect of old chemistry, but which has lost sight entirely of the higher aspects of Nature. A higher advancement of the science of chemistry will bring it again into contact with alchemy. Chemistry decomposes and recombines material substances in certain proportions; it purifies simple substances of all foreign elements, and leaves the primitive elements unchanged; but alchemy changes the character of things, and raises them up into higher states of existence. To exercise this power, not mere mechanical labour, but artistic skill is required. "A person who composes a chemical preparation by manual labour and according to certain rules is a chemist; the weaver who manufactures a cloth, and the tailor who makes a coat, may be called alchemists, because neither clothes nor coats are grown by Nature. The chemist imitates Nature, the artist surpasses her; the labourer lends his hands to Nature, so that she may accomplish something through him. The artist makes use of the material with which Nature provides him, and develops something that exists germinally in Nature. The painter who daubs a wall is a chemist; his work requires skill, but no genius. The artist who composes a picture is an alchemist, because he embodies an idea, and puts his own character into his work."

To understand correctly the meaning of the words alchemy and astrology, it is necessary to understand the intimate relationship and the identity of the Microcosm and Macrocosm, and their mutual interaction. All the powers of the universe are potentially contained in man, and man's physical body and all his organs are nothing else but products and representatives of the powers of Nature. The Microcosm and Macrocosm may not only "be compared together," but they are really and actually essentially one in their power, and one in the constitution of their elements.[2]

"If I have 'manna' in my constitution, I can attract 'manna' from heaven. 'Melissa' is not only in the garden, but also in the air and in heaven. 'Saturn' is not only in the sky, but also deep in the earth and in the ocean. What is 'Venus' but the 'Artemisia' that grows in your garden? What is 'iron' but 'Mars'? That is to say, Venus and Artemisia are both the products of the same essence, and Mars and iron are both the manifestations of the same cause. What is the human body but a constellation of the same powers that formed the stars in the sky? He who knows what iron is, knows the attributes of Mars. He who knows Mars, knows the qualities of iron. What would become of your heart if there were no sun in the universe? What would be the use of your 'vasa spermatica' if there were no Venus? To grasp the invisible elements; to attract them by their material correspondences; to control, purify, and transform them by the living power of the Spirit—this is true alchemy." (*Paragran.* i.)

The Seven Planets

The "Seven Planets" are the Seven Principles which constitute the universe, and which are at least "potentially" contained in everything. Paracelsus speaks of them in a very mystical language, as follows:

"There are seven elementary powers or principles—four lower ones belonging to mortal and changeable things (Sthula sharira, Linga sharira, Prana, and Kama), and a trinity of celestial power (Atma, Buddhi, Manas), which is also called the *quinta essentia*. The four elements (lower principles) can in no way interfere with the *quinta essentia*. The heavenly and the hellish power is not obedient to the four elementary powers, but each section stands for itself." (*De Mercurio*, vol. vi. p. 378)

This goes to show that to the spiritual kingdom belongs a state of consciousness different from the lower states of consciousness, and having nothing in common with them. Spirituality is, therefore, not to be considered as a state of high intellectual development, but it is an awakening to an entirely different and higher state of consciousness, which may take place in persons of high intellectual development, but far oftener in those who are unsophisticated and of a simple mind.

The "Seven Planets" are equally mysteriously described in his "Coelum Philosophorum":

1. ☿ *Mercury. Wisdom;* i.e., the knowledge of the soul that realises the truth, and which has nothing to do with the action of the intellect, that consists in collecting and comparing ideas. "All things are hidden within all things. One of them is their concealer, and at the same time their body and vehicle, external, visible, and movable. All things are revealed within this vehicle, for it is a corporified spirit; but the spirit thereof has no name." Translated into modern language this means: "Mercury represents divine wisdom. The whole of Nature is a vehicle and visible manifestation of the wisdom of God; but God Himself cannot be described. He is the universal life, the root of all consciousness and knowledge, and the will of divine wisdom."

2. ♃ *Jupiter.* Universal primordial *substance and power.* "Within the body of Jupiter are contained all the other six metals in a spiritual state, each always still deeper hidden and more remote than the one that precedes." This means that, of all the seven principles, each contains the other six either actively or potentially. Thus, even within a stone or an oyster there is a hidden spark of divinity, such as may become conscious and manifest in the constitution of man.

3. ♂ *Mars. Universal energy. The will.* "Mars, owing to its combative energy, is enabled to gain glory and to assume the place of the king. Care will have to be taken that he does not become captured. We must see how we can raise him up and combine ☉ and ☽ with ♄ in the place of Mars." This indicates that we should seek to attain a powerful will, but avoid letting that will become subservient to matter (♄). This is done by combining our imagination (☽) with wisdom (☉).

4. ♀ *Venus. Love,* identical with *Knowledge*; because true love is the spiritual recognition of the true self. "The six other metals have formed a corruptible external body with the quality of Venus; but all combustible things can be changed by the power of fire." This is to say that human love is at present bound up with many impurities, but when the true fire of love awakens, these impurities will burn away and leave us in possession of unadulterated wisdom.

5. ♄ *Saturn. The Life-principle.* Saturn says: "My six brothers have relegated me and expelled me from the spiritual kingdom. They have forced me to live in a corruptible form. I have to submit to be that which they refuse to be. My body is attracted to the earth, so that everything I embrace becomes earthly; but it would not be well for the world to know all the virtue hidden in me and all that I may accomplish." This means that the human mind (Manas) is the connecting-link between spirit and matter. If the inquisitive scientist were to know the divine life within his own constitution, and could develop it before he has attained innocence and virtue, he would become an incarnate devil instead of a god.

6. ☽ *Luna—Moon. Imagination.* "The principal thing to know in regard to Luna is its origin. It is the seventh metal, containing the six others in a spiritual state, and it is externally corporeal and material." This goes to show that *Luna*, in its external aspect,

means matter with its phenomena, which are always illusive as long as we do not know their true origin. If we wish to gain absolute knowledge of all things in Nature, we must attain the knowledge of God.

7. ☉ *Sol—Sun. The Life, or Wisdom.* "It is pure fire, and has within itself all the other six metals (principles)." Everything that exists is a manifestation and product of the one life in the universe, from which all things receive their vitality and powers; "for that which is visible is merely the vehicle, but the element therein is a spirit, and lives in all things as the soul lives in the body. This is the *prima materia* of the elements, invisible and incomprehensible, but nevertheless present in all; for *prima materia* is nothing else than the life itself in all creatures. That which is without life is no longer an element, but within the *ultima materia*, wherein is contained neither virtue nor energy." (*Philosophia ad Athenienses*, vol. viii)

The above extracts will be quite sufficient to show that the modern method of thinking scientifically, which deals only with external phenomena, and with comparing opinions referring to them, is quite insufficient for our initiation into the mysteries of alchemy, and that this study requires a mind capable to look upon the world not as being made up of many separate pieces, but as one great and indivisible organism, pervaded by co-existing spiritual powers, whose outward manifestation is the realm of phenomena. Alchemy studies not merely phenomena, but it is the science of the soul of all things.

What does material science know about things of the soul? Chemistry is a science which deals with the chemical combination, separation, and recombination of physical substances. Alchemy deals with the purification and combination of astral elements, and with the development of lower forms and lower states into higher ones. By chemistry we may purify physical substances from all foreign elements, and divest them of physical impurities, but their own element will not be changed. By alchemy we raise a principle into a higher and purer state of development. The processes in Nature by which combinations and decompositions of matter take place, such as putrefaction, caused by the contact of a substance with air, and the chemical combinations of two or more substances coming into contact with each other, are chemical processes. The growth of a tree out of a seed, the evolution of worlds, the development of precious metals out of an apparently worthless matrix, the growth of a foetus, the development of an animal or a human being, etc., are alchemical processes, because life itself enters into these processes, as a factor, and they would not take place without the action of life.[3]

Planets are states of mind, and as the mind has a higher and a lower aspect, consequently each planet has its two aspects correspondingly.

Mercury in its higher aspect is the symbol of wisdom, in its lower aspect that of the intellect.

Jupiter in its higher aspect represents majesty, in its lower aspect energy.

Mars represents spiritual power, but also in its lower aspect strength of passion, etc.

Venus in its higher aspect is divine love, identical with self-knowledge; in its lower aspect, desire.

Saturn is the life in the universe, and in another aspect it represents matter.

The Sun is the fountain of all life. The spiritual sun is the symbol of spiritual life and immortality, the physical sun the source of vitality.

The Moon in its higher aspect represents spiritual substance, the glorified soul; in its lower aspect it is the symbol of imagination and fancy.

"Separation is the cause of existence, the birth of things from the Mysterium magnum. It is the greatest wonder known to practical philosophy; it is a divine art. He who can attract things out of the *Mysterium magnum* (A'kasa) is a true alchemist." This power is possessed only by those who are spiritually developed.[4] Nature continually exercises that art through the organising power of the invisible astral body. "As the fowl produces a chicken with wings and legs out of the small microcosm contained in the shell of an egg, so the arcana of Nature are ripened by the processes of alchemy. Natural alchemy causes the pear to ripen, and produces grapes on a vine. Natural alchemy separates the useful elements from the food that is put into the stomach, transforms it into chyle and blood, into muscles and bones, and rejects that which is useless. A physician who knows nothing of alchemy can only be a servant of Nature, however well he may be versed in the science of external things; but the alchemist is her lord. If the physician cannot infuse vitality into decaying parts, he cannot effect a cure, but must wait until Nature accomplishes the task; but he who can guide the power of life can guide and command Nature."

Alchemy is described by Paracelsus as an art in which Vulcan (the fire of Nature) is the active artist. By this art the pure is separated from the impure, and things are made to grow out of primordial matter (A'kasa). Alchemy renders perfect what Nature has left imperfect, and purifies all things by the power of the spirit that is contained in them.

Sulphur, Mercury and Salt

"All things (man included) are composed out of three substances, and all things have their number, their weight, and their measure. Health exists when the three substances constituting a thing preserve their normal proportion of quantity and quality; disease results if this proportion becomes abnormal. These three substances are called *Sulphur, Mercury, and Salt*."[5] These three substances are not seen with the physical eye, but a true physician should see them nevertheless, and be able to separate them from each other. That which is perceptible to the senses may be seen by everybody who is not a physician; but a physician should be able to see things that not everybody can see. There are natural physicians, and there are artificially made physicians. The former see things which the latter cannot see, and the others dispute the existence of such things because they cannot perceive them. They see the exterior of things, but the true physicians see the interior. The inner man is the substantial reality, while the outer one is only an apparition, and therefore the true physician sees the real man, and the quack sees only an illusion."

"The three substances are held together in forms by the power of life.[6] If you take the three invisible substances and add to them the power of life, you will have three invisible substances in a visible form. The three constitute the form, and become separated only after the power of life deserts them. They are hidden by life, and joined together by life. Their combined qualities constitute the qualities of the form, and only when life departs their separate qualities become manifest. If the three are united in due proportions, health exists in the form; but if they become separated, the one will putrefy and the other will burn. Man does not see the action of these three substances as long as they are held together by life, but he may perceive their qualities at the time of the destruction of their form. The invisible fire is in the sulphur, the soluble element in the salt, and the volatile element in the mercury. The fire burns, the mercury produces smoke, and the salt remains in the ashes; but as long as the form is alive there is neither fire, nor ashes, nor smoke."[7]

"There are hundreds of different kinds of salt, sulphur, and mercury in the universe and in the human system, and the greatest arcana (potencies) are contained in them. All things are hidden in them in the same sense as a pear is hidden in a pear-tree and grapes in a vine. The superficial observer sees only that which exists for his senses, but the interior sight discovers the things of the future. A gardener knows that a vine will produce no pears, and a pear-tree no grapes. The ignorant speak of heat and cold, of dryness and moisture, of sweetness and acidity, of bitterness and astringency, without knowing the cause that produces such qualities; but the wise recognise in them the qualities of the stars" (*Paragranum*).

"Let no one be so foolish as to imagine that Alchemy can easily be understood and be made common property. If you want to make the sphere of Saturn run in harmony with earthly life, you may put all the planets therein. Of Luna, however, you must not take too much; only a little. Let it all run until the heaven of Saturn entirely disappears; then will the planets remain. They will have died in their corruptible bodies and taken an incorruptible perfect body. This is the life and spirit of heaven which causes the planets to live again and become corporified as before" (*Coelum Philosophorum*).

The remedy by which, according to Paracelsus, rejuvenation (regeneration) could be accomplished is something entirely different from what it has been supposed to be by his critics. It is not a compound of chemical substances, but an *Arcanum*, "an invisible fire, which destroys all diseases" (*Tinct. Phys., vii.*). "The *Materia Tinctura* is the greatest treasure in the world."[8]

Paracelsus was an enemy of endless prescriptions, and of all the daubing and greasing, quackery and nastiness, connected with the apothecaryship of his time. He says: "What shall I say to you about all your alchemical prescriptions; about all your retorts and bottles, crucibles, mortars, and glasses; of all your complicated processes of distilling, melting, cohibiting, coagulating, sublimating, precipitating, and filtering; of all the tomfoolery for which you throw away your time and your money? All such things are useless, and the labour for it is lost. They are rather an impediment than a help to arrive at the truth." But he was a practical alchemist. In the preface to his work entitled "Tinctura Physica" he says: "I have a treasure buried at the hospital at Weiden (Friaul), which is a jewel of such a value that neither Pope Leo nor the Emperor Carolus could buy it with all their wealth, and those who are acquainted with the spagyric art (alchemy) will confirm what I say."[9]

"True Alchemy which teaches how to make ☽ or ☉ out of the five imperfect metals, requires no other materials, but only the metals. The perfect metals are made out of the imperfect metals, through them and with them alone; for with other things is *Luna*, (phantasy), but in the metals is *Sol* (wisdom)."

Charms

The power of certain substances to absorb and to retain certain planetary influences is used for the purpose of investing them with occult qualities. Pure metals may be used by the alchemist for that purpose, and in this way amulets, "magic mirrors," and other things that will produce magic effects are prepared. Paracelsus says:

"The compositions of the *astra* of metals produce wonderful effects. If we make a composition of seven metals in the proper order and at the proper time, we will obtain a metal which contains all the virtues of the seven. Such a composition is called 'electrum.' It possesses the virtues of the seven metals that enter into its composition, and the electrum is one of the most valuable preparations known to secret science. The ordinary metals cannot be compared with it on account of its magic power. A vessel made of the electrum will immediately indicate it, if any poisonous substance has been surreptitiously put into it, because it will begin to sweat on its outside."

"Many wonderful things can be made of this electrum, such as amulets, charms, magic finger-rings, arm-rings, seals, figures, mirrors, bells, medals, and many other things possessing great magic powers, of which very little is publicly known, because our art has been neglected, and the majority of men do not even know that it exists."

"It would not be proper to explain all the virtues and powers of the electrum, because the sophist would begin to blaspheme, and the ignorant would become angry; the idiot would ridicule and the wicked misuse it; and we are therefore forced to be silent in regard to some of its principal virtues. But there are a few wonderful qualities which it possesses, and of which we will speak. We have observed them personally, and we know that we are speaking the truth. We have seen finger-rings made of the electrum that cured their wearers of spasms and paralytic affections, of epilepsy and apoplexy; and the application of such a ring, even during the most violent paroxysm of an epileptic attack, was always followed by immediate relief. We have seen such a ring begin sweat at the beginning of a hidden disease."

"The electrum is antipathetic to all evil influences, because there is hidden in it a heavenly power and the influence of all the seven planets. Therefore the Egyptians and Chaldeans and the Magi of Persia used it against evil spirits, and made great discoveries by its use. If I were to tell all I know about the virtues of the electrum, the sophists would denounce me for being the greatest sorcerer in the world."

"I will, however, say that I have known a person in Spain who possessed a bell made out of the electrum, and weighing about two pounds, and by ringing that bell he could cause various kinds of spectres and apparitions to appear, and they would obey his commands. Before using the bell he always wrote some words or characters on its inside. He then rang the bell, and immediately the spirits appeared in such a shape as he ordered them to take. He was even able to attract by the sound of that bell the spectres of men or animals, or to drive them away when they were not wanted; and whenever he wanted another spirit to appear he wrote some other characters on the inside of that bell. He refused to tell me the secret of these words and characters, but I meditated about it, and found it out myself."

"You need not be surprised to hear that such things are possible, because everything is possible, if it is consistent with natural laws. One man may call another man by his name, and order him to do certain things, and if the latter respects the former, or is awed by his superiority, he will obey his order without being forced to do so with a weapon or stick. On invisible beings the will of man has still more effect, and an inferior being can be made to obey the will of a superior one by the force of the mere thought of a word, because the lower is subject to the higher, and the inferior to the superior, and what else is the will but a power hidden in the thought (mind) of man, and becoming active through his imagination.[10] But the thought of man is as potent to impress a spirit as the spoken word is to impress the mind of a man, for spirits have no physical ears to hear physical sounds, and the voice is only needed for those who cannot hear in the spirit."[11]

"If the astral element in man can be sent into another man by the power of his Olympic spirit, such an astral element may also be embedded in metals and leave its influence in them, and thereby the metal can be raised into a higher state than the one into which it was put by Nature."[12]

The Electrum Magicum

The *electrum magicum* is prepared as follows:

"Take ten parts of pure gold, ten of silver, five of copper, two of tin, two of lead, one part of powdered iron, and five of mercury. All these metals must be pure. Now wait for the hour when the planets Saturn and Mercury come into conjunction, and have all your preparations ready for that occasion; have the fire, the crucible, the mercury, and the lead ready, so that there will be no delay when the time of the conjunction arrives, for the work must be done during the moments of the conjunction. As soon as this takes place melt the lead and add the mercury, and let it cool. After this has been done, wait for a conjunction of Jupiter with Saturn and Mercury, melt the compound of lead and mercury in a crucible, and in another crucible the tin, and pour the two metals together at the moment of such conjunction. You must now wait until a conjunction of the sun with either one or both of the above- named planets takes place, and then add the gold to the compound after melting it previously. At a time of a conjunction of the moon with the sun, Saturn, or Mercury, the silver is added likewise, and at a time of a conjunction of Venus with one of the above-named planets the copper is added. Finally, at a time of such a conjunction with Mars, the whole is completed by the addition of the powdered iron. Stir the fluid mass with a dry rod of witch-hazel, and let it cool."[13]

"Of this *electrum magicum* you may make a mirror in which you will see the events of the past and the present, absent friends or enemies, and what they are doing. You will see in it any object you may desire to see, and all the doings of men in daytime or at night. You will see in it anything that has ever been written down, said, or spoken in the past, and also see the person who said it, and the causes that made him say what he did, and anything, however secret it may have been kept."[14]

"Such mirrors are made of the *electrum magicum*; they are made of the diameter of about two inches. They are to be founded at a time when a conjunction of Jupiter and Venus takes place, and moulds made of fine sand are used for that purpose. Grind the mirrors smooth with a grindstone, and polish them with tripoli, and with a piece of wood from a linden-tree. All the operations made with the mirror, the grinding, polishing, etc., should take place under favourable planetary aspects, and by selecting the proper hours three different mirrors may be prepared. At a time of a conjunction of two good planets, when at the same time the sun or the moon stands on the 'house of the lord of the hour of your birth,' the three mirrors are to be laid together into pure well-water, and left to remain there for an hour. They must then be removed from the water, enveloped in a linen cloth, and be preserved for use."[15]

Palingenesis

Nothing in Nature is dead, and alchemy does not deal with inanimate things. The old alchemists were believers in the possibility of spontaneous generation, and by the action of psychical powers they created forms in which life became manifest. They could generate living beings in closed bottles, or by the Palingenesis[16] of plants or animals, cause the astral form of a plant or an animal to become visible again, and to resurrect from its ashes. One of the greatest secrets, however, is the generation of beings like men or women, that were generated without the assistance of a female organism, and which were called Homunculi. Paracelsus speaks about them as follows:

Homunculi

"Human beings may come into existence without natural parents. That is to say, such beings grow without being developed and born by a female organism; by the art of an experienced spagyricus (alchemist)."—*De Natura Serum, vol. i*

"The *generatio homunculi* has until now been kept very secret, and so little was publicly known about it that the old philosophers have doubted its possibility. But I know that such things may be accomplished by spagyric art assisted by natural processes. If the sperma, enclosed in a hermetically sealed glass, is buried in horse manure for about forty days, and properly 'magnetised' it begins to live and to move. After such a time it bears the form and resemblance of a human being, but it will be transparent and without a corpus. If it is now artificially fed with the *arcanum sanguinis hominis*[17] until it is about forty weeks old, and if allowed to remain during that time in the horse-manure in a continually equal temperature, it will grow into a human child, with all its members developed like any other child, such as could have been born by a woman; only it will be much smaller. We call such a being a homunculus, and it may be raised and educated like any other child, until it grows older and obtains reason and intellect, and is able to take care of itself. This is one of the greatest secrets, and it ought to remain a secret until the days approach when all secrets will be known."[18]

It seems to be useless to quote any more alchemistical prescriptions of Paracelsus, or of any other alchemist. To the uninitiated they are unintelligible; while the initiated, having the light of the spirit for his teacher, will not require them. But those who condemn the ancient occultists for their supposed ignorance and superstition would do well to remember that it requires a vastly greater amount of credulity to believe that great reformers in science and men possessed of wisdom, such as Paracelsus, Johannes Tritheim, Van Helmont, and others, should have consented to write whole volumes of such intolerable rubbish as such writings would certainly be if they were to be taken in a literal meaning, than to believe—as is actually the case—that great spiritual truths were thus hidden behind allegories that were intended to be understood only by those who possessed the key in their own hearts.

Although Paracelsus asserts that it is possible to make gold and silver by chemical means, and that some persons have succeeded in making it,[19] still he condemns such external experiments as useless in the end, and it seems to be more than probable that, even in such chemical experiments as may have succeeded, something more than merely chemical manipulations was required to make them successful.[20]

"The heavenly fire which comes to us from the sun, or acts within the earth, is not such a fire as is in heaven, neither like our fire upon the earth; but the celestial fire is with us a cold, stiff, frozen fire, and this is the body of gold. Therefore nothing can be gained from gold by means of our fire, except to render it fluid in the same sense as the sun renders fluid the snow and turns it into water." (Coelum Philos.)[21]

Astrology is intimately connected with medicine, magic, and alchemy. If we desire to make use of the influences of the planets for any purpose whatever, it is necessary to know what qualities these influences possess—how they act, and at what time certain planetary influences will be on the increase or on the wane. The quality of the planetary influences will be known to a man who knows his own constitution, because he will then be able to recognise in himself the planetary influences corresponding to those that rule in the sky; the action of such influences will be known if we know the qualities of the bodies upon which they act, because each body attracts those influences that are in harmony with it, and repels the others; the time when certain planetary influences rule may be found out by astronomical calculations, or by tables that have been prepared from such for that purpose; but the spiritually developed seer will require no books and no tables, but will recognise the conditions of the interior world by the states existing in his own mind.

Paracelsus was not—what is called to-day—a professional astrologer. He did not calculate nativities or make horoscopes, but he knew the higher aspect of astrology, by which the mutual relations of the Macrocosm and the Microcosm are known. He rejected the errors of popular astrology as he did those of other popular religions or scientific superstitions; and his system of astrology, if rightly understood, appears of a sublime character and full of the grandest conceptions. He says: "No one needs to care for the course of Saturn; it neither shortens nor lengthens the life of anybody. If Mars is ferocious, it does not follow that Nero was his child; and although Mars and Nero may both have had the same qualities, they did not take them from each other. It is an old saying that 'a wise man may rule the stars,' and I believe in that saying—not in the sense in which you take it, but in my own. The stars force nothing into us that we are not willing to take; they incline us to nothing which we do not desire.[22] They are free for themselves, and we are free for ourselves. You believe that one man is more successful in the acquirement of knowledge, another one in the acquisition of power; one obtains riches more easily, and another one fame. And you think that this is caused by the stars; but I believe the cause to be that one man is more apt than another to acquire and to hold certain things, and that this aptitude comes from the spirit.[23] It is absurd to believe that the stars can make a man. Whatever the stars can do we can do ourselves, because the wisdom which we obtain from God overpowers the heaven and rules over the stars."

He objected strongly to the use of ceremonies that were made for the purpose of attracting spirits by means of planetary influences. He says: "Whatever comes from the astral 'spirits' is sorcery. Such spirits are false, and we do not believe in them; but we believe in the power of that wisdom which rules heaven, and by which all the mysteries of Nature may be known. Sorcery has been called magic; but magic is wisdom, and there is no wisdom in sorcery. True science knows everything. The eternity of all things is without time, without beginning, and without an end. It is substantially present everywhere, and acts where it is not expected. That which seems to be incredible, improbable, and impossible will become wonderfully true in eternity."

"Man's mind is made up of the same elements as the stars; but as the wisdom of the Supreme guides the motions of the stars, so the reason of man rules the influences which rotate and circulate in his mind. The essence of man's sidereal body, which he attracts from the stars, is of a substantial nature; still, we consider it as being something spiritual on account of the ethereality of its substance, and on account of the great dimensions of its invisible body. The essences in man's sidereal body are intimately related to the sidereal essences of the stars, and the former attract the powers of the latter; but if a man is the master over his own mind, he can permit those attractions to take place in an irregular manner, or control his passions and repel influences which he does not desire.

"There is an attractive power in the soul of man, which attracts physical, mental, and moral diseases from the Chaos. The planetary influences extend through all Nature, and man attracts poisonous qualities from the moon, from the stars, and from other things; but the moon, and the stars, and other things also attract evil influences from man, and distribute them again by their rays, because Nature is an undivided whole, whose parts are intimately connected."

"The sun and the stars attract something from us, and we attract something from them, because our astral bodies are in sympathy with the stars, and the stars are in sympathy with our astral bodies; but the same is the case with the astral bodies of all other objects. They all attract astral influences from the stars. Each body attracts certain particular influences from them; some attract more and others less; and on this truth is based the power of amulets and talismans, and the influence which they may exercise over the astral form of the bearer. Talismans are like boxes, in which sidereal influences may be preserved."

"Three spirits, united in one, live and act in man; three worlds, united into one, throw their rays upon him; but all three are only the reflection, image, or echo of one primordial creation. The first is the essence of the elements; the second, the soul of the stars (the mind); they are caused by the life of the elements, but there is only *one life*, and the life that causes the instincts of man is contained in all elements in the stars as well as in vegetable and animal forms. The activity of the life-essence is modified in vegetable, animal, and human forms; it becomes the life of the earth, and the life of the earth is radiated back to the stars. Stars attract and repel each other; they have their sympathies and antipathies; and these living antipathies and sympathies, attractions and repulsions, could not exist if no vehicle of life existed between them."

"Primordial matter, forming the basis of the constitution of the human body, has absorbed influences from the stars, and they nourish the elementary (physical) body, and by means of these influences man's soul is connected with and united to the souls of the stars. Having three worlds in him and living in three worlds, man should learn to know the lower elements, understand the sidereal, and know the eternal."

"The body comes from the elements, the soul from the stars, and the spirit from God. All that the intellect can conceive of comes from the stars."[24]

"All knowledge comes from the stars (the Universal Mind). Men do not invent or create ideas; the ideas exist, and men are able to grasp them. If all professors of music in the world would die in one day, heaven, being the original teacher of music, would not die, and it would teach other persons this art."

"Many ideas exist which men have not yet grasped; many stars are still too far away to form a connection with the earth. The realm of stars and ideas is infinite, and therefore the source of inventions and discoveries is not yet exhausted."

"New stars appear and others disappear on the sky. New ideas appear on the mental horizon, and old ideas are lost. If a new comet appears on the sky, it fills the hearts of the ignorant with terror; if a new and grand idea appears on the mental horizon, it creates fear in the camp of those that cling to old systems and accepted forms."

"Physical man takes his nutriment from the earth; the sidereal man receives the states of his feelings and thoughts from the stars; but the spirit has his wisdom from God. The heat of a fire passes through an iron stove, and the astral influences, with all their qualities, pass through man. They penetrate him as rain penetrates the soil, and as the soil is made fruitful by the rain. Likewise man's soul is made fruitful by them; but the principle of the supreme wisdom of the universe penetrates into the centre, illuminates it, and rules over all."

"Hail may destroy the fruits of the earth, evil planetary influences be attracted by the soul of the earth and cause epidemic diseases, and the spiritual centre in man be devoid of wisdom, and darkness rule in its place. The earth, the animal kingdom, and physical man are subject to the government of the stars; but the spiritual man rules over the stars and over the elements, and conquers the worlds without and the world within by the wisdom that comes from God. Stones, plants, and animals obey the government of the mind, and man should obey the will and wisdom of God. The individual terrestrial life should correspond to the laws governing the universe; man's spiritual aspirations should be directed to harmonise with the will and wisdom of God. If this is attained, the inner consciousness will awaken to an understanding of the influences of the stars, and the mysteries of Nature will be revealed to his spiritual perception."

Chapter 9: Philosophy and Theosophy

Modern philosophy is a system of theoretical speculation, based upon reasoning from that which is believed to be true to the unknown, drawing logical deductions from accepted opinions and establishing new theories; but theosophy is the possession of spiritual knowledge obtained by practical experience. To be a philosopher it is necessary to have acute reasoning powers, and to calculate possibilities and probabilities; to be a true theosophist it is necessary to have the power of spiritual perception and to know the things perceived, irrespective of any possibilities, probabilities, or accepted opinions. A speculative philosopher occupies an objective standpoint in regard to the thing which he examines; the theosophist finds the character of that thing in himself. There is nothing in the Macrocosm of Nature that is not contained in man, because man and Nature are essentially one, and a man who is conscious of being one with Nature will know everything in Nature if he knows only himself. A philosopher having no knowledge of his own spirit can only speculate about things which he does not see; a practical theosophist, knowing his own spiritual state, does not need to speculate, because he sees the spirit of things and knows what he sees. Philosophy is the love of wisdom and the speculation thereon; theosophy is nothing more nor less than the *clear understanding* itself.

"There is a true and a false philosophy. As the froth in new-made wine swims upon the top and hides the true wine below, likewise there is a froth of sophistry and pseudo-philosophy swimming at the top of true philosophy; it looks like knowledge, but it is the outcome of ignorance, gilded and varnished to deceive the vulgar. It is like a parasite growing upon the tree of knowledge, drawing the sap out of the true tree and converting it into poison. The intellectual working of the brain alone is not sufficient to give birth to a physician; the true physician is not he who has merely heard of the truth, but he who feels the truth, who sees it before him as clearly as the light of the sun, who hears it as he would hear the noise of the cataract of the Rhine or the whistling of the storm upon the ocean, who smells it and tastes it, it being sweet to him as honey or bitter as gall. Nature produces diseases and effects their cures, and where, then, could be found a better teacher than Nature herself? That alone which we see and feel and perceive constitutes true knowledge, not that of which we are merely informed in books and which is not confirmed by experience."

"The knowledge of Nature as it is—not as we imagine it to be—constitutes true philosophy. He who merely sees the external appearance of things is not a philosopher; the true philosopher sees the reality, not merely the outward appearance. He who knows the sun and the moon has a sun and a moon in him, and he can tell how they look, even if his eyes are shut. Thus the true physician sees in himself the whole constitution of the Microcosm of man, with all its parts. He sees the constitution of his patient as if the latter were a clear crystal, in which not even a single hair could escape detection. He sees him as he would the stones and pebbles at the bottom of a clear well. This is the philosophy upon which the true art of medicine is based. Not that your physical eyes are able to show you these things, but it is Nature herself who teaches it to you. Nature is the universal mother of all, and if you are in harmony with her—if the mirror of your mind has not been made blind by the cobwebs of speculations, misconceptions, and erroneous theories—she will hold up before you a mirror in which you will see the truth. But he who is not true himself will not see the truth as it is taught by Nature, and it is far easier to study a number of books and to learn by heart a number of scientific theories than to ennoble one's own character to such an extent as to enter into perfect harmony with Nature and to be able to see the truth."

If "theosophy" means the clear perception and understanding of truth, there can be no true philosophy, religion, or science without theosophy, the understanding of truth being the only basis upon which all true knowledge rests.

No one can, therefore, be truly called a theosophist who does not possess the knowledge of his own divine self, which enables his person to know all things as only God knows them. This power is in possession of no mortal man, but belongs to the god in man. Only when man has found the god in him can he partake of divine wisdom.

Man is a mixed being; he is a centre or focus in which the three kingdoms—i.e., the three forms of manifestation of the primordial Will, the world of darkness or fire, the world of spiritual light, and that of external nature— are active, and in which the powers of either of these three kingdoms may become conscious and manifest. If he is a temple of the holy spirit, God will reveal His wisdom in him; if he is a dwelling of evil will, the devil will become personified in him; if the world of mind, intellect, emotion, etc.—i.e., the "heaven" of the external world—is reflected within his soul, and his mind becomes absorbed by it, he will be a child of the world.

It is most true and certain that if there were no natural world, Nature could not become manifested in man, and it is equally true that if there were no God and no devil—i.e., no supreme power for good and no power for evil in the universe—neither a god nor a devil could become revealed or personified in a man. Evil exists for the purpose of being conquered by good. Only in this way can knowledge be obtained.

There is no seed having the power to create itself the sunlight which it requires to enable it to grow, and in the same sense there is no man having himself the power to create a god by his own will and pleasure; but like acts upon like. The natural (physical or astral) principles in man are acted upon by the corresponding powers in Nature; the growth of plants is due to the power of the sun being active in them, and the spiritual unfoldment of the soul of man is also due to the power (the grace) of the God of the universe descending upon him.[1]

The knowledge of a man in regard to a truth, however learned and intellectual he may be, can be nothing else but a dream to one who does not recognise his own real existence in God. If we believe or accept the doctrine of another man who perceives the truth, it does not follow that we possess that truth as our own; it simply means that we consider his opinion worthy of our belief. A knowledge of the opinions of others may guide us in our researches as long as we cannot find the truth in ourselves, but such a knowledge is as liable to mislead us as to lead us right; the only key to arrive at the recognition and understanding of the truth is the perception and understanding itself. Opinions change, and creeds and beliefs change accordingly, but the knowledge which we find in our own experience stands as firm as a rock.

There is no such thing as a theoretical theosophy, because divine wisdom is not a matter of theory, but the divine knowledge of self. To know a thing we must see it and feel it and be identified with it ourselves. Things that transcend the physical power of sight can only be known if they are experienced and seen by the soul. Love or hate, reason and conscience, are unknown things to those who do not realise their existence. The attributes of the spirit are not only beyond the power of sensual perception, but they are beyond the power of intellectual comprehension; they can only be known to the spirit itself, and they are called occult because they cannot be understood without the possession of the light of the spirit. This spiritual light is an attribute of the spirit and beyond the reach of the merely intellectual but unspiritual mind.

"Man has two kinds of reason, angelic and animal reason. The former is eternal and of God, and remains with God; the latter is also, but indirectly, originating from God, and not eternal; for the body dies and its animal reason with it. No animal product can be victorious over death. Death kills that which is animal, but not that which is eternal. A man who is not a man as far as wisdom in him is concerned, is not a man but an animal in human shape." (*De Fundamento Sapientiae*)

To be able to understand good, it is necessary that man should experience evil, for without the knowledge of darkness the true nature of light could not be known; but no amount of evil experience will enable a man to know that which is good and divine if he is not in possession of the true understanding, which endows him with the power to profit by his experience, and which is not of his own making, but given to him as a gift by wisdom itself.

"The wise rules the stars in him, but animal man is ruled by his stars, which force him to do as he is directed by his animal nature. He who has escaped the gallows once will repeat his crimes; for he thinks that, having escaped his punishment once, he will escape it again. Such a person is blown about like a reed, and cannot resist the forces which are acting upon him, and the reason of this is, that he has no real self-knowledge, and does not know that there is in him a power superior to that of the stars (the lower mind). Wisdom in man is nobody's servant and has not lost its own freedom, and through wisdom man attains power over the stars."[2] (*De Fundamento Sapientiae*)

Knowledge

Intellectual reasoning may arrive at the door of the spiritual temple, but man cannot enter without perceiving that the temple exists and that he has the power to enter. This knowledge is called faith; but faith does not come to those who do not desire it, and a desire for divine wisdom is not created by man. Man's desires depend on the presence of an exciting cause, and that which attracts him strongest is the thing for which he has the greatest desire. It is not within the power of the animal or intellectual nature of man to desire or to love that which he does not know. He may have a curiosity to see the unknown God, but he can truly love only that which he feels, and of which he knows that it exists. He must realise the presence of the highest in his own heart before he can know it. The spiritual temple is locked with many keys, and those who are vain enough to believe that they can invade it by their own power, and without being shown the way by the light of wisdom, will storm against it in vain. Wisdom is not created by man; it must come to him, and cannot be purchased for money nor coaxed with promises, but it comes to those whose minds are pure and whose hearts are open to receive it. It is said that those who wish to become wise must be like children, but there are few amongst the learned who would be willing to undertake such a feat. There are few who would be able to realise the fact, even if they were willing to do so, that they themselves are without life, without knowledge, and without power, and that all life and consciousness, knowledge and power, come from the universal fountain of all, of which they are merely imperfect instruments for its manifestation. There are few amongst the learned capable of giving up their pet theories, their accepted opinions, their dogmatic reasoning and speculations about possibilities and probabilities, and sinking their own personal will entirely into the wisdom of God. Humanity resembles a field of wheat, in which each individual represents a plant, attempting to grow higher than the others and to bear more abundant fruit; but there are few who desire to be nothing themselves, so that God may take full possession of them and be all in and through them.

"The great majority of the 'investigators of theosophy' do not love wisdom, they only desire it; they desire to possess it for the purpose of adorning themselves with it; but wisdom is no man's servant—it comes only to those who, abandoning self, sacrifice themselves in the spirit of wisdom. Those who seek the truth for their own benefit and gratification will never find it, but the truth finds those in whom the delirium of 'self' disappears, and it becomes manifested in them."

The object of existence is to become perfectly happy, and the shortest way to become so is to be perfect and happy now, and not wait for a possibility to become so in a future state of existence. All may be happy, but only the highest happiness is enduring, and permanent happiness can be obtained only by attaining permanent good. The highest a man can feel and think is his highest ideal, and the higher we rise in the scale of existence and the more our knowledge expands, the higher will be our ideal. As long as we cling to our highest ideal we will be happy, in spite of the sufferings and vicissitudes of life. The highest ideal confers the highest and most enduring happiness, and the whole of Theosophy consists in the recognition and realisation of the highest ideal within one's self. This is to be accomplished only by the overcoming of the illusion of separate existence and the awakening of the soul to the essential unity of all things. It is a state of divine wisdom which can be attained in no other way than by the light of that wisdom becoming manifested in man.[3]

Spiritual Regeneration

As long as any one fancies his highest ideal to exist only outside of him, somewhere above the clouds or in the history of the past, he will go outside of himself to seek for it in dreamland or in the pages or history. This is not theosophy, but merely dreaming; for not that wisdom which exists outside of man but that which has taken root in him renders him wise. A child is not born from outside of its mother's womb, but from within, and the spiritual regeneration of the soul must be accomplished by that power which is existing within the soul itself.

Chapter 9: Philosophy and Theosophy

The spiritual regeneration of man requires the opening of his inner senses, and this, again, involves the development of the internal organs of the spiritual body, while the latter is intimately connected with the physical form. Thus this regeneration is not an entirely spiritual process, but productive also of great changes in the physical body. He who rejects, neglects, or despises his physical body, as long as he has not outgrown the necessity of having such a corporeal form, may be compared to the yolk in an egg wanting to be free from the white of the egg and the shell, without having grown into a bird.

"Philosophy" means love of wisdom, but not those who love wisdom for their own aggrandisement are its true lovers. Such people love only themselves, and desire wisdom as a means for parading with it; they desire to know the secrets of Nature and the mysteries of God, for the gratification of their scientific curiosity. "Theosophy" means the wisdom of God; in other words, the self-knowledge of God in man. It is not "man," but the god in man who knows his own divine self, and it therefore does not rest with the will and pleasure of man to become a theosophist, but this depends on the awakening of the divine spirit in him. Philosophy argues and deducts, speculates, makes additions and multiplications, and by logical reasonings seeks to prove that for such or such reasons this or that cannot be otherwise than so or so; but divine wisdom requires no arguments, no logic or reasoning, because it is already the self-knowledge of the One from whom all other things are deriving their origin. It is the highest and most exalted kind of rationality, for there can be nothing more rational than to know the divine fountain of All, by entering into its own understanding.

"All numbers are multiples of one, all sciences converge to a common point, all wisdom comes out of one centre, and the number of wisdom is one. The light of wisdom radiates into the world, and manifests itself in various ways according to the substance in which it manifests itself. Therefore man can exhibit reason in a threefold manner: as instinct, as animal reason, and spiritual intelligence. The knowledge which our soul derives from the physical and animal elements is temporal; that which it derives from the spirit is eternal. God is the Father of wisdom, and all wisdom is derived from Him. We may grow into knowledge, but we cannot grow or manufacture knowledge ourselves, because in ourselves is nothing but what has been deposited there by God. Those who believe that they can learn anything real and true without the assistance of God, who is Himself the truth and the reality, will fall into idolatry, superstition, and error. But those who love the luminous centre will be attracted to it, and their knowledge comes from God. God is the Father of wisdom, and man is the son. If we wish for knowledge we must apply for it to the Father and not to the son. And if the son desires to teach wisdom, he must teach that wisdom which he derived from the Father. The knowledge which our clergymen possess is not obtained by them from the Father, but they learn it from each other. They are not certain of the truth of what they teach, and therefore they use argumentation, circumvention, and prevarication; they fall into error and vanity, and mistake their own opinions for the wisdom of God. Hypocrisy is not holiness; conceit is not power; slyness is not wisdom. The art of deceiving and disputing, sophisticating, perverting, and misrepresenting truths, may be learned in schools; but the power to recognise and to follow the truth cannot be conferred by academical degrees; it comes only from God. He who desires to know the truth must be able to see it, and not be satisfied with descriptions of it received from others, but be true himself. The highest power of the intellect, if it is not illumined by love, is only a high grade of animal intellect, and will perish in time; but the intellect animated by the love of the Supreme is the intellect of the angels, and will live in eternity." (*De Fundamento Sapientiae*)

"All things are vehicles of virtues, everything in Nature is a house wherein dwell certain powers and virtues such as God has infused throughout Nature and which inhabit all things in the same sense as the soul is in man; but the soul is a creature originating of God and returns again to God. Natural (terrestrial) man is a son of Nature, and ought to know Nature, his mother; but the soul, being a son of God, ought to know the Father, the Creator of all." (*Vera Influentia Rerum*)

Faith

In regard to the true and the false faith Paracelsus says:—"It is not a faith in the existence of a historical Jesus Christ that has the power to save mankind from evil, but a faith in the Supreme Power (God), through which the man Jesus was enabled to act, and through which we also may act when it becomes manifested in us. The former 'faith' is merely a belief and a result of education; the latter is a power belonging to the higher constitution of man. Christ does not say that if we believe in His personal power to accomplish wonderful things we will be enabled to throw mountains into the ocean; but He spoke of our own faith, meaning the divine power of God in man, that will act through ourselves as much as it acted through Christ, if we become like Him. This power comes from God and returns to Him; and if one man cures another in the name of Christ, he cures him by the power of God, and by his own faith. That power becomes active in and through him by his faith, and not out of God's gratitude for his professed belief, or the belief of the patient that Christ once existed upon the earth."

"The power of the true faith extends as far as the power of God in the universe. Man can accomplish nothing by his own power, but everything can be accomplished through man by the power of faith. If we did not have faith in our ability to walk, we would not be able to walk. If we accomplish anything whatever, faith accomplishes it in and through us."

"Faith does not come from man, and no man can create faith or make himself faithful without faith; but faith is a power coming from God. Its germ is laid within man, and may be cultivated or neglected by him; it can be used by him for good or for evil, but it only acts effectively when it is strong and pure—not weakened by doubt, and not dispersed by secondary considerations. He who wants to employ it must have only *one* object in view. Diseases are caused and cured by faith, and if men knew the power of faith they would have more faith and less superstition. We have no right to call any disease incurable; we have only the right to say that we cannot cure it. A physician who trusts only in his own science will accomplish little, but he who has faith in the power of God acting through him, and who employs that power intelligently, will accomplish much."

"If any one thinks that he can cure a disease, or accomplish anything else, without the power derived from God, he believes in a superstition; but if he believes that he can perform such a thing because he is conscious of having obtained the power to do so, he will then be able to accomplish it by the power of the true faith. Such a faith is knowledge and power. True faith is spiritual consciousness, but a belief based upon mere opinions and creeds is the product of ignorance, and a superstition."[4]

Reincarnation

"The body which we receive from our parents, and which is built up from the nutriments it draws directly and indirectly from the earth, has no spiritual powers, for wisdom and virtue, faith, hope, and charity, do not grow from the earth. These powers are not the products of man's physical organisation, but the attributes of another invisible and glorified body, whose germs are laid within man.[5] The physical body changes and dies, the glorified body is eternal. This eternal man is the real man, and is not generated by his earthly parents. He does not draw nutriment from the earth, but from the eternal invisible source from which he originated. Nevertheless the two bodies are one, and man may be compared to a tree, drawing his nutriment from the earth, and from the surrounding air. The roots extend into the earth, and seek their nutriment in the dark, but the leaves receive their nutriment from the air. The temporal body is the house of the eternal, and we should therefore take care of it, because he who destroys the temporal body destroys the house of the eternal, and although the eternal man is invisible, he exists nevertheless, and will become visible in time, just as a child in its mother's womb is invisible before it is born, but after its birth it may be seen by all but those who are blind; and as everything returns after a while to the source from whence it came, so the body returns to the earth and the spirit to heaven or hell. Some children are born from heaven, and others are born from hell, because each human being has his inherent tendencies, and these tendencies belong to his spirit, and indicate the state in which he existed before he was born. Witches and sorcerers are not made at once; they are born with powers for evil.[6] The body is only an instrument; if you seek for man in his dead body, you are seeking for him in vain."

"The Philosopher's Stone"

But this physical body, which is believed to be of so little importance by those who love to dream about the mysteries of the spirit, is the most secret and valuable thing. It is the true "stone which the builders rejected," but which must become the corner-stone of the temple. It is the "stone" which is considered worthless by those who seek for a God above the clouds and reject Him when He enters their house. This physical body is not merely an instrument for divine power, but it is also the soil from which that which is immortal in man receives its strength. A seed requires the power of the sunshine to enable it to take from the earth the elements necessary for its growth, and in the same sense the spiritual body of man, receiving its nutriment from the spirit, could not unfold and develop if it were not for the presence of the physical body of man, with its elementary and elemental forces; for the physical body is comparable to the wood from which is produced the fire which gives light; there would be no light if there were nothing to burn. "The more there is wood to burn, the greater will be the combustion, and thus it is with the Lapis Philosophorum or Balsamo perpetuo in corpore humano."[7] "But it is not proper to say a great deal about the Lapis Philosophorum or to boast about its possession; the ancients have sufficiently indicated the way for its preparation to those who are not devoid of the true understanding; but they have spoken in parables, so that unworthy persons may not know the secret and misuse it. Look at a man; he is not a perfect being, but only a half a man as long as he has not been made into one with the woman.[8] After having become one with the woman (in him), then will he be not a half, but a whole." (*De Lapid. Philosoph.*)

The Church

The rock upon which the true (spiritual) church is founded is not to be found in Rome nor in Protestantism, nor in the realm of fancy, but in the power of faith. "It is the Word of Wisdom from which you should learn, and in that Word you will find neither statuary nor paintings, but only the universal spirit. If faith is preached to you, it is done for the purpose of implanting it into your heart, where it may take root and grow and become manifest to you; but if your faith is not in your heart, but in forms and ceremonies, and if you cling to these forms you may know that your heart is evil; because, although the forms and the ceremonies cause you to weep and to sigh, this sighing and weeping is worthless, because your sentiment comes from those images, and to those images will it return. All things return finally to the place from whence they took their origin, and as these things are perishable, the sentiments which they excite will perish with them. God only desires the heart and not the ceremonies. If you do not require the ceremonies, they will be useless in matters of faith as well as in the art of magic."

It is foolish to refuse to be guided by the church as long as one is not able to find one's own way; but to be thus guided is not the object of existence; we should strive to learn how to govern ourselves, instead of being continually dependent upon the help of another.

"I do not say that images should not be made, and that the suffering of Christ should not be represented in pictures. Such things are good to move the mind of man to the practice of piety, virtue, and veneration, and to those who are unable to read they are very useful and better than many a sermon. I am not speaking against the use of a thing, but against its misuses. Such things are useful if we know their true meaning and understand their effects." (*De Imaginibus*, iii.)[9]

"The saints are in heaven, and not in the wood out of which an image is carved. Each man is himself nearest to his own god. I contradict your old fathers because they wrote for the body and not for the soul; they wrote poetry, but not theosophy; they spoke flatteries instead of telling the truth. They were teachers of fashions and usages, not teachers of eternal life. The mere imitation of the personal usages of the saints leads to nothing but damnation. The wearing of a black coat, or the possession of a piece of paper signed by some human authority, does not make a man a divine. Those are divine who act wisely, because wisdom is God. A clergyman should be a spiritual guide for others; but how can a man be a spiritual guide if he merely talks about spiritual things and knows himself nothing about them? It may be said that the personal behaviour of a clergyman does not affect the truth of what he teaches; but a clergyman who does not act rightly does not possess the truth, and therefore cannot teach it. He can only, parrot-like, repeat words and sentences, and their meaning will be incomprehensible to his hearers, because he knows nothing about that meaning himself."

"Belief in opinions is no faith. He who foolishly believes is foolish. A fool who believes unreasonable things is dead in faith, because he has no real knowledge, and without knowledge there can be no faith. He who wants to obtain true faith must know, because faith grows out of spiritual knowledge. The faith that comes from that knowledge is rooted in the heart. He who ignorantly believes has no knowledge, and possesses no faith and no power.[10] God does not desire that we should remain in darkness and ignorance; on the contrary, our knowledge should be of God. We should be the recipients of divine wisdom. God does not rejoice to see fools, blockheads, and simpletons, who are ready to believe anything, no matter how absurd it may be; neither does He desire that only one wise and learned man should be in each country, and that the other people should follow him blindly, as the sheep follow a ram; but we should all have our knowledge in God, and take it out of the universal fountain of wisdom. We should know who and what God is, but we can learn to know God only by becoming wise, and we become wise when the wisdom of God becomes manifested in us. The works of God will become manifest to us through wisdom, and God will be most pleased if we become His image. To become like God we must become attracted to God, who is the universal fountain of all, and the power that attracts us is divine love. The love of God will be kindled in our hearts by an ardent love for humanity, and a love for humanity will be caused by a love of God. Thus the God of the Macrocosm and the God of the Microcosm act upon each other, and both are one, for there is only one God, and one law, and one Nature, through which wisdom becomes manifest." (*De Fundamento Sapientiae*)

"There is an earthly sun, which is the cause of all heat, and all who are able to see may see the sun, and those who are blind and cannot see him may feel his heat. There is an eternal sun, which is the source of all wisdom, and those whose spiritual senses have awakened to life will see that sun, and be conscious of his existence; but those who have not attained full spiritual consciousness may nevertheless perceive his power by an inner faculty, which is called Intuition. Animal reason is active in the animal soul, and angelic wisdom in the spiritual soul. The former sees by the light of Nature, which is produced by a reflection of the rays of the divine light acting in Nature; but the light of the spirit is not a product of Nature, but the supreme cause of all which in Nature becomes manifest. Nature does not produce a sage; she merely furnishes a natural vehicle for a sage. Nature is not perfect, but produces cripples and diseases, abnormalities and monstrosities, the blind and the lame; but that which comes from God is perfect. It is a germ which is planted in the soul of man, and man is the gardener and cultivator, whose business it is to surround it with the elements necessary for its growth, so that when the earthly tabernacle is broken, the spirit, attracted by His love, His eternal home, may return to it, having grown in knowledge, being clothed in purity and illumined by divine wisdom."

"The wisdom of God is not made up of pieces, but is only one. While we are on this earth we ought to keep our mirror in God, so as to be in every respect as a child is like its father. Thus we ought to be made out of the whole cloth, and not be patched up. The wise man in God has his wisdom in God, and he will teach in a way that nobody can contradict or resist him, and his teaching will harm no one, but bring joy and gladness and glory to all who will receive it." (*De Fundamento Sapientiae*)

Spirit passes into the body, and out of it, like a breath of air passing through the strings of an Aeolian harp. If we succeed in binding it there, we will create a source of undying harmony and create an immortal being. But to bind spirit we must be able to bind thought. Man is a materialised thought; he is what he wills. To change his nature from the mortal to the immortal state he must change his material mode of thinking, and even rise above the sphere of thought. He must cease to hold fast in his thoughts to that which is illusory and perishing, and hold on to that which is eternal. The visible universe is a thought of the eternal mind thrown into objectivity by its will, and crystallised into matter by its power. Look at the everlasting stars; look at the indestructible mountain-peaks. They are the thoughts of the universal mind, and they will remain as long as the thoughts of that mind do not change. If we could hold on to a thought we would be able to create. But who but the enlightened, who live above the region of mentality in the kingdom of spirit, can hold on to a thought? Are not the illusions of the senses continually destroying that which we attempt to create? Men do not think what they choose, but that which comes into their mind. If they could control the action of their mind by rising above it, they would be able to control their own nature and the nature by which their forms are surrounded.

But mortal man has no power to control the powers of Nature in him, unless that power becomes manifested in him. "We mortals are not from heaven, but from the earth; we did not drop down from heaven, but grew from the earth. Terrestrial powers are moving in us; but if we are reborn in the spirit, then will we move in celestial power. What is this aid, these powers of which I am writing, but celestial powers? Who gives and distributes them but God alone?" (*Morb. Invisib.*, v.). He who trusts in his own power will fail, and become a victim of his own vanity; he who expects salvation from others will be disappointed. There is no god, no saint, and no power in which we can put any confidence, faith, or trust for the purpose of our salvation, except the power of divine wisdom acting within ourselves. Only when man realises the presence of God within himself will he begin his infinite life, and step from the realm of evanescent illusions into that of permanent truth.

The realisation of eternal truth is caused by the "Holy Ghost," this being the light of self-knowledge, the spirit of truth. No man can create within himself that light, nor drag the spirit of truth down to his level, nor push himself by his own will into that light; he can only wait in peace until that spirit descends and becomes manifest in his soul. Thus the acquisition of wisdom consists in passively receiving the light from above, and in actively resisting the influences from below which hinder its manifestation.

Unselfishness

"Theosophy" is the wisdom of God in man, and therefore cannot be appropriated by any person. It cannot become manifested in man as long as there exists in him the delusion of "self," because that "self" is a limited thing, which cannot grasp the infinite indivisible reality. For this reason "love"—that is to say, the abandonment of "self"—is the beginning of wisdom. This doctrine, however, is generally misunderstood. It does not teach that *I* should merely desire nothing for myself; but it teaches that there should be no conception of "I" in my mind that loves or desires anything. Only when that illusion of "self" has disappeared from my heart and mind, and my consciousness arisen to that state in which there will be no "I," then will not *I* be the doer of works, but the spirit of wisdom will perform its wonders through my instrumentality. (*Philosophia Occulta*)

In this also exists the difference between divine love and "altruism." Altruistically inclined persons are usually not selfish, but possessed by the idea of "self." Not from God, but from their own illusion of selfhood, are their works emanating. They are themselves the doers of their works, and are proud of their own goodness and wisdom; but their good works, being the product of an illusion, are illusive, and therefore impermanent. The altruistic humanitarian sees in other human beings his brothers and sisters; but God, dwelling in the soul of the wise, sees in every vehicle of life and in every creature His own divine self.

Appendix

Adepts

There are Adepts of various grades. There are such as live like normal men in their physical bodies, and who are able to send their astral spirit out of their bodies during their sleep to any place they choose, and on awakening, their astral spirit returns again into the body to which it belongs; and there are others who have no physical bodies, because they have arrived at a state of perfection in which such bodies are no longer required for their purposes.[1] "There are persons who have been exalted (*verzuecht*) to God, and who have remained in that state of exaltation, and they have not died. Their physical bodies have lost their lives, but without being conscious of it, without sensation, without any disease, and without suffering, and their bodies became transformed, and disappeared in such a manner that nobody knew what became of them, and yet they remained on the earth. But their spirits and heavenly bodies, having neither corporeal form, shape, nor colour, were exalted to heaven, like Enoch and Elias of old."[2] (*Philosoph.*, v.)

"There is a great difference between the physical and the ethereal body. The former is visible and tangible, but the latter is invisible and intangible. The body eats and drinks; the spirit lives in faith. The body is evanescent and destructible; the spirit eternal. The body dies; the spirit lives. The body is conquered by the spirit; the spirit is victor. The body is opaque, clouded; the spirit transparent and clear. The body is often sick; the spirit knows no disease. The body is dark, but the spirit is light, and sees into the hearts of the mountains and the interior of the earth. The body executes acts which the spirit orders. The body is the mumia; the substance of the spirit is the balsam of life. The former comes from the earth, but the spirit from heaven."[3] (*Philosoph.*, iv.)

Creation

The unmanifested Absolute cannot be conceived otherwise than as a mathematical point, without any magnitude, and such a point in becoming manifest in all directions would necessarily become a sphere. If we imagine such a mathematical point as being self-conscious, thinking, and capable to act, and desirous to manifest itself, the only thinkable mode in which it could possibly accomplish this would be by radiating its own substance and consciousness from the centre towards the periphery. The centre is the Father, the eternal source of all (John i. 4); the radius is the Son (the *Logos*), who was contained in the Father from eternity (John i. 1); the power of the father revealed in the light of the son from the incomprehensible centre to the unlimited periphery is the Holy Ghost, the spirit of truth, which is manifested externally and revealed in visible Nature (John xv. 26). We cannot conceive of a body without length, breadth, and thickness; a circle or a sphere always consists of a centre, radius, and periphery. They are three, yet they are one, and neither of them can exist without the other two.[4] God sends out His thought by the power of His will (the Iliaster divides itself). He holds fast to the thought, and expresses it in the

Word, in which is contained the creative and conservative power, and His thought becomes corporified, bringing into existence worlds and beings, which form, so to say, the visible body of the invisible God. Thus were the worlds formed in the beginning by the thought of God acting in the Macrocosm (the Universal Mind), and in the same manner are forms created in the individual sphere of the mind of man. If we hold on to a thought we create a form in our inner world, and we might render it objective and material if we knew our own creative power. A good thought produces a good, and an evil thought an evil form, and they grow as they are nourished by thought or "imagination."

Generation

All beings are the product of the creative power of the imagination.[5] This imagination may proceed (1) from Nature, (2) from man, (3) from God.

There are consequently three modes in which men may come into existence:

1. Natural men, the result of sexual intercourse between men and women. The imagination of the parents creates the sperm; the matrix furnishes the conditions for its development. "They are born of flesh, and their destiny is to serve as vehicles for the Spirit." (St. John iii. 6)[6]

2. God-men, the products of the imagination and will of the divine Logos, the incarnating spiritual entities (St. Matt. i. 23; St. Luke i. 35). "They are already born of the Spirit." (St. John i. 14)[7]

3. Primordial men, without fathers or mothers and without sex, produced by the thought of God in the matrix of Nature (Hebrews vii. 3). "They are the true images of the Creator, the children of God, without sin and without knowledge." (Luke iii. 38) Being attracted to matter, and desiring to enjoy material pleasures, they gradually sink into matter and learn to know good and evil.[8]

Initiation

"Initiation," or "baptism," is the growth of the spiritual principle, which is germinally contained in every man, into consciousness. "Two germs grow into one man. One comes from the Spirit, the other germ comes from Nature; but the two are one. One becomes conscious of Nature, the other one may become conscious of the Spirit. One is the child of Adam, the other the son of Christ. There are a few whose spiritual consciousness is awakened to life, who have died in Adam and are reborn of Christ;[9] those who are reborn know themselves, and are thus initiated into the kingdom of the Spirit.

"Initiation is therefore a matter of growth, and cannot be obtained by favour. Ceremonies are only external forms. The true baptism is the baptism of fire, the growth into the spirit of wisdom, the victory of the spirit over the animal nature of man."[10]

We know that nobody can enjoy the possession of any external sense, such as sight, hearing, etc., unless he has organs adapted for that purpose. The same is true in regard to the inner senses of man, which also require the organisation of a spiritual but nevertheless substantial body; and as the physical body generates its organs in the womb of its mother, so the spiritual body becomes generated in the astral body of man.

"The form of man must be adapted to his plane of existence. A horseshoe of iron has a form adapted to its purpose, and so has a goblet of silver. Nature has many strange children, and man must have his shape, and also that wherein he is made. Therefore

Christ says, 'He who is with Me denies himself.' This means that he must rise superior to that which belongs to Nature in him. He must take his cross upon his shoulders, namely, the cross which Nature has put upon him. Take Nature upon your shoulders and carry her, but do not identify yourself with her. Love your neighbour, and free yourself of that carnal reason which forces you to be a servant of self." (*De Arte Presaga*)

Mediumship

"Nature can teach everything belonging to Nature; she derives her knowledge from the Spirit. But Spirit and Nature are one, for Nature is a light that comes from the Spirit. If Nature learns from the Spirit, the one becomes divided into two: the disciple asks questions, and answers them himself. In a dream the dreamer and the person he dreams of are one; and in temptation the tempter and the tempted are one."

"The light of Nature is the light that comes from the Spirit. It is in man—is born with him, and grows up with him. There are some persons who live in this interior light, but the life of others is centred in their animal instincts, and they grope in darkness and error. There are some who write wiser than they know, but it is wisdom that writes through them, for man has no wisdom of his own; he can only come into contact with wisdom through the light of Nature that is in himself."

"Those who live in their animal instincts are not wise, and that which they write is inspired by their animal reason. Some animals are murderous and others are greedy; some are thievish and others are lewd; but all the elements of the animal kingdom are in the soul of man, and whenever such elements become alive in him they dominate over his reason, and man becomes like a reasoning animal, and writes as dictated by his animal reason."

"That which a man writes is not created by him, but it existed before him, and will exist after him; he only gives it a form. Therefore that which he writes is not his but another's; he is only the instrument through which truth or error expresses itself. There are those who write mechanically, and such writing may come from three causes; intellectual writing may come from over fifty-seven causes, and the writing of the Word of God may come from ten causes. A person who writes should know the cause from whence his ideas come, for only he who knows wisdom can write wisely."[11] (*De Fundamento Sapientiae*)

Occult Phenomena

Action at a Distance.—"The (spiritual) breath of man reaches very far; for the breath is his spirit, and he may send his spirit many hundred miles away, so that it will accomplish all that the man himself could have accomplished. Such a breath travels as fast as the wind, or as a ball shot out of a gun, and delivers its message." (*Philosoph. Tract.*, iii.)

Disappearance of Objects.—"Visible bodies may be made invisible, or covered, in the same way as night covers a man and makes him invisible, or as he would become invisible if he were put behind a wall; and as Nature can render something visible or invisible by such means, likewise a visible substance may be covered with an invisible substance, and be made invisible by art."[12] (*Philosoph. Sag.*, i.)

Palingenesis.—"If a thing loses its material substance, the invisible form still remains in the light of Nature (the astral light); and if we can reclothe that form with visible matter, we can make that form visible again. All matter is composed of three elements—*sulphur, mercury, and salt.* By alchemical means we may create a magnetic attraction in the astral form, so that it will attract from the elements (the A'kasa) those principles which it possessed before its mortification, and incorporate them and become visible again."[13] (*De Resuscitationibus*)

Occult Letters.—"If the elementary body can write a letter, and send it by a messenger to somebody in a month, why should not the ethereal body of an Adept be able to write a letter and to send it to its destination (by an element spirit) in an hour?"[14] (*Philosoph, Sag.,* i. cap. 6).

Transformations.—"There is a species of magic by which living bodies can be formed and one body be transformed into another, as was done by Moses."[15] (*Philosoph. Sag.*)

Transmutations.—"An instance of transmutation may be seen in wood which has become petrified. The form of the wood remains unchanged; nevertheless it is no longer wood, but a stone." (*De Transmutationibus*)

Passage of Matter through Matter.—"Things that are done by visible means in the ordinary manner may be done by invisible means in an extraordinary way. For instance, a lock can be opened with a key; a cut be made with a sword; the body be protected by a coat-of-mail. All this may be done by visible means. You may grasp a man with your hand without making a hole in him, and take a fish out of water without leaving a hole in the water; or you may put something into water, and if you withdraw your hand no hole will be left in the water. By the necromantic art something can be put through a body or into a body, and no hole will be left in the latter."[16] (*Philosoph. Sag.,* i. 4)

Thought-Transfer

"By the magic power of the will a person on this side of the ocean may make a person on the other side hear what is said on this side, and a person in the East thus converse with another person in the West. The physical man may hear and understand the voice of another man at a distance of a hundred steps, and the ethereal body of a man know what another man thinks at a distance of a hundred miles and more. What can be accomplished by ordinary means in a month (such as the sending of messages) can be done by this art in one day. If you have a tube a mile long, and you speak through it at one end, a person at the other end will hear what you say. If the elementary body can do this, how much easier will it be for the ethereal body, which is much more powerful (in relation to other ethereal bodies) than the former!"[17] (*Philosoph. Sag.,* i. cap. 60)

Spirits of the Departed

"If a person dies, it is only his body that dies; the human soul does not die,[18] neither can it be buried, but it remains alive, and knows whatever it knew before it became separated from the body. It remains the same as it was before death: if a man has been a liar in his life, he will be one after death; and if he has been well experienced in a certain science or art, he will know that science or art; but a human soul that knew nothing about a certain thing during its life will not be able to learn much about it after death."

"If we desire to enter into communication with the spirit of a deceased person, we may make a picture representing that person, and write his name and the questions we wish to ask him upon it, and put that picture under our head after retiring to rest; and during our sleep the deceased appears to us in our dreams and answers our questions. But the experiment must be made in a spirit of unfaltering faith, full of confidence that it will succeed, else it will fail, because it is not the picture that brings the spirit, but our faith that brings us into communication with it; and the picture is only made for the purpose of assisting the imagination, and to make it more powerful."[19] (*Philosoph.*, v.)

"Men have two spirits—an animal spirit and a human spirit—in them.[20] A man who lives in his animal spirit is like an animal during life, and will be an animal after death; but a man who lives in his human spirit will remain human. Animals have consciousness and reason, but they have no spiritual intelligence. It is the presence of the latter that raises man above the animal, and its absence that makes an animal of what once appeared to be a man. A man in whom the animal reason alone is active is a lunatic, and his character resembles that of some animal. One man acts like a wolf, another like a dog, another like a hog, a snake, or a fox, etc. It is their animal principle that makes them act as they do, and their animal principle will perish like the animals themselves. But the human reason is not of an animal nature, but comes from God, and being a part of God, it is necessarily immortal." (*De Lunaticis*)

The Elixir of Life[21]

Paracelsus, as well as his predecessors, such as Galen, Arnold, De Villanova, Raimund Lullius, etc., laboured studiously to discover a remedy for the prolongation of life. He did not believe in the possibility of rendering the physical body immortal, but he considered it the duty of every physician to attempt to prolong human life as long as it could be prolonged, because it is only during life upon the earth that man can acquire knowledge and improve his character; after death he acquires nothing new, but enjoys his possessions. Paracelsus, like Roger Bacon, Verulam, and others, maintained that the human body could be rejuvenated to a certain extent by a fresh supply of vitality, and it was his aim to find means by which such a supply could be obtained. He says:

"If we could extract the fire of life from the heart without destroying the heart, and draw the quintessence out of inanimate things, and use it for our purpose, we might live for ever in the enjoyment of health, and without experiencing any disease. But this is not possible in our present condition. We cannot reverse the laws of Nature, and whatever dies a natural death cannot be resuscitated by man. But man may mend that which he himself has broken, and break that which he himself has made. All things have a certain time during which they exist upon the earth. The saints have a certain time during which they exist, and also the wicked. If a man's time to stay is over, he will have to leave. But many die before their time is over, not by a visitation of Providence, but because they are ignorant of the laws controlling their nature."

"Metals may be preserved from rust, and wood be protected against the rot. Blood may be preserved a long time if the air is excluded. Egyptian mummies have kept their forms for centuries without undergoing putrefaction. Animals awaken from their winter sleep, and flies, having become torpid from cold, become nimble again when they are warmed. A tree will sometimes bear no fruit for twenty years, and then begin again to bloom and bear fruit as it did when it was young; and if inanimate objects can be kept from destruction, why should there be no possibility to preserve the life-essence of animate forms?"

"Life itself comes from heaven. It is an emanation of the Supreme Power of the universe, and it is therefore eternal and unchangeable; but it requires a substantial vehicle for its manifestation. Material forms are earthly, and, like all earthly substances, they are subject to dissolution and change. To prolong the process of life, we must try to protect the material form in which life is active against all injurious influences that may act upon it. We must therefore attempt to eradicate all physical and psychical diseases, and to prevent all evils that are caused by age, occupation, or accidents. We should protect man against all evil influences acting upon him during the foetal state, in infancy, youth, manhood, and old age; we should defend him against injurious influences coming from the astral plane; cause him to avoid immoderate eating and drinking, fatigue of body or mind, excessive joy or grief, or mental excitement of any kind. We must protect him against infectious or epidemic diseases, whether they are of a physical or moral character, and employ such remedies as have been provided by Nature for such purposes."

"Such a remedy is the *Primum Ens,* the source of all life. As the fabulous halcyon becomes rejuvenated and its own substance renewed by drawing its nutriment from the Primum Ens, so may man rejuvenate his constitution by purifying it so that it will be able to receive without any interruption the life-giving influence of the divine spirit."[22]

"But the vehicle that forms the medium through which life acts consists of elementary substances that are found in Nature, and which form the quintessence of all things. There are some substances in which this quintessence is contained in greater quantities than in others, and from which it can more easily be extracted. Such substances are especially the herb called melissa and the human blood."

The Primum Ens

The "*Primum Ens*" of a thing is its first beginning, its Prima Materia, an invisible and intangible spiritual substance, which can be incorporated in some material vehicle. "He who wants to separate the *Primum Ens* from its *Corpus* (vehicle) must have a great deal of experience in the spagyric art. If he is not a good alchemist his labour will be in vain." (*De Separat. Per.*)

"The *Primum Ens Melissae* is prepared in the following manner:—Take half a pound of pure carbonate of potash and expose it to the air until it is dissolved (by attracting water from the atmosphere). Filter the fluid, and put as many fresh leaves of the plant melissa into it as it will hold, so that the fluid will cover the leaves. Let it stand in a well-closed glass, and in a moderately warm place, for twenty-four hours. The fluid may then be removed from the leaves, and the latter thrown away. On the top of this fluid absolute alcohol is poured, so that it will cover the former to the height of one or two inches, and it is left to remain for one or two days, or until the alcohol becomes of an intensely green colour. This alcohol is then to be taken away and preserved, and fresh alcohol is put upon the alkaline fluid, and the operation is repeated until all the colouring matter is absorbed by the alcohol. This alcoholic fluid is now to be distilled, and the alcohol evaporated until it becomes of the thickness of a syrup, which is the Primum Ens Melissae; but the alcohol that has been distilled away and the liquid potash may be used again. The liquid potash must be of great concentration and the alcohol of great strength, else they would become mixed, and the experiment would not succeed."[23]

Primum Ens Sanguinis

To make the *Primum Ens Sanguinis* take blood from the median vein of a healthy young person, and let it run into a warm bottle that has been weighed upon scales, so that the exact quantity of the blood used will be known. Add to this blood twice its quantity of alcahest, close the bottle, and permit it to remain in a moderately warm place for about fourteen days, after which the red fluid is to be separated from the sediment, filtered, and preserved. This is the *Primum Ens Sanguinis*, and it is used in the same manner as the *Primum Ens Melissae*.

The Alcahest

The celebrated Alcahest is an universal medicine whose preparation was also known to Helmont and to some Rosicrucians. It was considered by them as one of the greatest mysteries. It is prepared as follows:

"Take freshly prepared caustic lime, if possible still warm; powder it quickly in a dry place, and put it into a retort. Add as much absolute alcohol as the powder will absorb, and distil the alcohol at a moderate heat, until the powder in the retort is left perfectly dry. The distilled alcohol is now to be poured again upon the lime, and distilled, and this operation repeated ten times. Mix the powder with the fifth part of its own weight of pure carbonate of potash. This must be done very quickly and in a dry atmosphere, so that it will not attract any moisture. Insert the mixture of the two powders into a retort and heat it gradually, after putting about two ounces of absolute alcohol into the recipient. White vapours arise from the powder, and are attracted by the alcohol, and the heating is to be continued as long as this takes place. Pour the alcohol from the recipient into a dish, and set it on fire. The alcohol burns away, and the alcahest remains in the dish. It is an excellent medicine, and is used in the same manner as the *Primum Ens Melissae*.[24] On account of the great powers contained in the limestone, Paracelsus says that "many a man kicks away with his foot a stone that would be more valuable to him than his best cow, if he only knew what great mysteries were put into it by God by means of the spirit of Nature."[25]

Zenexton

One of the greatest sympathetic remedies of Paracelsus, for the possession of which he was envied a great deal, and the preparation of which he kept very secret, was his Zenexton. His disciple, Oswald Sroll, in his "Basilica Chemica," pp. 210-213, describes its preparation as follows:

"Make an instrument of good steel, by which you may cut some small tablets of the size of a penny, and whose composition will be given below. The instrument consists of two discs, which can be connected together by a middle piece in the shape of a ring, forming a hollow space between the two discs, and the latter are provided with handles. Upon the inner side of one disc is engraved a snake, and the inner side of the other represents a scorpion, so that the substance which is to be put into the hollow space between the two discs will receive the impression of the snake on one side and of the scorpion on the other. The instrument is to be made at a time when sun and moon are together in the sign of Scorpion.[26] By this process the upper bodies will be joined to the lower ones in an inseparable sympathetic union."

"The substance of which the tablets are made is prepared as follows:—Take about eighteen live toads, dry them by exposing them to the sun and the air, and powder them. They must be dried very quickly, else they will rot. Take a number of menstrual cloths from young girls; white arsenic, auro-pigment, half an ounce of each; roots of *Diptamus albus* and *Tormentilla erecta*, of each three drachms; one drachm of small pearls; red corals, pieces of hyacinths and smaragds, half a drachm of each; oriental saffron, forty grains; and a few grains of musk and amber. Powder all fine, mix it all together, and make a paste out of it with rosewater and gum-tragacanth. Make a paste out of it at the time when the moon is in the sign of Scorpion, cut into tablets, and seal them with the instrument. Dry the tablets, cover them with red silk, and wear them by a string around your neck, but they ought not to touch the bare skin. Such an amulet protects the wearer against the plague, sorcery, poison, and evil astral influences; it draws poisons out of the body, and absorbs them entirely."

Notes

Chapter 1

1. At present a place of pilgrimage.
2. Van Helmont, "Tartari Historia."
3. Conrad Gesner, "Epist. Medic." lib. i fol. I.
4. Urtstisitis, "Baseler Chronik.," bk. vii. chap. xix, p. 1527.
5. "Libr. Paragranum," Preface.
6. "Libr. Paramirum," Preface.
7. Appropriate terms for the subjects referred to are only found in Eastern languages, especially in Sanskrit.

Chapter 2

1. It is an element in the life of the "great snake" Vasuki, that according to Hindu mythology encircles the world, and by whose movements earthquakes may be produced.—H.P.B.
2. They are the Devas of fire in India, and bulls were sometimes sacrificed to them.—H.P.B.
3. For instance, each metal has its elementary matrix in which it grows. Mines of gold, silver, etc., become exhausted, and after centuries (or millenniums) they may be found to yield again a rich supply; in the same way the soil of a country, having become infertile from exhaustion, will after a time of rest become fertile again. In both cases a decomposition and a development of lower elements into higher ones takes place.
4. This division takes place in consequence of the opposite attraction of matter and spirit. After it is accomplished, the astral body will be dissolved into its elements, and the spirit enter into the spiritual state. See A.P. Sinnett, *Esoteric Buddhism*.
5. See "Magic, White and Black; or, The Science of Finite and Infinite Life", by Dr. F. Hartmann.
6. A case is cited in which a plastic operation was performed on a man's nose by transplanting on it a piece of skin taken from another person. The artificial nose answered its purpose for a long time, until the person from whom the piece of skin was taken died, when the nose is said to have rotted. Cases are also known in which persons have felt a pain caused by the pressure of a stone upon a recently amputated leg that, without their knowledge, had been buried, and the pain instantly ceased when the stone was removed. This sympathy existing between man's consciousness and his body is the cause that the astral form of a dead person may keenly feel any injury inflicted upon his corpse. The "spirit" of a suicide may feel the effects of a *post-mortem* examination as severely as if he had been cut up while alive.
7. Ruland says about them: "Umbratilia transmutata sunt in hominem conspectum ab astris et suis ascendibus occultis oblata, quae non sicus lemures apparent oculis, idque per magiam efficaciam."—Lexic. Alchemic., Alchemic., p. 466.
8. Well-authenticated cases of vampires may be found in Maximilian Perty's works and in H. P. Blavatsky's "Isis Unveiled."
9. They assist "physical mediums" to lift material objects without any visible means.

Chapter 3

1. From ὑλη, forest, and *astra*, stars or worlds.
2. The λογος.

3. By the breath (out-breathing) of Brahma.

4. This means that Life is the cause of matter and force. Force and matter are originally identical; they are only two different modes of one and the same cause or substance which is called Life, and which is itself an attribute or function of the supreme cause of all existence. Modern discoveries go to prove the unity or identity of matter and energy. Recent researches in chemistry, and comparisons made between the chemical, musical, and colour scales seem to indicate that the cause of the difference between the heterogeneous single bodies is not caused by an essential difference of the substances of which they are composed, but only a difference in the number of their atomic vibrations.

5. "Mysterium" is everything out of which something may be developed, which is only germinally contained in it. A seed is the "mysterium" of a plant, an egg the mysterium of a living bird, etc. If Eastern mythology says that the universe came out of an egg put into the water by Brahma (Neuter) or Ideation, it implies the same meaning as the Mysterium magnum of Paracelsus; because the egg represents the mysterium, the water the life, and the spirit hatches out of it the Creative God, Brahma (Masculine).

6. It seems that Paracelsus anticipated the modern discovery of the "potency of matter" three hundred years ago.

7. The Yliaster of Paracelsus corresponds to the Ev of Pythagoras and Empedocles, and it was Aristotle who spoke first of the form *in potentia* before it could appear *in actu*—the former being called by him "the privation of matter." (Note by H. P. Blavatsky.)

8. This doctrine, preached 300 years ago, is identical with the one that has revolutionised modern thought after having been put into a new shape and elaborated by Darwin; and is still more elaborated by the Indian Kapila, in the Sankhya philosophy. (Note by H. P. Blavatsky.)

9. Everything, whether it may manifest itself as matter or as force, is essentially a trinity.

10. This description of the sympathy existing between Man and Eternal Nature recalls to memory the old ἔντοπαν and the συμπνοια μια, συρρια μια, συμπαδεια παντα of Hippocrates, and it especially reminds us of the "Timaeus" of Plato and the "Emerides" of Plotin, in which works the whole of Nature is represented as a living and rational being (ζῶον), having come into existence by the will of the Supreme Cause. The head of man is there pictured as being an imitation of the peripheric constitution of the world. The basis of the natural philosophy of Paracelsus is the evidently existing correspondence, correlation, and harmony between the human constitution and the constitution of the starry world, including all terrestrial things, and this philosophy is almost identical with that of Plato, which speaks of the formation of all things in the inner world according to eternal patterns existing in the realm of the pure Ideal.]

11. For instance, fishes in the water, blood-corpuscles in the blood, animalcule in putrid fluids, bacteria in impure air, etc. etc.

12. Each Elemental may know the mysteries of that element to which it belongs.

13. The *Astral body* (Linga-sharira) of minerals, plants, and animals.

14. Astral protoplasm.

15. Perhaps this may serve as a clue to explain the action of homoeopathic medicines.

16. See Appendix: "Palangenesis of Plants."

17. Thus a man in whom Supreme Wisdom or God has become fully manifest is a god to the extent of his wisdom, and the power which he can exercise will extend as far as the power manifested through him will reach. A man will become an incarnation of good or evil according to the degree in which the good or evil existing in the Universe becomes manifested through him. But as no one can become a Christ by merely speculating upon the doctrines of Christ without practicing them, so nobody can come into possession of practical knowledge by merely accepting a creed or a belief in the scientific opinions of others without any experience of his own.

18. One mind.

19. "Liber Paramirum," cap. 2. This is the fundamental doctrine of the teachings of Paracelsus.

The Macrocosm and the Microcosm may not only be "compared together," but they are one in reality, divided only by form, which is an essentially Vedantic doctrine.

20. This fundamental truth of occultism is allegorically represented in the interlaced double triangles. He who has succeeded in bringing his individual mind in exact harmony with the Universal Mind has succeeded in reuniting the inner sphere with the outer one, from which he has only become separated by mistaking illusions for truths. He who has succeeded in carrying out practically the meaning of this symbol has become one with the father; he is virtually an adept, because he has succeeded in squaring the circle and circling the square. All of this proves that Paracelsus has brought the root of his occult ideas from the East.

21. If the individual mind is one with the Universal Mind, and if the possessor of the individual mind wishes to find out some secret of Nature, he does not require to seek for it outside of the sphere of his mind, but he looks for it in himself, because everything that exists in Nature (which is a manifestation of the Universal Mind) exists in and is reflected by himself, and the idea of there being two minds is only an illusion; the two are one.

22. It would be difficult to find many practitioners of medicine possessed of genuine powers of true spiritual perception; but it is a universally recognized fact that a physician without intuition (common sense) will not be very successful, even if he knew all medical books by heart. We should be guided by wisdom but not by opinions. The opinions of others may serve us, but we should not be subservient to them.

23. Von Eckartshausen describes this inner sense as follows: "It is the centre of all senses, or the inner faculty of man, whereby he is able to feel the impressions produced by the exterior senses. It is the formative imagination of man, whereby the various impressions that have been received through the outer senses are identified, and brought into the inner field of consciousness. It is the faculty through which the spirit interprets the language of Nature to the soul. It changes bodily sensations into spiritual perceptions, and passing impressions into lasting images. All the senses of man originate in one sense, which is sensation."

24. In Babbitt's "Principles of Light and Colour," it is demonstrated that each ray of colour has a certain therapeutic influence on the human system; Blue acting soothingly on the circulation of the blood; Red stimulating; Yellow acting as a purgative, etc. He gives some interesting examples of correspondences between the colours and medicinal qualities of certain flowers, plants, drugs, etc., with the action of the above-named colour-rays.

25. Eckartshausen has made such a herbarium: he gives the names of medical plants and the names of the planets with which they are sympathetically connected.

26. Dr. J. R. Buchanan, in his "Therapeutic Sarcognomy," makes practical use of this sympathetic relationship existing between the various parts of the human body.

27. Thus Paracelsus employed not only the vital magnetism (mesmerism) of human beings, but also that of animals and plants, for the cure of disease.

28. "The Spirit of God moved upon the face of the waters." (Gen. i. 2)

29. The true doctrine has also been taught by Jacob Boehme, an uneducated shoemaker but illuminated seer, from whom all of our great philosophers have borrowed ideas. He says: "The constellation is the outspoken Word. It is the instrument through which the holy, eternally speaking Word speaks and produces objective forms. It is like a great harmony of many voices and musical instruments. They are interacting powers, wherein the essence of sound (Akasha) is the substance, and this is taken up by the Fiat and causes corporeity. This substance is the astral spirit. In it the elements become coagulated (corporified), and thus forms are born, comparable to the hatching of an egg brooded over by a hen." (*Myster. Magn.*, xi. 26)

30. "Heaven"—the interior kingdom, the mind.

Chapter 4

1. It is taught that primordial man also had within himself the power to propagate his own species, while he was in an ethereal state; but when he became more material the female element became partly separated from him and woman came into existence.

2. This Spirit is the same spiritual ray that has overshadowed man in his previous incarnation and afterwards become withdrawn into the divine essence, from which it issues again. It is, therefore, not a new Spirit, but the same that incarnated before.

3. This is not to be understood as if some astral form in the human shape were waiting to crawl into the body of the child, but that the spiritual element gradually develops and becomes active in the child, in proportion as the human instrument through which it desires to act enables it to manifest that activity. An incarnation generally becomes complete only when the child has attained its seventh year.

4. There is a difference between individuality and personality; personality being a changeable mask which the individual ray produces.

5. This is not to be understood as if the astral influences were creating the divine soul of man. Man's spirit is from God; his astral qualities are developed by the astral influences, and his elementary (physical) body grows out of the elements by which it is surrounded.

6. Those anatomists, physiologists, and other scientists who claim to know all about the constitution of man, because they have studied the organisation, of his physical body, and deny the existence of a soul and spirit, know only a part and in fact the most unimportant part of the constitution of man.

7. This doctrine of Paracelsus is identical with the one taught by the ancient Brahmins and Yogis of the East; but it may not necessarily be derived from the latter, for an eternal truth may as well be recognised by one seer as by another, in the East as well as in the West, and two or more spiritually enlightened persons may perceive the same truth independently of each other, and describe it each one in his own manner. The terms Microcosm and Macrocosm are identical in their meaning with the Microprosopos and Macroprosopos, or the "Short-face" and "Long-face," of the Kabala. (Note made by H. P. Blavatsky.)

8. This "end of the world," *i.e.*, of external bisexual generation, will be when man has again found the woman within himself from whom he has become separated by his descending from his spiritual state and becoming gross and material. "The Lord is not without the woman;" that means to say that the paradisaical Man (the Karana sharira) is still male and female in one; but man, having ceased to be "the Lord," and become a servant to the animal kingdom in him, has ceased to recognise the true woman in him, his heavenly bride, and seeks for the woman in that which is external to him. Therefore man cannot enter into his original state of unity and purity except by means of the celestial marriage (within his soul) such as takes place during the process of spiritual regeneration. (See Jacob Boehme.)

9. What else can this "Ens proprietatis" mean but the human monad reincarnating itself, and being in possession of all the tastes, inclinations, talents, and temperament acquired during its former existences as an individual being?

10. Aboriginal spiritual Man (male and female in one) has been created by the will of God being active within divine wisdom; but the woman was made out of a "rib" (a power) of man. Therefore man and woman are not equals, except as far as their animal constitution goes: "The matrix from which man originated was the whole world (the limbus); but woman came out of the matrix of man. Thus man made unto himself a matrix, the woman, who is now to him as much as a whole world, and the spirit of the Lord is within her, informing and fructifying her. No one has seen it; but nevertheless it is in the matrix of woman. Therefore they ought not be used for whoredom; for the spirit is in them, coming from the Lord and returning to Him." (*Paramirum*, iv.)

11. That which Paracelsus calls the semen, or seed of man, is not that which is known as semen to

modern physiologists, but a semi-spiritual principle to which the sperma merely serves as a vehicle and instrument for propagation; or, to express it in other words, the fructifying principle does not exist in the sperma, but in the spirit (the will and imagination) of man, or what is also called "the tincture." The sperma merely serves as a vehicle, in the same sense as the body of a man is a vehicle for the manifestation of his interior spirit. (See De Gener. Hom.)

12. The universal matrix, into which the spiritual monad, having passed through the *Devachanic* state, finally enters, and from which it is again attracted into new incarnations.

13. Thus the *matrix* attracts the seed of both persons, mixed with the sperm; and afterwards it expels the sperm, but retains the seed. Thus the seed comes into the matrix." *(Gebaerung)*

"*The matrix*," however, does not mean merely the womb of a woman; the whole body of the woman is a mother, a "*matrix*." *(De Morbor. Matric.)*

14. It might be objected, that if this were true, a man having lost a leg could beget only one-legged children; but such a superficial reasoning would be caused by a misunderstanding of the true nature of man. The invisible man is the essential man, the physical body only the outward expression. If the physical body loses a limb, it does not follow that the soul-body loses it likewise; but if there is a congenital malformation, such as supernumerary fingers or toes, they may be reproduced in the child; because nature has a tendency to acquire habits and to repeat them.

15. This creative and formative power of the imagination may be used to advantage for the purpose of producing male or female offspring at will, as has also been proved by experiments made in cattle-breeding. If the desire or passion, and consequently the imagination, of the female is stronger than that of the male during coition, male children will be produced. If on such an occasion the imagination of the male is stronger than that of the female, the child will be of the female sex. If the imagination of both parties is equally strong, a "hermaphrodite" may possibly be the result.

16. It will perhaps be difficult to state an example to prove this assertion; neither has it been disproved.

17. The effects of the mother's imagination on the development of the foetus are well known to the people. Hare-lip, acephali, moles, etc., may be caused by the effects of a morbid imagination.

18. If a child, as is often the case, manifests the same tastes, talents, and inclinations as those of his father or as other members of the same family, it does by no means necessarily follow that these tastes, etc., have been inherited by it from his parents, and the contrary often takes place. A similarity of tastes, etc., between the child and his parents would rather go to show that the monad, having developed its tendencies in a previous incarnation, was attracted to a particular family on account of an already existing similarity of his own tastes with those of its future parents.

19. Numerous cases are known in which persons of great learning have become simpletons in their old age; others, where such persons, in consequence of a short sickness, lost all their memory, and had to learn to read again, beginning with the A B C.

20. "As there is a love between animals so that they long to dwell and cohabit together as males and females, so there is such an animal love among men and women, which they have inherited from the animals. It is a deadly love, which cannot be carried higher, and belongs merely to the animal nature of man. It springs from animal reason, and as animals love and hate each other, so does animal man. Dogs envy and bite each other, and in so far as men envy and fight each other they are the descendants of dogs. Thus one man is a fox, another a wolf, another a bear, etc. Each one has certain animal elements in him; and if he allows them to grow in him, and identifies himself with them, he is then fully that with which he is identified." *(De Fundamento Sapientiae)*

21. This goes to account for cases of vampirism, when the elementary of a dead person is still attracted to the object of its affections and obsesses him or her. (Incubi and Succubi: "Spirit-husbands and "Spirit-brides")

22. It is not the flesh and bones of a man which form attachments and make and break promises, but the internal, carnally minded man; and this man will be bound by his attachments and

promises long after the house in which he has lived (his body) will have ceased to exist. In regard to this subject, Paracelsus regards it as dangerous to give further details.

23. See A. P. Sinnett's "Esoteric Buddhism."

24. Speaking of the day of the resurrection, Paracelsus refers to a great mystery, alluded to in St. John's Revelation, and more plainly spoken of by the Eastern Adepts, when at the end of the Seventh Round all the higher recollections of the various personalities with which the spiritual monad has been connected during its many objective existences, and which have not become exhausted in Kama-loca, but have been preserved in the Astral Light, will re-enter the field of consciousness of the spiritual (divine) man.

25. It ought to be kept in mind that whenever Paracelsus speaks of the terrestrial or "earthly" man, he does not refer to the elementary (physical) body, but to the carnal part of the mind (the lower manas). Therefore, he says, "the body thinks, but the spirit wills." The elementary body does not think; it is merely a corpse, without the "inner man", and the shadow of the latter. It is as such of so little importance that it may not be at all missed, if we leave it either during a trance or after its death.

26. If clairvoyance were at present a normal faculty of mankind, and if men could see the astral forms of the dead hovering over the graves and decomposing in the air, graveyards would soon be abolished, and cremation take the place of burial.

27. Thus there seems to be a scientific reason for offering sacrifices upon the graves of the dead, as is the custom in China.

28. The last thoughts and desires of a dying person, and their intensity, will, to a great extent, determine the locality to which such a sidereal body may be attracted. Some places have been known to be haunted for a great number of years.

29. It appears from this sentence that the phenomena of "Modern Spiritualism" are not a new revelation, but were known and explained three hundred years ago. "Oh, the soul of poor Galen! If he had remained faithful to truth, his Manes would not now be buried in the abyss of hell, from whence he wrote me a letter. Such is the fate of all quacks!" (*Paragranum*, Preface)

30. This sentence may seem to throw discredit upon the practices of modern spiritualists, but not all the practices of spiritualists consist in dealing with the sidereal bodies of the dead. Such practices do not deserve the name Spiritualism, but ought to be looked upon as Spiritism, and when the laws upon which our modern Spiritualism and Spiritism are based are known, it will be easy enough to make a distinction. Spiritualism means a dealing with spiritual intelligences; Spiritism, a dealing with unintelligent or semi-intelligent invisible forms. A spiritualist enters into the sphere of a spirit; that is to say, he enters *en rapport* with a certain mind, and writes or speaks in the spirit of the latter, making himself a medium through which the intelligence of the latter can act, and by which means he may obtain great truths. The spiritist permits an invisible entity to enter bodily into his own physical form and submits his body to the will of the invisible stranger.

31. The fact that such material objects are occasionally brought by invisible powers is known to all who have examined the phenomena of Modern Spiritism; but no scientific researcher will ever discover how this is done as long as he does not believe in the existence of Elementals, in regard to which little is publicly known.

32. According to the teachings of the Eastern Adepts, each of the seven principles of man may again be subdivided into seven, and each soul has therefore a sevenfold constitution. In other words, each of the seven qualities contains also the other six. (See Jacob Boehme.)

33. So-called *Astral Bells*, known to all practical occultists.

34. The Evestrum appears to be identical with the Linga shariram, or Astral body of the Eastern occultists. The Trarames is the power which acts on the open sense of hearing of the astral man.

35. They have often been seen and described as the spirits of the dead by mediums and clairvoyants. The "Evestra" are merely states of mind, or thoughts, having become endowed with a certain amount of will, so as to render them more or less self-conscious, and, as it were,

independent of the person from whom they originate, as is shown in cases where a man would be glad to get rid of some idea by which he is possessed, but cannot drive it away from his mind. Such thoughts will remain impressed on the astral light of a room which that person inhabited, and such an image may even become visible and objective. A case is known where a man became insane and was sent to an insane asylum, where he was kept for over a year. He suddenly became well and went home; but afterward he heard that his "ghost" was still haunting the cell which he had occupied in the asylum, and that it was there living, overthrowing the furniture, etc. He became curious to see his own "ghost," and in spite of all the warnings of his friends, he went back to that cell, saw his "ghost," and was again observed by it, so that he died insane.

36. The Soul of the Universe. According to Jacob Boehme, it is the awakened life of the inner world, perturbing Nature.

37. Direct emanations of the Universal Mind; Thought bodies.

38. The transcendental bodies of the Dhyan-Chohans collectively.

39. See Professor Denton's "The Soul of Things." Every atom and molecule, every ephemeron, must have its Evestrum, whether the compounds are regarded as organic or inorganic.

40. The Astral Plane.

41. The sphere of the Universal Mind.

42. The writings of Paracelsus, such as have been preserved, in regard to the description of the Astral world, are exceedingly mixed up, and written in a style which renders their meaning almost incomprehensible.

43. This means that it is not advisable to try to develop astral sight or to deal with the inhabitants of the astral plane as long as we have not the power to rise above that plane. When our true spiritual powers become active in us, we shall also be able to see all that is below that state of existence, and incur no danger from it.

44. Those are in error who claim that there is nothing supernatural; for although all things exist in Nature, Nature itself is not God. God is not outside, but above and beyond Nature; not in regard to locality, but in regard to His superiority.

45. The thoughts of great minds remain for ages like stars on the mental horizon of the world.

46. "The spirit educates the body (the internal the external man), and may seduce it to commit sins, for which the body has to suffer; but the body can neither instruct nor seduce the spirit. The body eats and drinks, but the nourishment of the spirit is faith. The body perishes, the spirit is eternal. The body is subdued by the spirit, but not the spirit by the body. The body is dark, the spirit light and transparent. The body is subject to disease; the spirit remains well. Material things are dark to the body, but the spirit sees through everything. The body (mind) speculates; the spirit (the will) acts. The body is Mumia, the spirit is *balsam*. The body belongs to death, the spirit to life. The body is of the earth; the spirit from heaven and God." (*Phil. Tract.*, iv.)

47. The seventh principle.

48. Premature deaths from crime, suicide, and accidents cause their victims to become earthbound spirits, until the time of their natural dissolution arrives.

49. See F. Hartmann, "Premature Burial," London, 1896.

50. Spirit-communications from suicides go to confirm this fact.

51. The vehicle of life (the astral body).

52. The Eastern esoteric doctrine teaches the same: The astral form, or *Caballi*, of suicides, or of one who died an unnatural premature death, cannot immediately be dissolved, but will linger and wander in the earth's atmosphere (Kama-loca) for the period that was allotted to its body's life by natural law. The astral bodies (spirits, so called) of suicides are those who appear nine times out of ten in spiritual seances, when they will assume any celebrated name, or even the appearance of certain well-known persons, whose images are well impressed in the aura around those present. They are the most dangerous of all the Elementaries. See "Key to Theosophy."

53. Jacob Boehme says: "Death is a breaking up of the three kingdoms in man. It is the only

means by which the spirit is enabled to enter into another state and to become manifest in another form. When the spirit dies relatively to its selfhood (personality) and its self-will becomes broken in death, then out of that death grows another will, not according to that temporal will, but according to the eternal will." (Signal, xvi. 51)

Chapter 5

1. Boehme says: "When the soul has passed through death, it is then in the essence of God. It remains with the works which it has produced here, and in this state it will behold the majesty of God and see the angels face to face. In the unfathomable world where the soul is, there is no end or object which that soul would have to attain. Where the carrion is, there will the eagles assemble." (All that the soul desires will come to it.)—Forty Questions, xxi. 3.

2. Boehme says: "The majority of souls depart from their terrestrial forms without the body of Christ (divine love), but being connected therewith only by a small thread." Such souls, having but little spirituality, will not exist in such glorious bliss as those whose spirituality has been unfolded upon the earth and who loved God above all.

3. Sensation is an attribute of life. If life resides in the astral body, the astral body will have sensation, and as long as that body is connected sympathetically with the dead physical body, it may even feel any injury inflicted upon the latter. The physical body, if it is inanimate, has no sensation; the latter belongs to the inner man. Wherever the centre of consciousness is established, there is sensation.

4. Books might be filled with reliable accounts of obsessions, of haunted houses, and instances in which such ghosts have been seen are exceedingly numerous. Some persons, that may not be able to see them, may feel them instinctively, or even physically, like a cold wind, or like a current of electricity passing through the body (see "Borderland").

5. Chinese and Hindus have been known to kill themselves for the purpose of revenge, so that their soul may cling to their enemies and trouble their minds or drive them to suicide. It is also well proven that wars are often followed by numerous suicides occurring in the victorious army.

6. Such a case of vampirism is personally known to me. A young man killed himself on account of his passion for a married lady. The latter loved him, but did not encourage his advances on account of her matrimonial obligations. After his death his astral form became attracted to her, and as she was of a mediumistic temperament, he found the necessary conditions to become partly materialised and trouble her every night. It required a long-continued effort until she finally became rid of the Incubus. If our practitioners of medicine were better acquainted with occult laws, many "mysterious" cases that come under their observation might become clear to them, and they would obtain a deeper insight into some causes of mania, hysteria, hallucination, etc.

7. Fragment, "De Animabus Mortuorum." A great part of this fragment has been lost. All such spirits are the products of imagination and will. If a person has an evil imagination he creates a corresponding form in his mind, and if he infuses that form with his will he has then created a "spirit," which will attract similar influences.

8. Paracelsus recommends the wearing of red corals as a remedy against melancholy. They are said to be ruled by the influence of the sun, while those of brown colour are under the influence of the moon. The red ones are disagreeable not only to Phantasmata, but also to Monsters, Incubi, Succubi, and other evil spirits; but the brown corals are agreeable to and attract them. I know of some cases of melancholy, depression of mind, hypochondria, etc., that have been successfully treated by the wearing of red corals, while other articles employed for the same purpose had no effect, and the cure could therefore not be attributed merely to the belief of the patient The ignorant will find it easier to ridicule such things than to explain them.

9. The word "imagination" ought not to be mistaken for empty fancy; it means the power of the

mind to form into a substantial image the influences which are actually present.

10. It is here not the question of merely visible and tangible things, but of the products of the mind, which are also substantial, and which may become visible and tangible under certain conditions. "The invisible body as well as the terrestrial body act each in its own way. That which the visible body performs is done with its hands; the inner man works by means of his imagination and will. The works of the former appear to us real; those of the latter like shadows." (*Morb. Invisib.*, iii.)

11. Mediaeval occult literature and that of Modern Spiritualism contain many examples of Incubi and Succubi, some having appeared visibly and tangibly; others, though unseen, were touched and felt. Such cases are at the present day much more numerous than is commonly believed, but they can only "materialise" if the necessary conditions are given. They are therefore only felt during a state of sickness, and after the recovery of the patient they disappear, because they cannot draw the elements necessary for materialisation out of a healthy constitution. Such Incubi and Succubi are the products of a physically and morally diseased state. The morbid imagination creates an image, the will of the person objectifies it, and the nerve aura can render it substantial to sight and touch. Moreover, having once been created, they attract to themselves corresponding influences from the astral soul of the world.

12. Animal instincts cannot be suppressed, and the "flesh" cannot be "mortified," except by awakening a higher psychical activity in the place of the lower ones, or by an exaltation of the spiritual nature over the animal principle in man. Abstinence in acts is useless for spiritual development, unless it is followed by abstinence in thought. Enforced celibacy does not make a priest; a true priest is a saint, and saints are persons who have outgrown their carnal desires.

13. This is the kind of "spirit" created by the followers of P. B. Randolph, according to the instructions given in his book called "Eulis."

14. They cannot, however, become visible, unless they can draw some of the astral essence from the person or persons in whose presence they desire to appear; in other words, persons must be mediumistic to produce such manifestations of form.

15. John Scheffler says: "If you could see the horrible monsters by which you are surrounded you would be sick from disgust."

16. Paracelsus gives here a very good description of some of the modern spirit-materialisation. The "airy appendix" (astral form) usually comes out of the left side of the medium, in the region of the spleen. Mediums need not necessarily be depraved persons, but there must be some fault in their organisation, else the combination of their principles would be too strong to part with some of their astral substance. Materialising mediums may be very good people, but solitary lives and vicious habits lead to the development of such mediumship, which proves to be very injurious in the end.

17. By "praying" is meant the exercise of the spiritual will. "Oh, you stupid and foolish priest, who know absolutely nothing; because you imagine to be able to drive away evil spirits with sweet-smelling incense, such as is enjoyed by good and evil spirits alike. If instead of your incense you were to take asafoetida, then might you succeed in driving away the evil spirits and the good ones besides." (*Philos. Occulta*)

18. It often happens that bodily diseases are the cause of morbid desires. A disease of the skin (pruritus vaginae or scroti) causes erotic desires; a displacement of the womb, an erosion, ulcer, or inflammation of the os uteri, cause mental depression and hysteria; piles cause melancholy, etc., etc.; but all such causes are, in their turn, the effects of previous causes having a psychical origin, and they establish the conditions by which elementary influences act.

19. Experiments that have been made in London, with the inhalation of various ethers, chloroform, nitrous oxide gas, and hydrocarbonates, have had the effect of producing such "hallucinations." Before these gases were known, fumigations of poisonous substances were used for such purposes. The receipts for the materials used for such fumigations were kept very secret, on account of the abuse that might have been made of such a knowledge, and in consequence of which

a person may be even made insane. One of the most effective fumigations for the purpose of causing apparitions were, according to Eckartshausen, made of the following substances: Hemlock, Henbane, Saffron, Aloe, Opium, Mandrake, Solanum, Poppy-seed, Asafoetida, and Parsley. The fumigations to drive away evil spirits were made of Sulphur, Asafoetida, Castoreum, and more especially of Hypericum and Vinegar. Carbolic Acid was not known at that time.

20. This is confirmed by Swedenborg in his description of "Hell," and also by Jacob Boehme. The animal soul of the departed takes the form and shape of that animal whose character predominated in his constitution.

21. There is a never-ending chain of births and transformations taking place in the world of causes (spirits), as in the world of effects (forms). The lives of some such entities extend over enormous periods of time; others have only a short individual existence. According to the Brahminical teachings there are seven main classes of spirits, some of them having innumerable subdivisions: 1. Arupa Devas (formless spirits), planetary spirits—the intelligent sixth principle of the planet whose product they are. 2. Rupa Devas (having forms). High planetary spirits. Dhyan-Chohans. 3. Pisachas and Mohinis—male and female Elementaries consisting of the astral forms of the dead, that may be obsessed by Elementals, and cause Incubi and Succubi. 4. Mara rupas: forms of desire or passion. Souls doomed to destruction. 5. Asuras: Elementals (Gnomes, Sylphs, Undines, Salamanders, etc.). They will develop into human beings in the next Manvantara (cycle of evolution). 6. Beasts. Elementals having animal forms, monstrosities. 7. Rakshasas or demons. Souls of sorcerers and of men with great intelligence, but with evil tendencies. Criminals for the advancement of science, dogmatists, sophists, vivisectionists, etc., furnish material for the development of such "devils." The Asuras are often called Devas, and are worshipped in many places of India. They are the guardian spirits of certain places, gardens, houses, etc., and have temples of their own. There are many thousand varieties. (See *Isis Unveiled*.")

22. They are evidently a different class of "familiar spirits" than the "invisible guides" mentioned above. The spirit which each child receives at its birth, and who attends to the person during his terrestrial life, is his own spiritual self, the "Karana sharira."

23. Nectromancy is not to be confounded with Necromancy. See chapter 2.

24. The Count Saint Germain could read sealed letters, and the same was repeatedly done by H. P. Blavatsky in the presence of the author.

25. The whole of the universe is an expression of consciousness, and there are, therefore, innumerable states of conscious and intelligent will in the world; some in visible and others in invisible form; some shapeless, like currents of air; others undefined, like mists or clouds; others solid, as rocks; some impermanent; others permanent, like the stars.

26. The rationale on which divination, geomancy, the practice of the divining-rod, etc., is based, is that by means of such practices a knowledge in regard to certain things, such as already exists in the spirit of man, may come to the understanding of the intellect of his own personality. The inner man cannot, under all circumstances, communicate his knowledge to the external man, because the consciousness of the two is not identical; but the spirit may influence the nerve aura of the person and control the muscles of his body, and thus guide his hands.

27. Those who have some experience in modern spiritualism will recognize the truth of this description. Spiritualists should not act upon the advices of spirits, if such advices are against their own reason, and scientists should not rely on the opinions of others, if such opinions are against common sense.

28. Man in his aspect as a terrestrial being, and if we leave the divine principle out of our consideration, is himself an elemental spirit of Nature, composed of all the four elements; but as he lives and breathes in the air, he may be called an elemental of the air walking upon the earth.

29. There is nothing very strange in the belief that such "spirits" exist, if we only keep in mind that the best part of ourselves is an invisible spirit of unknown dimensions, occupying and overshadowing a limited material form.

30. The "soul" of the elements; i.e., their ethereal aspects.

31. It is not credible that a person has entered with his physical body into the Venus mountain or Untersberg, or any other such renowned places of which popular tradition speaks. Neither have the witches and sorcerers of the Middle Ages been at the witch-sabbath in their physical bodies, and it seems equally improbable that a person should ever have entered physically the abodes of disembodied adepts. But the physical body of a man is not the man; it is only his external shadow, and wherever man's consciousness is, there will he be present himself. But while he is there, he does not miss his exterior body, of which he has no more use than of a part of his clothing purposely laid away, and on reawakening to physical consciousness he may well believe that he had been to such a place in his physical form.

32. "If anyone marries a water-nymph, and she deserts him, he ought not to take another wife, for the marriage has not been dissolved. If he marries another woman he will shortly die." (*De Nymph.*)

33. Italicore Catacca (Mermaid).

34. The "devil" is evil spiritual will. The devil has no power over man; but if man allows a devil within himself to grow, then will the great Devil aid the little devil to grow and nourish him with his own substance. (See "The Doctrines of Jacob Boehme.")

Chapter 6

1. Magic is the knowledge of how to employ spiritual powers; but it is self-evident that nobody can employ any spiritual powers unless he has come into their possession by the awakening of his own spirituality; nor can any one become spiritual by merely imagining himself to be so. It is therefore not surprising that in an age in which the very meaning of the term 'spiritual' became incomprehensible to the learned, the meaning of 'magic' has become also a mystery."

2. The word "supernatural," as employed by Paracelsus, does not imply anything beyond Nature as a whole, because nothing exists beyond the All, but it means that which transcends Nature in her lower aspect, or a higher or spiritual aspect of Nature than the merely mechanical and physiological part of her work. If, for instance, we follow our instincts, we act naturally that is to say, according to the demands of our animal nature; but if we resist natural impulses by the power of will and reason, we employ powers belonging to a higher order of Nature. If we avoid to do evil on account of the evil consequences which it would cause to ourselves, we act naturally; but if we avoid it on account of an inherent love of principle, we act in the wisdom of God.

3. The will is only free when it is free from the delusion of self and its desires.

4. All sciences are false if they are godless; that is, if they seek for the first origin of anything anywhere else but in divine truth.

5. All phenomenal science springs from a knowledge of phenomena, and is therefore only relative and subject to change.

6. During sleep the soul, so to say, separates itself to a certain extent from the body, and lives in its own sphere. If a man does not remember his soul experiences after his body awakens, it is because the union of his personal mind with his spiritual understanding has not yet taken place.

7. There is nothing to prevent any person from seeing by this inner light of Nature, except the errors, prejudices, and misconceptions which are caused by the illusions of the senses, and which are intensified by an education in a system of philosophy which mistakes these errors for fundamental truths. The truth can only be found where it is. A knowledge of the supreme power of the universe cannot be obtained by denying its existence. Life cannot be found in an empty form.

8. Here Paracelsus does not refer merely to the faculty of ordinary clairvoyance, but to the true inner comprehension, to the "spirit of Nature" which reveals all things in its own light. It is, in other words, the Holy Ghost or the true spiritual understanding within the higher region of the mind, above the "constellation."

9. Such modes of divination are well known to modern spiritualists.

10. The astral duplicate of the writing is seen by the astral sense.

11. Man possesses that power from birth, but the majority lose it afterwards by neglecting to use it, and in consequence of concentrating all their attention upon the illusions of the material plane. Moreover, the organs for the finer perceptions become paralysed and atrophied by the use of alcoholic drinks.

12. Dreams or visions of a true spiritual origin make usually a very strong impression, and are then not easily forgotten.

13. Thus, for instance, we may dream of a death and burial, and the cause of that dream may be that one of the animal elementals in our own constitution has died, or, in other words, that we have become free from some degrading idea or element, an event which is surely a cause for joy.

14. All such practices have a certain scientific reason. The experiments of Reichenbach with the magnetic or odic emanations of persons and objects have shown the great effect they have upon sensitive organisms; but to try such experiments upon hardened sceptics and habitual deniers is like testing the powers of a magnet upon a piece of wood.

15. For this reason pregnant women should during the time of their pregnancy have beautiful surroundings and think noble and beautiful thoughts.

16. If we do not think that which we speak, our words will be empty talk. He who thinks many things disperses his power in many directions; he who thinks and wills only one thing is powerful.

17. This passage refers to the excursions of witches on the Hartz Mountains and other places, often spoken of in the witch trials. Many supposed witches were burnt to death for having confessed that they had attended at such meetings.

18. It is well known that the corpses of women having died of puerperal fever are very infectious, and dissecting wounds received in such cases are especially dangerous. The passage implies that the invisible astral substance may draw contagion from the poisonous body, and spread it by the power of an evil will.

19. This means that we should be able to feel the truth with our souls, without reasoning about it from an objective standpoint. We should realise the truth by being one with it, and not examine it as if it were something strange and separate from ourselves.

20. Even physical sight depends on the imagination. If we behold an object, it is not scientific to say, "I see;" but we ought to say, "I imagine to see."

21. This, however, no man can do by exercising his own self-will; but it is accomplished by the divine will in him, into which he must enter himself, it being that of his higher self.

22. The term "spirits" refers here to intelligent souls.

23. It may happen that the spirit of a person will go to a distant place while the body is asleep, and act intelligently there, and that the man, after awakening from his sleep, remembers nothing about it. But an adept, in whom spiritual consciousness is his normal state, can do so knowingly and consciously, and remember all about it after his spirit (Majavi-Rupa) returns to his body.

24. Any one may make successful scientific experiments with thought-transference. Similar scientific experiments for long distances will be more difficult, on account of the differences of time, place, and conditions, and because spiritually enlightened persons, possessing great power of impressing their thoughts at great distances, are at present not easily found.

25. It has been proved by many experiments that a person thrown into a mesmeric sleep by a mesmeriser may be requested to do certain things after he awakens from his sleep, and that after he awakens he will perform such actions, although he will not remember what has taken place during his sleep. It is therefore very fortunate that, in the present state of morality of our modern civilisation, such powers are not generally known, and that they are not often in the possession of those who wish to abuse them.

26. Faith is not based upon any intellectual comprehension, but it is the true spiritual understanding. It is not a belief in some external aid, but the inner consciousness of the possession

of power. If Joshua Davidson broke his leg by jumping from a two-story window for the purpose of proving his faith to himself, it was because he superstitiously believed that some external power would protect him in his fall, and he knew nothing of the power of the god, his own self. His faith was an artificial and not a natural one. He knew nothing about God; that is to say, he had no divine will; he placed his confidence in the say-so of the theologians, but not in his own perception of truth.

27. They are now called "hypnotisers."

28. It may be remarked that the processes given below would not be effective if employed by any one who is not in possession of power to make them effective, and we see, therefore, no cause why they should not be published. Those who possess such evil powers know these things already.

29. If the representatives of modern erudition would take some trouble to inquire in an unsophisticated manner among the country populations of Europe, they would he surprised at the great amount of evil that is still caused by sorcery, either consciously or unconsciously employed. Such things are all caused by natural means, but with whose character our modern sceptics are not acquainted.

30. We would not advise any reader to make any such experiment, because, apart from the immorality of such a practice, it is known to every occultist that if such an evil power is once propelled, and is not of sufficient strength to penetrate the soul-sphere of his object, and to accomplish its purpose, it rebounds with a destructive effect to the source from whence it was projected.

31. The term "miracles" means natural feats produced by spiritual power. If a person acts against his own natural instincts—if he, for instance, performs an act of unselfishness without any hope of reward such an act may be called a supernatural act. The natural law for self is selfishness, and if a man causes his selfish nature to act in a manner that goes against the interests of that nature, he acts in the strength of a power that is beyond his selfish nature and supernatural to it, although that power is not outside of him. Spirit may manifest itself in Nature, but it is not produced by Nature. God is the original cause of all things; Nature is an effect, God is the will; Nature its manifestation.

32. What a great field would be opened to the delight of our "physiological institutes" and vivisectors for the gratification of their morbid scientific curiosity if this art were taught, or if they believed in its possibility! Fortunately the scepticism of the fool is his own best protection against the evils that would arise from premature knowledge, and also the best protection for mankind against the injury he would otherwise inflict. But that such things can be done will be clear to every intelligent student of mediaeval witchcraft, and they are still done this very day, several such cases having recently come within the personal knowledge of the author.

33. Absolute good cannot be evil, but requires the presence of relative evil to become manifest.

34. However much this may be disputed in theory by superficial reasoners, it is nevertheless accepted in practice even by the most sceptical practitioners of medicine. A physician who has no confidence or faith in his own ability will not accomplish much. Moreover, physicians often have each one his own favourite remedy, which will act successfully, if employed by one, and fail in the hands of another, and this can be explained by the fact that one physician has more faith in his own favourite remedy than in that of another.

35. "The whole world is like a man and a woman, and has also its anima and its *spiritus imaginationis*; only much stronger and more powerfully than man." The spirit orders, the will (matter) obeys; thought (imagination) directs, the soul (the body) executes and produces, be it intellectually or without intelligence.

36. The "spirit" of a thing is represented by the sum of its qualities.

37. The odic or "magnetic" body, containing the life-principle.

38. One reason why anyone who desires to develop his spirituality should, if his condition otherwise permits it, adopt a vegetarian diet, is that the flesh of animals exercises a stimulating effect upon the lower and animal instincts, which ought to be overcome instead of being aroused.

The scientific explanation of this action of flesh is, that each material thing is an expression of its soul, and that it contains some of the qualities of that soul or life (Kama), and communicates them to a certain extent to those in whom it is taken up.

39. Those who are to a certain extent acquainted with modern spiritualism will know that usually at the beginning of a strong "physical manifestation" a cold draught of air is felt, and sometimes even a corpse-like odour pervades the air of the room where the seance is held. This is caused by the presence of the astral body of the dead bringing with it the elements if its surroundings, such as are connected with its Mumia, from the grave. If it is the "spirit" of a drowned person, the air in the room will appear to become damp and musty, or perhaps a sprinkling of spray may take place. Moreover, if the "spirit" of a person who was a great drunkard manifests itself, the air may become pervaded with the odour of alcohol.

40. The final fate of sorcerers and black magicians has often been alluded to in writings on occultism. The organisation of spiritual forces which they create, and in which their consciousness and sensation rests, is very strong; but as it does not receive its life from the Supreme Spirit, it is not immortal, and its dissolution will therefore be painful and slow, but certain.

41. *Note.* I have taken especial pains to investigate this subject, and I have come to the conclusion that, if such persons make a bargain with evil spirits, they usually do this effectually, not by any talk or ceremonies, but by entering into a state of harmony of feeling (coming en rapport) with such evil entities, and they may do this unconsciously or unknowingly in their normal state, or it may be that only the sidereal man knows that such a compact exists. Such "sorcerers" are often evil-disposed but ignorant persons, who perhaps do not even know that they possess such powers, and they "bewitch" persons simply by the power of their ill-will, guided by some unseen intelligence, and without being themselves conscious of their success; but in other instances they know it. The fact that such sorceries do occur will not be doubted by any one who has investigated the subject. They occur to a great extent among the country people in Europe, and especially in Roman Catholic countries. In Bavaria and Tyrol the country people are always suspicious of strangers, whom they believe capable of bewitching their cattle. They will not permit such strangers to enter their stables if the latter do not pronounce a blessing on entering it; and if they are afraid of the evil power of some neighbour, they will, under no circumstance, lend any article to him or accept anything from him.

Several cases of "bewitched cattle" and "blue milk" are known to me personally, of which I will mention the following as an example:

At a farm-house not far from Munich the milk became one day "blue"; after having been deposited in the usual place it began to darken, became lightly blue, and that colour after a while deepened into an almost inky darkness, while the layer of cream exhibited zigzag lines, and soon the whole mass began to putrefy and to emit a horrible odour. This occurred again and again every day, and the farmer was in despair. Everything was attempted to find out the cause of the trouble; the stable was thoroughly cleaned, the place where the milk was kept was changed, a different food was given to the cattle, and samples of the milk were sent to Munich to be examined by chemists; the old milk-pots were replaced by new ones, etc., but nothing produced a change in the existing state of affairs.

At last my sister, the Countess S———, who resided in the neighbourhood, hearing of these things, went to that farm-house to investigate the matter. She took with her a clean, new bottle, and filled it with the milk as it came from the bewitched cows. This milk she took home with her and deposited it in her own pantry, and from that day the trouble in the house of her neighbour ceased, and all the milk in her own house became blue.

Here again everything was tried to find out the cause, but without any success, until, about three months afterwards, some old lady living about 300 miles distant effected another spell by her own occult powers, using some slips of paper, on which she wrote something, and in consequence of which the trouble ceased. Before it ceased, however, something strange happened. Before daybreak, as the milkmaid was about to enter the stable, some black thing like an animal rushed out of the half-opened door, knocked the milk-pail and the lantern out of her hands, and disappeared. After this all went well again.

On another occasion, in a similar case which took place in the same neighbourhood, the owner of the bewitched cattle was advised to take a sample of the milk from each cow, to mix them in a pan, to boil it over a slow fire, and to whip it with a rod while it was boiling down, and to throw the rest away. This advice he followed, and on the next day a person of ill repute was met, having his face covered with bloody streaks, as if they had been inflicted with a rod. This man could give no satisfactory account of the origin of his marks, and it is supposed that he was the punished sorcerer. The trouble then ceased. These examples go to corroborate what Paracelsus says about the Mumia.

42. This was a common belief during the Middle Ages, and many a poor old woman has been burned to death for having been suspected of being a witch. This, however, does not invalidate the statements of Paracelsus. In women, on the whole, the will is more active than in men, and they are less liable to exercise self-control. A woman having become disappointed in love and embittered with the world becomes a suitable instrument for the powers of evil to act through her organism. Woman is more powerful for good and for evil than males, because she represents will and substance, and man only the imagination.

43. Poisonous and malicious animals are forms of life in which an evil quality of the poisoned will in Nature has become manifest.

44. The more the physical body is active, the more will it need material food. The more the astral body is active, the more will it attract nutriment from the astral plane. The more divine love is active in man, the more will his soul receive of the substance of Christ. Each of these three states has its own functions and qualities.

45. According to Paracelsus, the characteristic signs by which witches can be known, or which justify the suspicion of a person being a witch, are as follows:
   1. They avoid the company of men and lead solitary lives.
   2. They especially venerate certain days, such as Thursday, Friday, and Saturday.
   3. They avoid sexual intercourse.
   4. They often have special marks, such as certain deformities and physiognomical characteristics.
   5. They practise certain ceremonies, and seek to associate with those who practise such arts.

46. The weak-minded people of our present civilisation know nothing about an imagination that comes from the heart. They live entirely in their brains, in moonshine and fancy. What Paracelsus calls the imagination of the heart, and H. P. Blavatsky the "doctrine of the heart," is the self-conscious will enlightened by intelligence.

47. Fear makes a person negative and liable to be infected. During the time of epidemic diseases, those who are not afraid of being infected are the least liable to become their victims. He who is confident that he cannot be affected by sorceries is not liable to become their victim. "He who fears thinks of nothing but evil. He has no confidence in God (in himself); he only imagines diseases and death, and thus he creates diseases in his imagination, and ultimately makes himself sick." (*De Pestilitate*, ii.)

Chapter 7

1. Is not even now the scientific world continually engaged in seeking for means by which man may lead an intemperate and immoral life without becoming subject to the natural consequences thereof? Are not even now many of our doctors poisoning the imagination of their patients by frightening them instead of seeking to instil hope and confidence into their minds?

2. Those who study the effects of vaccination without prejudice will easily find that nothing is done in that practice except substituting a slowly developing and far more dangerous disease for a

more acute and less dangerous one. The reason why this is not generally known is because the diseases inoculated by vaccination often appear only a long time after its performance, and their cause is therefore not recognised. Thus a lifelong suffering from eczema is often the consequence of vaccination. As to the celebrated Pasteur cures, it is said that of all his patients, ninety-six per cent have died, while the remaining four were probably not infected, and would have remained well anyhow.

3. Here comes in the advantage of intellectual education, but an educated intellect without any self-perception of truth belongs to the devil.

4. Recent experiments go to prove that sensation may be externalised. Thus, for instance, a man may surround himself with an invisible shell or aura by projecting his own odic emanations to a certain distance from his body; so that, while his body becomes insensible to pain, the pain will be felt when the aura around him is touched. This goes to show that sensation exists in the odic aura (Prana), and not in the physical form. (Compare E. Du Prel, *Die sympathetische Kurmethode*.)

5. We should sympathise with the patient, but not with his disease. We should not confirm him in his morbid fancies, or encourage him in believing himself sick. The majority of sick people lack the energy necessary to cure themselves. In such cases we should show them energy instead of a helpless commiseration.

6. Modern medicine, with its hypnotism, and suggestion, seems to be about to learn the first letters of the alphabet of the system of Paracelsus.

7. It is the Pranamaya of Sankaracharya.

8. Such as are caused by overloading the stomach with food, constipation of the bowels, obstructions, etc.

9. This mode of reasoning is as applicable to the state of medical science today as it was at the time of Paracelsus.

10. It would be interesting to find out how many chronic diseases and lifelong evils are caused by vaccination. If the organism contains some poisonous elements, Nature attempts to remove it by an expulsive effort caused by the action of the spirit from the centre toward the periphery, and producing cutaneous diseases. If by vaccination a new herd is established to attract the diseased elements (Mumia), the manifestation of the poison on the surface of the body may disappear, but the poisonous elements will remain in the body, and some other more serious disease will manifest itself sooner or later.

11. This invisible Mumia, that may be transferred from one living being to another, is nothing else but the vehicle of life, or "animal magnetism."

12. Paracelsus, not Mesmer, is the original discoverer of so-called Mesmerism.

13. It is nothing uncommon, especially in Mohammedan countries, to see packages lying in the road tied together with a string. On opening them, hair, bloody rags, excrements, etc., will be found. Such packages are laid there by some sick persons or their friends; they contain the Mumia of the sick, and it is intended that he who opens the package should get the disease of the patient, and the latter get well. Occasionally such a magnet is buried under the doorstep of an enemy, so as to cause him to walk over it and become sick. It is dangerous for sensitive persons to handle such things. The mode of curing diseases by transplanting the virus into trees has been used by the successors of Paracelsus, Tentzel, Helmont, Flood, Maxwell; and others practised them to a great extent, and acquired great reputations. They give some of the following instructions:—Many diseases may be cured by way of sympathy, by employing the warm blood of the patient as a magnet for the Mumia. The blood may be extracted by venesection or cupping, and made to run into lukewarm water or milk, and this is given to a hungry dog to eat. The process can be repeated several times, until the patient recovers.

14. The excrements of the patient may be dried as described above, and pulverised; they are tied up in a cloth and applied as a poultice, until they are penetrated with sweat from the patient, and the powder is then mixed with earth and inserted into a flower-pot, and a plant bearing the signature

of the patient's disease is planted into it. After the plant has grown a while it is thrown into running water in cases of fevers and inflammations, but in cases of a humid character or in lymphatic affections it should be hung into smoke.

15. An intelligent physician will neither accept nor reject the sympathetic cures to which the directions given above refer, although they may seem to be absurd and based upon superstition. The term "superstition" signifies a belief in something of which we have no knowledge, but if we understand the rationale of a thing the superstition ends.

16. Have those who ridicule this statement ever employed the hypericum in cases of hallucination?

17. The knowledge of the therapeutic use of the magnet has not advanced much since the days of Paracelsus. Baron Reichenbach investigated the subject in a scientific manner, but the result of his experiments is still ignored by the medical profession as a whole.

18. If we remember that the blood corpuscles, and consequently also the nerve aurae, contain iron, this statement appears very rational.

19. This might perhaps be translated as a congestion of blood to the brain caused by overworking the brain, or overloading it with a bad nervous aura.

20. This means: astral causes or origins, causes from poisons or impurities, causes that spring from morbid conditions in the body, spiritual causes, and such as come through the action of the moral law (*Karma*).

21. Those who are Jacks of all systems are usually masters of none.

22. Such influences consist in certain states of electricity, magnetism, miasmas, and other forces, for which modern science has no names and modern languages no words, but which we may call modifications of *Prana*.

23. It is not the physical body of the planet that acts upon the physical body of man, but the astral influence of the planet acting upon the astral form.

24. What the noxious influence of the moonlight is in the external world, the same is the influence of a morbid imagination in man.

25. Diseases often appear without any assignable cause. In acute diseases the patient often grows suddenly worse, or he may grow suddenly better, and no cause can be assigned to it. Such changes are usually attributed to catching cold where no cold has been caught, to mistakes in the diet where no such mistakes have been made, or they are attributed to meteorological changes, of whose action upon the human system therapeutic science knows less today than at the time of Paracelsus, because it is fashionable among certain people to reject everything which they cannot see, as being unworthy of their consideration.

26. For instance, elder-berries (*Sambucus*).

27. We ought not to forget that each planet corresponds to a certain state of the mind. Thus ♄ represents a melancholy, ♂ a fiery temper, ☽ a dreamy disposition, ♃ ambition and pride, ☿ intelligence, ♀ love and desire, ☉ wisdom.

28. Let the vivisectionists consider that question.

29. That which is divine in man is only one, and has only one aspect; all other things have two aspects, a material and an ethereal one.

30. It would be interesting to collect statistics of crimes, showing exactly the time when they have taken place, comparing the latter with the time of the conjunctions of the planets existing at the same longitude and latitude, and also compare them with the constellations that ruled at the time of birth.

31. Useless to say that our druggists know nothing about such things, and do not observe them.

32. The physician of the nineteenth century will hardly fail to recognise among these remedies many that are habitually used in modern medicine, although there is hardly any other reason for their employment known but that experience has taught that they are useful.

33. The ascendency of a star means the increase of a power.

34. The quality of the influences acting upon the patient.

35. This doctrine is corroborated by modern discoveries. Amputations of limbs are followed by a state of atrophy of certain parts of brain-substance, which seems to indicate that the force which shapes the limbs has its centre in the brain. If certain parts of the brain were destroyed, the limbs would begin to atrophy. If we apply this mode of reasoning to the Macrocosm, we find that all the essences and ethers that go to make up the organs of the Macrocosm are also contained in its centre, the sun; and if a certain element were taken away from the sun, the planets could not continue to exist in their present condition. If a certain element that goes to form the legs of men were suddenly taken away from the universal storehouse of the Macrocosm (the *Limbus*), human beings would be born without legs; if no principle of reason existed, there would be no use for brains, etc.

36. "That which is born from our thoughts is a spirit." (*Paramir.*,i.)

37. To think is to act on the plane of thought, and if the thought is intense enough, it can produce an effect on the physical plane. It is very fortunate that few persons possess the power to make it act directly on the physical plane, because there are few persons who never have any evil thoughts entering into their mind.

38. Here is the whole philosophy of what is now called "hypnotic suggestion outlined. Men's thoughts constantly act upon each other, be it knowingly or without their knowledge, and the stronger overcomes and overawes the weaker; but the strength of the thought depends upon the force of the will by which it is endowed, and the strength of will depends upon the amount of its consciousness.

39. Here again is a glorious new field of activity for the enterprising vivisectionist; but unfortunately he in whom such evil forms of will-power (elementals or devils) have come into existence will not get rid of them easily, and he will be himself the greatest sufferer in the end.

40. The will of God.

41. The word eternal does not signify a time without end, but a state in which time is not measured, and in which it therefore does not exist.

42. A misunderstanding of the doctrine of Karma may give rise to an erroneous belief, which may be productive of serious harm. There are great numbers of religious fanatics in the East, and some in the West, who would not make an attempt to pull a person out of a burning house, even if they could easily do so, because they believe that if it is the will of God, or his *Karma*, that he should perish in the fire, it would be wrong to interfere with that law, and to frustrate the purpose of God. They should remember that if it was the will of God which caused such a person to fall into danger, it must also have been the will of God which sent them near, and enabled them to save; and if they neglect to do their duty and suffer him to perish, they are arrogating to themselves the prerogatives of gods. They then act against the law, and will become responsible for their act. God acts through man, and a man who does not respond to His call, and refuses to obey the Divine command, spoken within his heart, is a useless instrument, and will be rejected.

43. The word surgery is here applied in a sense somewhat different from its modern acceptation.

44. So are light, heat, electricity, etc. Each of them is an individual, and nevertheless universally existing, energy.

45. Sankaracharya says: The first necessary requisite for the attainment of real knowledge is the possession of the power to distinguish the enduring (spirit) from the non-enduring (matter). That which hinders man to see the truth is the delusion of self.

46. The true physician acts in harmony with natural laws; the quack tries to oppose Nature by means of his own inventions. The true physician will aid Nature to throw off the germs of disease; the quack will try to force Nature to retain the poison and to prevent its outward manifestation. (Compare William Tebb, Leprosy and Vaccination. London, 1893.)

47. Not due to unexhausted *Karma*.

48. "An Arcanum is incorporeal and indestructible of eternal life, superhuman and beyond Nature. In us is the *Arcanum Dei* and the *Arcanum Naturae*; the *Arcanum* is the virtue of a thing

in its highest potency; the *Arcanum Hominis* is that power of man which is eternal in him." (*Archidoxes, De Arcanis*)

Chapter 8

1. "Hermes said that the soul alone is the medium by means of which spirit and body are united." (*Generat. Rerum., i.*)

2. "Man, being the son of the Microcosm, has in him also all the mineral elements." (*De Peste*)

3. Johannes Tritheim, Abbot of Spanheim, one of the greatest alchemists, theologians, and astrologers, a learned and highly esteemed man, makes some remarks in his book (printed at Passau, 1506) that may help to throw some light on the perplexing subject of alchemy. He says: "The art of divine magic consists in the ability to perceive the essence of things in the light of Nature, and by using the soul-powers of the spirit to produce material things from the unseen universe (A'kasa), and in such operations the Above (the Macrocosm) and the Below (the Microcosm) must be brought together and made to act harmoniously. The spirit of Nature is a unity, creating and forming everything, and by acting through the instrumentality of man it may produce wonderful things. Such processes take place according to law. You will learn the law by which these things are accomplished, if you learn to know yourself. You will know it by the power of the spirit that is in yourself, and accomplish it by mixing your spirit with the essence that comes out of yourself. If you wish to succeed in such a work you must know how to separate spirit and life in Nature, and, moreover, to separate the astral soul in yourself and to make it tangible, and then the substance of the soul will appear visibly and tangibly, rendered objective by the power of the spirit. Christ speaks of the salt, and the salt is of a threefold nature. Gold is of a threefold nature, and there is an ethereal, a fluid, and a material gold. It is the same gold, only in three different states; and gold in one state may be made into gold in another state. But such mysteries should not be divulged, because the fool and scoffer will laugh at it, and to him who is covetous they will be a temptation."

[*Notice.* I wish to warn the reader, who might be inclined to try any of the alchemical prescriptions contained in this book, not to do so unless he is an alchemist, because, although I know from personal observation that these prescriptions are not only allegorically but literally true, and will prove successful in the hands of an alchemist, they would only cause a waste of time and money in the hands of one who has not the necessary qualifications. A person who wants to be an alchemist must have in himself the "magnesia," which means the magnetic power to attract and "coagulate" invisible astral elements. This power is only possessed "by those who are "Initiates." Those who do not know what this expression means are not "reborn" (or initiated), and it cannot be explained to them. But he who is initiated will know it, and needs no instruction from books, because he will know his instructor.]

4. Spiritual development is not dependent on intellectual acquirements and there are sometimes persons that are ignorant in worldly things, but who nevertheless possess great spiritual powers.

5. This does not, of course, refer to the chemical substances known to us by these names. "No one can express or sufficiently describe the virtues contained in the three substances; therefore every alchemist and true physician ought to seek in them all his life unto his death; then would his labour surely find its just reward." (*De Morte Rerum*)

6. "The sophist says that nothing living can come out of dead substances, but no substance is dead, and they know nothing about the alchemical labour. The death of a man is surely nothing but the separation of the three substances of which his body is composed, and the death of a metal is the taking away of its corporeal form." (*De Morte Rerum*)

7. "The three Substances are three forms or aspects of the one universal will-substance out of which everything was created; for the unmanifested Absolute in manifesting itself reveals itself as a trinity of cause, action, and effect; father, son, and the holy ghost; body, soul, and spirit.

"It is therefore, above all, necessary that we should realise the nature of the three Substances as they exist in the Macrocosm and recognise their qualities, and we shall then also know their nature and attributes in the Microcosm of man. That which burns and appears fiery to the eye is the Sulphur, it is of a volatile (spiritual) nature; that which is of a material nature is the Salt; and the Mercury is that which may be sublimated by the action of the fire. It is invisible in its condition of *Prima materia*, but in its ultimate state it may be seen; and as the whole constitution of man consists of these three Substances, consequently there are three modes in which diseases may originate, namely, in the *Sulphur*, in the *Mercury*, or in the *Salt*. As long as these three Substances are full of life they are in health, but when they become separated disease will be the result. Where such a separation begins there is the origin of disease and the beginning of death. There are many kinds of Sulphur, of Mercury, and of Salt; that which belongs to Sulphur should be made into Sulphur, so that it may burn; what belongs to Mercury should be made to sublimate and ascend; what belongs to Salt should be resolved into Salt."

"To explain the qualities of the three Substances it would be necessary to explain the qualities of the *Prima materia*; but as the *Prima materia mundi* was the *Fiat* (*Logos*), who would dare to attempt to explain it?"

8. The "*tinctura physicorum*" is a great alchemical mystery. Hermes Trismegistus of Egypt, Onus of Greece, Hali, an Arab, and Albertus Magnus of Germany were acquainted with it. It is also called the Red Lion, and is mentioned in many alchemical works, but was actually known to few. Its preparation is extremely difficult, as there is the presence of two perfectly harmonious people, equally skilful, necessary for that purpose. It is said to be a red ethereal fluid, capable of transmuting all inferior metals into gold, and having other wonderful virtues. There is an old church in the vicinity of Kenysten, a town in the south of Bavaria, where this tincture is said to be still buried in the ground. In the year 1698 some of it penetrated through the soil, and the phenomenon was witnessed by many people, who believed it to be a miracle. A church was therefore erected at that place, and it is still a well-known place of pilgrimage. In regard to the material (if it may be so called) used for the preparation of this great medicine, Paracelsus says: "Be careful not to take anything from the lion but the rose-coloured blood, and from the white eagle only the white gluten. Coagulate (corporify) it according to the directions given by the ancients, and you will have the *tinctura physicorum*. But if this is incomprehensible to you, remember that only he who desires with his whole heart will find, and to him only who knocks strong enough the door shall be opened."

9. If we remember that the wise ones will lay up their treasures in heaven, the above passage becomes easily comprehensible.

10. The power that man may silently exercise over animals is well known.

11. It does not require the sound of our voice to bring the image of some object before our imagination, and if we see the image of a thing in our mind, and realise its presence, it actually exists for us, and thus a spirit may be brought into a form by the power of imagination.

12. This remark throws some light on alchemical processes, and goes to show that it is not the "magnetism" of the planets alone, but also the soul-essence of the operator, that is to be bound, and the two connected together in the metal by the process described below.

13. All the above-mentioned conjunctions take place in our solar system in the course of thirteen successive months, but the directions refer to conjunctions of principles contained in the Microcosm of man.

14. That is to say, you may come *en rapport* with the astral light, which is the sensorium of the world, and in which the "memory" or impression of everything is preserved.

15. It would be useless to give detailed descriptions of processes that cannot be followed out by any one who does not possess the necessary magic (magnetic) power, and those who possess the power will hardly require such descriptions, in which allegories are strangely mixed with truths.

16. See Appendix.

17. Without this arcanum the experiment would not succeed, nor the form become visible.

18. Paracelsus has been reproached for his belief in the possibility of generating homunculi; but a deeper insight into the processes of Nature will show that such a thing is not necessarily impossible. Modern authorities believe it to be not impossible. Moleschott thinks that we may perhaps yet succeed in establishing conditions by which organic forms can be generated; Liebig is of the opinion that chemistry will yet succeed in making organic substances by artificial means. Goethe says in his "Faust":

"And such a brain, that has the power to think,
Will in the future be produced by a thinker."

Where no germ is present such a generation would certainly be impossible; but chickens can be artificially hatched out, and perhaps homunculi may be developed. There seem to be some historic evidences that such things have been accomplished, as the following account will show:

In a book called "The Sphinx," edited by Dr. Emil Besetzny, and published at Vienna in 1873 by L. Rosner (Tuchlauben, No. 22), we find some interesting accounts in regard to a number of "spirits" generated by a Joh. Ferd, Count of Kueffstein, in Tyrol, in the year 1775. The sources from which these accounts are taken consist in masonic manuscripts and prints, but more especially in a diary kept by a certain Jas Kammerer, who acted in the capacity of butler and famulus to the said Count. There were ten homunculi or, as he calls them, "prophesying spirits" preserved in strong bottles, such as are used to preserve fruit, and which were filled with water; and these "spirits" were the product of the labour of the Count J. F. of Kueffstein (Kufstein), and of an Italian Mystic and Rosicrucian, Abbe Geloni. They were made in the course of five weeks, and consisted of a king, a queen, a knight, a monk, a nun, an architect, a miner, a seraph, and finally of a blue and a red spirit. "The bottles were closed with ox-bladders, and with a great magic seal (Solomon's seal?). The spirits swam about in those bottles, and were about one span long, and the Count was very anxious that they should grow. They were therefore buried under two cart-loads of horse-manure, and the pile daily sprinkled with a certain liquor, prepared with great trouble by the two adepts, and made out of some 'very disgusting materials.' The pile of manure began after such sprinklings to ferment and to steam as if heated by a subterranean fire, and at least once every three days, when everything was quiet, at the approach of the night, the two gentlemen would leave the convent and go to pray and to fumigate at that pile of manure. After the bottles were removed the 'spirits' had grown to be each one about one and a half span long, so that the bottles were almost too small to contain them, and the male homunculi had come into possession of heavy beards, and the nails of their fingers and toes had grown a great deal. By some means the Abbe Schiloni provided them with appropriate clothing, each one according to his rank and dignity. In the bottle of the red and in that of the blue spirit, however, there was nothing to be seen but 'clear water'; but whenever the Abbe knocked three times at the seal upon the mouth of the bottles, speaking at the same time some Hebrew words, the water in the bottles began to turn blue (respectively red), and the blue and the red spirits would show their faces, first very small, but growing in proportions until they attained the size of an ordinary human face. The face of the blue spirit was beautiful, like an angel, but that of the red one bore a horrible expression.

"These beings were fed by the Count about once every three or four days with some rose-coloured substance which he kept in a silver box, and of which he gave to each spirit a pill of about the size of a pea. Once every week the water had to be removed, and the bottles filled again with pure rain-water. This change had to be accomplished very rapidly, because during the few moments that the spirits were exposed to the air they closed their eyes, and seemed to become weak and unconscious, as if they were about to die. But the blue spirit was never fed, nor was the water changed; while the red one received once a week a thimbleful of fresh blood of some animal (chicken), and this blood disappeared in the water as soon as it was poured into it, without colouring or troubling it. The water containing the red spirit had to be changed once every two or three days. As soon as the bottle was opened it became dark and cloudy, and emitted an odour of rotten eggs.

"In the course of time these spirits grew to be about two spans long, and their bottles were now almost too small for them to stand erect; the Count therefore provided them with appropriate seats. These bottles were carried to the place where the Masonic Lodge of which the Count was the presiding Master met, and after each meeting they were carried back again. During the meetings the spirits gave prophecies about future events that usually proved to be correct. They knew the most secret things, but each of them was only acquainted with such things as belonged to his station: for instance, the king could talk politics, the monk about religion, the miner about minerals, etc.; but the blue and the red spirits seemed to know everything. (Some facts proving their clairvoyant powers are given in the original.)

"By some accident the glass containing the monk fell one day upon the floor, and was broken. The poor monk died after a few painful respirations, in spite of all the efforts of the Count to save his life, and his body was buried in the garden. An attempt to generate another one, made by the Count without the assistance of the Abbe, who had left, resulted in failure, as it produced only a small thing like a leech, which had very little vitality, and soon died.

"One day the king escaped from his bottle, which had not been properly sealed, and was found by Kammerer sitting on the top of the bottle containing the queen, attempting to scratch with his nails the seal away, and to liberate her. In answer to the servant's call for help, the Count rushed in, and after a prolonged chase caught the king, who, from his long exposure to the air and the want of his appropriate element, had become faint, and was replaced into his bottle not, however, without succeeding to scratch the nose of the Count."

It seems that the Count of Kufstein in later years became anxious for the salvation of his soul, and considered it incompatible with the requirements of his conscience to keep those spirits longer in his possession, and that he got rid of them in some manner not mentioned by the scribe. We will not make an attempt at comment, but would advise those who are curious about this matter to read the book from which the above account is an extract. There can be hardly any doubt as to its veracity, because some historically well-known persons, such as Count Max Lamberg, Count Franz Josef v. Thun, and others, saw them, and they possessed undoubtedly visible and tangible bodies; and it seems that they were either elemental spirits, or, what appears to be more probable, homunculi.

19. The following is a prescription how to make artificial gold, taken from an old alchemistical MS., and a marginal note says that an experiment tried with it proved successful:—Take equal parts of powdered iron, sublimated sulphur, and crude antimony. Melt it in a crucible, and keep it in red heat for eight hours. Powder it, and calcinate it until the sulphur is evaporated. Mix two parts of this powder with one part of calcinated borax, and melt it again. Powder and dissolve it in common muriatic acid, and let it stand in a moderate heat for one month. The fluid is then to be put into a retort and distilled, and the fluid that collects in the recipient (the muriatic acid) is returned into the retort and again distilled, and this is repeated three times; the third time a red powder will be left in the retort (probably a mixture of muriate of iron with antimonium oxide). This powder is to be dissolved in the menstruum philosophicum, (made by pouring chloride of antimony into water, filtering, and evaporating the fluid to a certain extent, to make it stronger). The solution is to be evaporated again, and the remaining powder mixed with its own weight of corrosive sublimate of mercury. This powder is to be dissolved again in the menstruum philosophicum (diluted muriatic acid), and distilled until a red oily substance passes into the receiver. If you obtain this oil, you may take some newly prepared chloride of silver, saturate it gradually with the oil, and dry it. Put one part of this powder into five parts of molten lead, separate the lead again from the silver (by cupellation), and you will find that one-third of the silver has been transformed into gold.

20. There is a considerable amount of historical evidence of a trustworthy character that goes to prove that pure gold has been artificially made, but it is, to say the least, doubtful if this was done in a way that could be successfully imitated by one who is not an alchemist. According to a trustworthy report, coming from a source whose veracity is not doubtful, a certain alchemist was kept imprisoned by the Prince-Elect of Saxony at a fortress at Dresden in the year 1748, because the

Prince wanted to obtain through him artificial gold. This adept produced four hundred pounds of gold by alchemical means, and finally escaped from the prison in some unexplained manner. Flamel is said to have made artificial gold on April 25, 1382.

21. Tiffereau has repeatedly succeeded in transmuting inferior metals into gold, by exposing for a long time solutions of chemically pure silver or copper to the sunshine in tropical countries, and he presented a considerable quantity of such gold to the Academy of Science in Paris. The gold thus obtained differed in some respects from the natural gold (Tiffereau, "L'Or," Paris). One of the best modern treatises on Alchemy in its physical aspects is August Strindberg's "Sylva Sylvarum" (Paris, 1896), which goes to show that all chemical substances are only modes of vibration of one primordial substance, and can be changed one into another by changing the state of etheric vibration.

22. It is not divine man, but the elements in the body of man, which attract corresponding influences from the powers of macrocosmic Nature.

23. If they come from the spirit, the spirit must have pre-existed, and have acquired them in a previous incarnation.

24. By "stars" (*astra*) Paracelsus does not refer to the physical bodies of the planets, but to mental states existing in the Cosmos, and which are represented by the stars.

Chapter 9

1. God is the supreme will of the universe, or, as Boehme calls it, the will of divine wisdom. It is therefore a divine will, and it could not be divine if it were not free and subject to nothing. This does not imply that God is something external to Nature, but that He is superior to it.

2. Everybody knows that the thinking faculty is not our own self, but that there is something in us which has the power to think or to let thinking alone. This something is higher than the intellectual realm, and therefore higher than all of its "stars."

3. God is the greatest power in the universe, because He is the source and sum of all powers in their highest mode of manifestation. God is therefore absolute consciousness, absolute love, and absolute wisdom. If we wish to accomplish anything great, the first requirement is the presence of God, because He is man's understanding and power, and resides in man. But God cannot be approached by an intellect that is without love. God is love, and is only attracted by love. We cannot know the principle of love unless we love it with our heart, and the more we desire it, the more will we be able to comprehend with the heart what this principle is. The love of God is therefore a power transcending the lower nature of man; it cannot develop itself out of the animal elements of man, but it is a gift from the universal fountain of love, in the same sense as sunshine cannot grow out of the earth, but comes from above. Gods lives in the hearts of men, and if we desire to love Him, we must love all that is good in humanity. The love of humanity is the beginning of the knowledge of God. The intellect is the greatest possession of mortal man, and an intellect that rises to the source of all knowledge by the power of love may know God and all the mysteries of Nature, and become godlike itself; but an intellect without love leads into error, grovels in darkness, and goes to perdition. An intellect combined with love for the supreme good leads to wisdom; an intellect without love leads to the powers of evil.

4. This is the curse of all dabblers in the divine mysteries, that when they begin to believe that there is something superior to the merely animal man, this belief opens the door for superstition and idolatry; for, having no knowledge of the power of the divine will within their own self, they are devoid of the true faith, which is divine self-confidence. They therefore put their trust, not in the one true God, but in the gods which they have created within their own imagination. They seek in outward things for that which they cannot find within their own empty shells. They neglect their duties as men and revel in dreams wherein there is nothing real. Some put their faith in doctors and priests, others in herbs and roots, still others in magic spells and incantations; but

the wise know that the first step on the road to spiritual unfoldment is the fulfilment of one's duties as a man; for no god can grow out of a man unless the man has become truly that which he ought to be. In this fulfilment of one's duty and becoming true to one's nature as man rests the germ of true happiness, and from this germ is evolved the regenerated man in whom heaven exists and who lives through eternity.

5. Where should that germ come from, if it had not existed before, and how did it attain its divine qualities?

6. They are born with the tendencies which they acquired in former lives upon the earth, or upon some other planet. The personified devils we meet in the world are the "materialised" forms of devilish powers existing upon the astral plane.

7. The balsam of life (a man without sexual power is unfit for initiation).

8. Man and woman are both one in the Lord. The "man" is the spirit and "woman" the soul.

9. Thus it would also be better for our modern would-be theosophists if, instead of running after external "Mahatmas" and seeking salvation from them, each one were to strive after knowing the real Mahatma existing within his own soul.

10. There is a false faith that comes from ignorance (Tamas) and a false faith that originates from selfish desire (Rajas); but the true faith springs from wisdom (Sattwa), and is itself the way for its attainment.

Appendix

1. See H. P. Blavatsky, *The Voice of the Silence*, (*Nirmanahaya's*)

2. C. von Eckartshausen speaks in his "Disclosures of Magic" (1790) about the Adepts as follows: "These sages, whose number is small, are children of light, and are opposed to darkness. They dislike mystification and secrecy; they are open and frank, having nothing to do with secret societies and with external ceremonies. They possess a spiritual temple, in which God is presiding.

"They live in various parts of the earth, and do not meddle with politics; their business is to do as much good to humanity as is in their power, and to drink wisdom from the eternal fountain of truth. They never quarrel about opinions, because they know the truth. Their number is small. Some live in Europe, others in Africa, but they are bound together by the harmony of their souls, and they are therefore as one. They are joined together, although they may be thousands of miles apart from each other. They understand each other, although they speak in different tongues, because the language of the sages is spiritual perception.

"No evil-disposed person could possibly live among them, because he would be recognised immediately, for he would be incapable of being illuminated by wisdom, and as a mirror covered with mire cannot reflect the light, likewise such a soul cannot reflect the truth. But the more the soul of man grows perfect, the nearer does it approach to God, and the more will its understanding grow and its love be exalted. Thus may man enter into sanctification; he may communicate with perfect beings in the spiritual kingdom, and be instructed and guided by them. He will be a true child of God. All Nature will be subject to him, because he will be an instrument to carry out the will of the Creator of Nature. He knows the future, the thoughts and the instincts of men, because the mysteries of eternity are open before him.

"But the plans of the worldly-wise will come to nought. That which took the followers of false science centuries to accomplish will be wiped out by a single stroke of the finger of God, and a nobler generation will come, which will worship God in spirit and in truth."

3. There are three kinds of knowledge: 1. External knowledge, or scientific opinions in regard to external things (Gal. vi. 3). This knowledge leads to error, because it concentrates all the attention upon the illusory exterior of things, and keeps the mind in ignorance in regard to interior truths. 2. Knowledge received by entering into the mysteries of Nature; comprehension of truths independent of the opinions of others. It is the beginning of wisdom (*Sirach* i. 16). 3. Wisdom, or

the knowledge of the Supreme Cause of all effects obtained by knowledge of self (*Book of Wisdom*, vii. 17-27). This is the wisdom of Solomon.

There are three kinds of knowers: 1. The theorists, who deal with opinions and with illusory appearances; the opinionated and dogmatists, sceptics, materialists, etc., who continually quarrel about their different opinions. 2. Those who are able to recognise interior truths objectively by the power of their interior perception. 3. The Adepts, who are united with God, and know everything because they know themselves, by the power of the Holy Ghost being manifest in themselves (Prov. ix. 7).

4. The doctrine of the Trinity is found in all the principal religious systems: in the Christian religion as Father, Son, and Spirit; among the Hindus as Brahma, Vishnu, and Siva; the Buddhists call it Atma, Buddhi, and Manas; the Persians [Zoroastrians] teach that Ormuzd [Ahura Mazda] produced light out of himself by the power of his word. The Egyptians called the First Cause Ammon, out of which all things were created by the power of its own will. In Chinese, Kwan-shai-gin is the universally manifested Word, coming from the unmanifested Absolute by the power of its own will, and being identical with the former. The Greeks called it Zeus (Power), Minerva (Wisdom), and Apollo (Beauty); the Germans, Wodan (the Supreme Cause), Thor (Power), and Freia (Beauty). Jehovah and Allah are trinities of Will, Knowledge, and Power; and even the Materialist believes in Causation, Matter, and Energy.

5. There are three kinds of imagination: passive imagination, active thought, creative thought.

6. There are three kinds of birth: the birth of the flesh, of the soul, and of the spirit; and each birth has three stages: generation, germination, and fructification. The first birth is the natural birth of man; the second is the awakening of the soul, and the attainment of its power (Ephes. iv. 13) to control the desires and passions; it is, so to say, an invisible fire, penetrating the whole of the body. The third birth is the regeneration of the spirit, its awakening to spiritual consciousness. The last stage is attained by very few (i Cor. xv. 47 ; St. John iii. 6). 1 Krishna, Buddha, Christ.

7. Krishna, Buddha, Christ.

8. "Adam." The failures of the Dhyan-Chohans.

9. The "flesh of Adam" forms the animal elements of the soul, but the flesh of Christ is the spirit (the sixth principle). All the animal principles existing in Nature exist germinally in the soul-essence of man, and may grow there and develop into entities. The whole of the animal creation is thus represented in the soul of man, because the growth of an animal passion means the growth of an animal principle in the soul. If such passions are conquered by the power of the spirit, these animal "creatures" will die and be expelled from the organism of the soul, in the same way as a decayed part of the physical body becomes separated from the physical organism; and as such processes going on in the physical form may be observed during the waking state, likewise the corresponding processes going on in the organism of the soul may be observed during a dream.

10. There are three kinds of baptism, by which three different names are received. The first baptism is only an external form, and the name is optional; the second is the baptism with the "water of truth," or the awakening of the soul to a recognition of the truth, by which a new name is received, expressing the quality and destination of the individual (1 Moses xvii. 5); the third is the baptism with the "fire of the spirit," and the name which it confers expresses the power of the perfect and immortal divine man. (St John's Revelation ii. 17)

11. There are three distinct classes of mediumship: mechanical mediumship, in which the physical forces of the medium are used by extraneous influences (obsession, physical manifestations, etc.); emotional mediumship, by which the energies of the soul of the medium are stimulated and his feelings and his thoughts aroused (trance speaking and writing); spiritual mediumship, in which wisdom manifests itself through transcendentally conscious man (ecstasy, illumination).

12. It is said that "darkness is absence of light." We may say with equal truth that "light is absence of darkness;" light and darkness are certain states of the cosmic ether (A'kasa). Light is "spirit," darkness is "matter." Both have positive qualities (Gen. i. 4).

13. Plato, Seneca, Erastus, Avicenna, Averroes, Albertus Magnus, Caspalin, Cardanus, Cornelius Agrippa, Eckartshausen, and many others wrote about the palingenesis of plants and animals. Kircher resurrected a rose from its ashes in the presence of Queen Christina of Sweden, 1687. The astral body of an individual form remains with the remnants of the latter until these remnants have been fully decomposed, and by certain methods known to the alchemist it can be reclothed with matter and become visible again.

14. The value of a letter should be determined by the quality of its contents, and not by the manner in which it has been received.

15. Exod. vii. 10.

16. Such manifestations of occult power may be witnessed frequently in spiritualistic séances. The reason why they seem incomprehensible to us is because we habitually look upon form as something real instead of seeing in it an illusion, and because our accepted opinions in regard to the constitution of matter are fundamentally wrong.

17. The earthly atmosphere may be, so to say, perforated by a tube or wire, carrying an electric current, and the ether (A'kasa) be "perforated" likewise by a current of spiritual force. An electric current passes unimpeded through the earth; a thought current passes unimpeded through the A'kasa.

18. The human soul is threefold: the animal, intellectual, and spiritual soul. The imperfect elements of the soul die; that which is perfect remains alive. Life is threefold: the organic life, the life of the soul, and that of the spirit.

19. There are three sources of faith: opinion, belief, and knowledge.

20. The human spirit has a twofold aspect, a human and a divine one.

21. The writings attributed to Paracelsus in regard to this subject that are known at present are partly spurious, partly fragmentary, and the translations incorrect. The extracts given below of his writings on the Elixir of Life are taken from an original MS, in private possession.

22. Compare *Five Years of Theosophy*, ch 1 "The Elixir of Life."

23. Lesebure, a physician of Louis XIV. of France, gives, in his "Guide to Chemistry" ("Chemischer Handleiter," Nuremberg, 1685, p. 276), an account of some experiments, witnessed by himself, with the Primun Ens Melissae as follows:—"One of my most intimate friends prepared the Primum Ens Melissae, and his curiosity would not allow him to rest until he had seen with his own eyes the effect of this arcanum, so that he might be certain whether or not the accounts given of its virtues were true. He therefore made the experiment, first upon himself, then upon an old female servant, aged seventy years, and afterwards upon an old hen that was kept at his house. First he took, every morning at sunrise, a glass of white wine that was tinctured with this remedy, and after using it for fourteen days his finger and toe nails began to fall out, without, however, causing any pain. He was not courageous enough to continue the experiment, but gave the same remedy to the old female servant. She took it every morning for about ten days, when she began to menstruate again, as in former days. At this she was very much surprised, because she did not know that she had been taking a medicine. She became frightened, and refused to continue the experiment. My friend took, therefore, some grain, soaked it in that wine, and gave it to the old hen to eat, and on the sixth day that bird began to lose its feathers, and kept on losing them until it was perfectly nude; but before two weeks had passed away new feathers grew, which were much more beautifully coloured; her comb stood up again, and she began again to lay eggs."

In the "Life of Cagliostro" some such rejuvenating medicine is mentioned, and the names of some persons who succeeded in the experiment are given. These and similar facts have neither been proved nor disproved by science, but are waiting for an investigation. The judges at the trial of Cagliostro, before the tribunal of the Inquisition at Rome, were only intent to convict him; but he who can read their report "between the lines" will find a great deal that speaks in favour of Cagliostro, and much that has not been explained.

24. We give these and the following prescriptions as curiosities, for what they are worth. They

contain great truths, but only those who know will be able to understand and to prepare them. Those who go to the apothecary's shop to get these remedies prepared will be disappointed.

25. The alchemistical writings of Paracelsus are as obscure for the uninitiated as those of any other alchemist, but to the initiated they are plain enough. He gives, however, many plain directions in regard to the treatment of special diseases, and which can easily be followed out The reason why the doctrines of Paracelsus are not more extensively followed out by modern physicians is, that his system is, unfortunately, little known, and still less understood. The time will come when the resurrected doctrines of Paracelsus will create again a revolution in medical science, as the man Paracelsus did three hundred years ago.

26. This takes place in the Macrocosm during the time of the new moon, occurring each year between October 23 and November 23.

Printed in Great
Britain
by Amazon